WHAT DOESN'T KILL YOU . . .

www.**penguin**.co.uk

WHAT DOESN'T KILL YOU . . .

My Life in Motor Racing

Johnny Herbert

BANTAM PRESS

LONDON • TORONTO • SYDNEY • AUCKLAND • JOHANNESBURG

TRANSWORLD PUBLISHERS
61–63 Uxbridge Road, London W5 5SA
www.penguin.co.uk

Transworld is part of the Penguin Random House group of companies
whose addresses can be found at global.penguinrandomhouse.com

Penguin
Random House
UK

First published in Great Britain in 2016 by Bantam Press
an imprint of Transworld Publishers

A CIP catalogue record for this book
is available from the British Library.

ISBN 9780593078389

Typeset in 12.5/15.5pt Ehrhardt by Falcon Oast Graphic Art Ltd.
Printed and bound by Clays Ltd, Bungay, Suffolk.

Penguin Random House is committed to a sustainable
future for our business, our readers and our planet. This book
is made from Forest Stewardship Council® certified paper.

To Rebecca, Chloe
and Aimelia

One

THERE IS A MUCH-USED but totally ridiculous saying that goes 'Never ASSUME, because when you ASSUME, you make an ASS of U and ME'. Rubbish, isn't it? The reason I'm including it is because when it comes to me and motorsport, people nearly always assume that I either come from a family steeped in automotive history, or, at the very least, have a father who was an out-and-out petrol-head and who had me karting from the age of one. Not true, I'm afraid. My dad was neither a Keke Rosberg nor an Anthony Hamilton. In fact he was, and still is, Bob Herbert, a retired electrician from Essex who, until I'd been karting a few years, didn't know a carburettor from a carbonara. I suppose that makes an ASS out of U (although not you personally) but not ME. You see, I told you it was rubbish.

In all seriousness, they're absolutely right to assume I've got form, as the vast majority of professional and even amateur racing drivers will have been influenced by family somewhere along the way, and usually quite early on. Indeed, at the time of writing, I can't think of one driver on the F1 grid who isn't a product of either some premeditated parental enthusiasm or, more directly, racing genes, nor can I think of too many who've come before. If the passion's there it rarely gets a chance to skip a generation, which is why so many racers have some kind of motorsport family tree.

I, on the other hand – John Paul Herbert, born 25 June 1964 – was the first member of my entire family – the Romford Herberts or, on my mum Jane's side, the Ingatestone Coxes – to have taken so much as a passing interest in motorsport, let alone made a career in it. In fact, and this is God's honest truth, before I won my first trophy in karting back in the mid-seventies, the closest any of us had ever come to enjoying success on four wheels was when I unexpectedly rocked my pushchair from one end of the garden to the other, impressing not only my speech-less parents but also several of their friends. There were no trophies that day though, just a few cries of 'How the bloody hell did he do that?' We all have to start somewhere, I suppose.

Irrespective of how you actually get involved in motorsport, there is one thing we racers all have in common, regardless of standard or the number of wheels involved, and that is a vivid and unforgettable recollection of the first time we sat behind (in my case) the wheel of a kart. You don't have to be a Lewis Hamilton or a Valentino Rossi to appreciate that feeling, and I'd hazard a guess that many of you reading this book will now be grinning like Cheshire cats as you recall yours.

My own experience is still breathtakingly vivid, to the point where I can still remember what people said to me and what they were wearing. I'm not going to bore you with that of course (although flares and wide collars were definitely at play), but what I will tell you is that the month was August, the year 1971, and the location a disused airfield just outside St Ives in Cornwall.

We used to go to Cornwall a lot when I was a child and I remember it used to take us about seven hours to get there. Seven flipping hours! These days you can probably do it in about four, with a bit of luck and a following wind, but back then there were far fewer motorways, and cars, although often brimming with character, were, shall we say, often somewhat underpowered. I don't know what the record is for saying 'Are we there yet?' on that particular journey but between my younger sister Sarah and me we must have gone well into four figures. Mum and Dad used to be ever so patient. Sometimes we'd get as far as Basingstoke before they started swearing at us.

The reason we started going to St Ives, apart from it being hundreds of bloody miles away on the other side of the country, is because my dad's sister Sheila and her husband Pete had started working down there and so we used it as an opportunity to visit them. They were running an old karting track that had been built on the runway of the aforementioned disused airfield and we stayed in a holiday complex just a short walk away. I say track, it was just a few old tyres that had been fashioned into a standard snake-like circuit and I don't recall being especially drawn to it. It was something new, though, so one afternoon while we were down there I thought I'd ask Dad if I could give it a go.

'Yes, all right,' he said. 'Watch yourself, though. Those things look bloody dangerous.'

After taking absolutely no notice of him whatsoever I went to see my uncle Pete and he set me up in a kart. The thing is, because I was so small he had to put four or five big cushions behind me just so I could reach the pedals. It must have looked ridiculous, and it certainly wasn't the last time it would happen. God bless Health and Safety 1970s style!

Once again, I don't remember feeling particularly excited or anything, it was just something to do. I'd probably do this for a few minutes, get bored, then go for a swim or kick a ball around with my dad. I recall Uncle Pete explaining how the kart worked and telling me all the dos and don'ts, but even though I can recollect what he said I didn't actually take any notice of him. 'Yes, Uncle Pete. No problem, Uncle Pete.' Typical seven-year-old boy, I suppose. Then, once I'd given him the thumbs up and he was happy, off I went.

You know what it's like when you ride a bike for the first time without stabilizers, the sensations of excitement and freedom you feel from being able to do something on your own? Well, that's exactly how I felt on my first few laps in the kart, the difference being that I never needed the stabilizers. The feeling I got through my hands, my arms, my toes, my legs, and even my bum, was just very natural. Straight away I felt completely at home, and within just a few laps I had instinctively begun to gauge not only the strengths and weaknesses of the kart but also the grip of the tyres. I also took the racing line, or something there or thereabouts – once again, courtesy of instinct. I didn't have to *think* about anything. The speed, such as it was, didn't faze me one little bit, and instead of fear I experienced frequent rushes of adrenalin. OK, the kart was just an old banger, but it still got up to about 40mph and I was only seven years old.

Instead of bombing round for ten minutes and then going for a swim like I'd originally planned, I ended up spending not just the rest of the day on track but the rest of the holiday. Every morning, straight after breakfast, Dad would take me from the chalet to the airfield and deposit me with Uncle Pete. Then, once Pete had filled up a kart for me, he'd just leave me to it. Talk about endurance racing. I must have done at least ten thousand laps and didn't make a single pit stop.

I wasn't the only one driving, by the way. Over the course of the holiday I was joined by a succession of challengers, mainly adults and teens, and, without wanting to sound like too much of a bighead, I thrashed them. No one could get anywhere near me, and the more I drove, the more confident I became; and the more confident I became, the more chances I took; and so it went on. By the end of the holiday I was quite a competent little driver. I even managed to persuade Uncle Pete to untie the throttle for a few laps. They'd been tied up to prevent excessive speed and I'd been nagging him to release mine ever since about the third lap.

'I want to go faster, Uncle Pete, I want to go faster!'

'You're only seven, Johnny. Fifty miles an hour is too fast for a seven-year-old.'

And 40mph isn't?

God I loved the seventies.

As enjoyable and as natural as my first experience in a kart had felt, I never thought for a moment that it was something I could do at home. For a start you needed a kart, and that August of 1971 was the first time any of us had ever laid eyes on one. We'd been to see some banger and caravan racing at Brands Hatch once, but that had as much to do with destruction as it did speed and agility, and was almost circus-like. Great fun, though. No, as far as I was concerned there were definitely no karts in Essex. It was a Cornish pastime.

Throughout the following year my theory concerning the natural habitat of karts was all but confirmed as the only time I ever saw one, let alone drove one, was in Cornwall. But despite being starved of the excitement karting had given me, including all those rushes of adrenalin which had been a completely new experience, I chose not to repeat my mini Le Mans the following year and decided to limit myself to just a few sessions. The logic was (it does take me occasionally) that because it was something I would only do on holiday, what would be the point in torturing myself? Do a few laps, have some fun, then walk away and forget about it. Actually, that's quite a mature attitude for a young 'un.

Not long after we arrived back from St Ives, after that second summer karting there, Mum suggested that karts may have been spotted outside Cornwall and that if she and Dad could find one, perhaps it might go some way to keeping little Johnny off the streets. This I found a bit puzzling, as little Johnny was never actually on the streets in the first place. I was quite a shy boy and tended to keep myself to myself, so I suppose they were trying to get me interested in something *before* I began to hang around bus stops and swear at old ladies. Either way, who was I to complain? I was going to get a kart.

Dad eventually found one for sale in the *Exchange & Mart*. It was in Redhill, which is close to Gatwick airport, and had been advertised by a local clergyman. We all climbed into the car and went down to see it one Saturday afternoon.

When we first saw the kart parked up in the vicar's garage we thought it might have been built by the man himself (we were clueless, remember), but His Reverence assured us that God's Go-kart, as I later christened it, had in fact been manufactured some time in the late 1950s or early 1960s. He didn't say by whom or in which country but one thing's for sure: there'd been little divine intervention at play in either its design or its build. It was quite an eccentric-looking thing, like something out of *Wacky Races*. The kart itself resembled an old bed-frame; the seat, which was solid iron, had been welded on to the chassis, and the wheels, which were small, narrow, and fitted with old Carlisle tyres, had been welded directly on to the axle. The fuel tank was situated just behind the driver's head, and at one point during its life it had been powered by two JLO engines. One of these was now in a carrier bag, which, when the vicar handed it to my dad, was accepted with an unconvincing cry of 'Ha! I'll soon have that fixed.' The other one was in good working order.

Since then I've seen photos of the great Graham Hill driving something similar, but on that Saturday none of us had any idea what we were looking at. What this vicar had been doing with the kart I didn't know. I had visions of him giving his sermon and then ripping off his dog collar and going wheel to wheel with some other ecclesiastical petrol-heads. We thought it best we take it off him. Not having the nerve to haggle with a clergyman, Dad handed over the £35 he was asking and off we went back to Romford.

I should stress that at this point (I'd only recently turned eight) I still had no desire either to race karts, watch Formula 1 or start stalking Jackie Stewart. I viewed the kart as something to thrash around in once every couple of weeks, something to help prevent me from turning into a juvenile delinquent. It would be the following year before I drove a kart in anger, and several months after that before I saw my first Grand Prix. Stalking Jackie Stewart would have to wait a bit longer than that – about twenty-five years to be exact. I'd get him, though.

My actual passion at the time, if you can call it that, was football. Was I any good at it? No, not really. I was too shy either to ask for the ball or even kick it very hard, and although I was the only left-footer in the team they always used to play me out on the right. Not much logic there. So, while all the other kids would be running around and screaming like hell for the ball, I'd be standing gingerly on the right wing, saying, 'Erm, excuse me, would you mind passing it to me, please? No? OK, that's fine.' Then, before I knew it, everyone would charge past and I'd be left standing there like a lemon. Not so much a shrinking violet, more a shrinking Herbert.

The teachers at my school also thought, like my mum, that I had the potential to go off the rails, which is why I started playing football in the first place. They thought I was becoming rebellious, when in fact I just found it very difficult to con-centrate. I wasn't capable of beating up a teacher any more than I was capable of throwing a piece of chalk, but I was even less capable of paying attention in class, and the teachers mistook this, understandably perhaps, for unruly behaviour. I suppose it was in a way, but it certainly wasn't intentional. If I stood up in class and worked – which I was often allowed to do – I was OK, but the moment I sat down that was it, I was away with the proverbial fairies.

'Stand up again, would you, Herbert? You're clearly no longer with us.'

'Yes, sir.'

Five minutes later, when my legs had grown tired I'd sit back down again, and drift off. When the teachers became really annoyed I'd be removed from the class and sent to one of the offices. Then, a few minutes later, in they'd come and I'd get a proper talking to (obviously I wouldn't pay any attention), after which I'd have to stand on my chair for a bit. It all sounds a bit bizarre, doesn't it? I suppose it was in a way. They just didn't know what to do with me.

In the end, as opposed to just tutting and making me stand on chairs, somebody thought it might be a good idea if I became involved in some kind of team sport. As I said, I was very shy and quiet back then so they probably thought I needed bringing out of my shell a bit, and perhaps I did. And so, without any further ado, I was forced on to the school football team. I was asked to take part in a practice match first and afterwards we all lined up so they could choose the team. The fact that my name was called out first did tend to arouse suspicion, especially as I'd been about as much use as Taki Inoue on a speed awareness course. Positive discrimination, I think they call it now, although at the time my team-mates only agreed with one half of the description. Discrimination, yes. Positive, most definitely not. 'What a load of bloody rubbish' was one comment, followed by 'But sir, he looks like a girl!'

The only thing that was going to stop me from getting beaten up was scoring a goal in my first match – and, would you believe it, I did exactly that. Just two minutes into the game I passed back to our goalie, and he wasn't there. Bugger.

I learned three new words that afternoon, and although I didn't know what they meant at the time I had a feeling that I should never, ever repeat them in front of my mum. Instinct, you see. We racing drivers live by it.

To be fair, I did manage to score one at the right end some time in the second half so to a certain extent I redeemed myself. It wasn't a pretty goal by any stretch of the imagination, but they all count. From memory I kicked the ball, it hit the goalie, bounced back out to me, I kicked it again, it hit the post, came back out again, and then went in off my knee. Lionel Messi, it was not. More Lionel Blair, really.

I remember somebody came up to me afterwards and said, 'You can go for your hat-trick now, John.' And so a footballing god was born.

Although I was admittedly often appalling on the ball – and it's quite important in the traditional game of Association foot-ball not to be – I was able to read a game very well indeed. In addition to having pretty good spatial awareness I could always position myself perfectly to make a pass. The passes didn't always reach their intended targets, but these skills – once again, none of which I even had to think about – just about kept me in the team and prevented the games teacher from being lynched.

What I never did manage to cultivate in football, besides ball control and other basic skills of the game, was that ruthless streak you need in pretty much any sport. Tackling always felt unnatural, and if I ever had the ball in front of goal I'd usually give it to somebody else and let them have a shot rather than have a go myself. It wasn't because I was terrified of missing. I just wasn't all that bothered.

With the benefit of hindsight, I probably had much of what is required to succeed in football: speed, agility, spatial aware-ness and an ability to read the game. But what I lacked, namely ruthlessness and skill, are as fundamental to that sport as they are to motor racing, so without them I was always going to be a bit lower division.

Luckily, in karting things were very different, although the tenacity, perseverance and ruthlessness I needed to augment my natural talent and enable me to progress developed over a period of time. Once it was there, however, it never left me.

In the mid-1970s, the nearest circuit to us was near Tilbury Docks, which is about twenty miles down the road from Romford, so after we got God's Go-kart we started going down there on a Saturday. Just like Uncle Pete did in Cornwall, Dad would fill it up and away I'd go. I remember coming down the straight on the first day we took it there when all of a sudden one of my wheels started to overtake me. I thought, *That wheel's bloody fast!* When I realized it was one of mine I looked round and saw that it had just sheared off. Fortunately Dad was able to weld it back on again so the pit stop only lasted about an hour, which was quite quick for Team Herbert.

The Tilbury track, like all of them back then, was jam-packed at the weekend, but there was only one kid on the circuit driving something you could have slept in. The rest of them all had karts with two-stroke engines and fat Goodyear tyres. That didn't matter, though. They were all practising for races that would take place the following day, whereas I was just letting off a bit of steam.

Gradually, however, as had happened in St Ives, the more people I had on the track with me the more competitive I became, and the more competitive I became the more tenacious and merciless I was behind the wheel. After a few months I was like a child possessed come Saturday morning, and the fact that everyone else on the track had more grip and more horsepower than I did simply galvanized me and made me even more determined.

One of the things we as a family always loved about karting

was the social side. To level things up a bit with Sarah, my sister, Mum and Dad had decided to buy her one of those little Monkey Bikes, so while I put in the laps on the track, she would tear around on that while Mum and Dad got to know the other parents. This, I think, is how they were persuaded to invest in a better kart. They could see that I really enjoyed it, and because it was fulfilling its remit of keeping me off the mean streets of downtown Romford they were agreeable when some of the other parents suggested an upgrade. There may also have been a touch of 'keeping up with the Joneses' involved, and why not? I was driving a prop from *Bedknobs and Broomsticks* that was only a few years off requiring a starting handle and, because I was quite good, I think they were curious to see what would happen if I had parity with the others.

In the end, Mum and Dad met a karter at Tilbury who wanted to pack it in; he was looking for a buyer for his kart, a Deavinson Sprint with a K88 engine. It cost Mum and Dad about £150, and when we went to collect it he ended up handing over all his trophies too. These went straight on to the shelves in my bedroom, and they helped to create just a little bit of aspiration. They looked great, but at the end of the day they weren't mine. Perhaps one day I could win a few of my own, then? One thing was for sure, though: with karting now about to take up even more of my and my family's time (and money) I could at last consign football to the bin. Poor old Don Revie must have been gutted.

The most noticeable difference between the Deavinson Sprint and the bed-frame, apart from performance, was size. Even though it was at the smaller end of what was now available, the Sprint was quite a lot bigger than God's Go-kart and one or two adjustments had to be made. I was a shortarse – still am, in fact, there's no use beating about the bush – so the first thing Dad had to do was put tobacco tins just in front of the pedals so that my feet could rest on them. Then, to stop my heels slipping off the tins, he made some little aluminium guards to go around them. This, by the way, was after he and Mum had pushed my seat as far forward as it would go and then stuffed it with all kinds of soft furnishings. My God, it was comfy. It was like going to bed!

Trophies weren't the only supplementary benefits that came with the new kart, by the way. It had a number on the front when we got it, one that I decided to stick with, and which served me well throughout my years as a racing driver. That number, for anyone who doesn't know, is 69. It was only when I was well into my teens that its well-known sexual connotation was made aware to me (only verbally, I might add). Back then I was absolutely mortified, whereas today I think it's hilarious.

The first ever suggestion that I should try my hand at racing the new kart happened one Saturday at Tilbury not long after we got it. The idea came from the father of a boy called Jackie Brown, who at the time was one of the biggest talents in junior karting. His dad was a motorsport fanatic and he knew a thing or two. 'He's pretty good you know, Bob,' he said to my dad. 'Why don't you get him in a race?'

'But he's not even eleven yet,' Dad responded. 'You have to be twelve, don't you?'

'Don't worry about that. Just hand in the licence.'

'What about the birth certificate? You're supposed to hand that in too, aren't you?'

'Just say you forgot it. That's what most people do.'

If only Jackie Brown's dad had known what he was doing – unleashing a Herbert into the hitherto contented world of competitive karting.

'Really?' said Dad. 'And you think that would work?'

'Why not?' he replied. 'It's worth a try.'

You were supposed to get a signature from the clerk on your licence after every race but you could only get that signature if you'd handed in your child's birth certificate. Luckily for us, one of my uncles had decided to take up karting about the same time as me, so when he got the clerk's signature, my dad would then trace it on to my licence.

Sorry, I meant to say forge – Dad would *forge* the signature on to my licence.

I think you had to get a total of six signatures to get your full junior licence back then and we managed to get those, or something resembling them, in one week! It was a bit of a baptism of fire to tell you the truth, doing six races in a week, but I loved it. The big boys were all at the front and as a novice I was somewhere at the back. I got a couple of trophies though, for sixth place, and again it all came easily to me. There were still no thought processes involved, and I never once attempted to familiarize myself with the nuances of a new track. I just jumped in, raced my backside off, slid around a bit, then got out and went to play with the other kids. Fear was still a complete stranger to me. In fact, the first time I remember experiencing any fear as a driver was when I entered Formula 3000. And it's not as if there wasn't anything to be scared of on a karting racetrack. If you've got twenty-eight karts all on cold tyres, accidents are almost guaranteed, and that's not taking into account mechanical problems, the weather, or driver error. There was very little protection too, so once you were out there pretty much anything could happen. But even when I did have the odd accident it never bothered me. I just got up, got back in if I could, and carried on. I was completely unhindered by any distractions.

The only time I ever thought *I'm not sure about this* was one weekend at Beccles in Suffolk, which is now the Ellough Park Raceway. These days it's quite a challenging track, but back then it was relatively straightforward and we fancied an easy weekend. The trouble was, everyone else seemed to have had exactly the same idea, so by the time the Herberts arrived at the old airfield it was jam-packed. Although daunted, it didn't take me long to come round and in the end I came a very respectable fourth, which, bearing in mind I'd probably only had my full fraudulent junior licence a few weeks, wasn't at all bad. I was also just turning eleven, remember, and the vast majority of boys I was driving against were between thirteen and fifteen. There were other youngsters present of course, and from what Jackie Brown's dad had said there could well have been one or two other illegal minors, but although modesty forbids me from going on about it, I was absolutely bloody brilliant and the best by a mile.

People often say that crime doesn't pay, that if you have committed some kind of transgression during your lifetime the chances are it'll catch up with you. Well, I'm afraid to say that Bob Herbert, Romford's premier master forger, could only evade the authorities for so long. His short-lived but nevertheless grubby little life of crime finally came to an abrupt end shortly after a weekend meeting at the now defunct track in Morecambe.

Morecambe was essentially a links track as it was based right on the cliff edge, and Dad won't mind me telling you that this terrified him. On one side of the track, running along the cliff, was a dirt lane and if you didn't manage to make it round the hairpin there was only a row of tyres and a picket fence separating you and the Irish Sea.

'You're not racing here, John,' said Dad. 'Half of it's a bloody death trap.'

'Aww, come on, Dad. We've come all this way. I want to race!'

You couldn't meet a more careful man than my dad, but even though the idea of my having an accident didn't grab him much, the idea of my whingeing at him all day appealed even less. So before he could inspect the rest of the track and have us all head for home I set about trying to change his mind.

'Oh, all right then,' he gasped after five minutes of gentle but continuous carping. 'We'll see how it goes. Just promise me you'll shut up.'

'Yes, Dad.'

Job done.

Because we were now committed to travelling quite a lot, Mum and Dad had splashed out on an old ten-foot caravan which we used to take with us to meetings. These always lasted the full weekend, so in order to make the first heat we often had to arrive on the Friday night.

When you consider the advantages of me karting competitively, the career that came after it speaks for itself, but there were certainly plenty of other pluses. For a start we ended up spending a lot of time together as a family, which might not have been the case had we been stuck at home. Sarah and I would have been off playing with our friends a lot of the time and even Mum and Dad might have been off doing their own thing. I'm not saying it was all perfect, and they do say that familiarity can breed contempt, but for the majority of the time we all got on well and we had some great times together.

The meeting up at Morecambe was a big event, and some of the more experienced senior runners even had gearboxes. In fact, I'm pretty sure it was an international meeting for the seniors, and because it was all just that little bit more professional, the attitudes towards things like rules and regulations were more stringent. People had been eyeing me up all weekend, and although nobody actually came up and said that I couldn't race, a lot of questions were being asked.

Looking back, how the hell we got away with it for as long as we did I'll never know. I was small for my age – I was probably small for half my age – and because of my slight frame and long golden locks I looked more like Cinderella than I did a mini James Hunt. One report from that Morecambe meeting read 'all

21

you could see was a helmet flying round. The body underneath it was too small to be visible.' The only reason you could see the helmet was because we couldn't find one small enough. Dad had bought the smallest one he could lay his hands on but because it was still so big Mum had had to cut out the hood from a very thick winter coat and I used that as a balaclava. Even then, my head rattled around in it like a pea in a whistle.

A few days after Morecambe, where I finished top eight in the juniors, Dad received a letter from the RAC asking to see a copy of my birth certificate. The chap who ran the Morecambe event had written to them expressing his concerns about my age, so they were obliged to follow it up. He probably regrets not doing it now (crime never really leaves you), but what Dad should have done is Tipp-Ex out the original birth date, change it to something that would have worked, photocopy the birth certificate, and then send them the copy. They hadn't asked for the original so we'd have been home and dry. I think Dad thought about doing it but chickened out. To be honest, if it were me, I'd have done exactly the same.

Without any kind of credible (or legal) riposte, Dad had to hold up his hands and tell the RAC that he wasn't able to produce the document, and so, after a twelve-week trial at the Old Bailey costing millions, the RAC banned me from competing until I came of age. It wasn't so much a punishment when you think about it; they simply asked us to abide by the rules. They did, however, write to every track in the country asking them not to accept John Herbert's entry until 25 June 1976.

At last, we were infamous!

Two

NOT BEING ABLE TO compete at karting was a complete pain in the arse. My confidence had been growing almost daily and that third place at Morecambe had been a revelation. They'd had some of the best juniors in the country there and I'd more than held my own. Then again, if Dad hadn't played 'hide the birth certificate' in the first place I wouldn't even have been there, so I suppose I should have counted myself lucky. All that newfound tenacity and determination must have been getting to me. I now felt like a bona fide racer and had become competitive in thought, word and deed. I'd been a hair's breadth away from winning at Morecambe, so even though I'd been racing there illegally, being banned on the cusp of your first win was enormously frustrating. Patience may well be a virtue but it's not something we racing drivers are known for. The other downer was that I'd miss out on the social life, and it wasn't just me who was going to suffer, the whole family would. Travelling to karting events had become a big part of the Herberts' lives and we all loved it.

'I'll tell you what,' Dad said one day. 'Why don't I take up racing instead? Just while John's suspended. That way we can keep going to the events.'

Mum wasn't convinced. 'Don't be silly, Bob. You can't drive a kart.'

And with that, the gauntlet was thrown down. Within about a week Dad had gone out and bought himself an old Zip Kart complete with a helmet, some overalls, a balaclava and some gloves.

'What do you think about that then?' he said to Mum. 'I'll show you who can't drive a kart.'

He wasn't kidding.

And so, as opposed to simply parking up the caravan and waiting for time to tick by, we went straight back on the road. I continued to practise as often as I could so as not to get rusty, and Dad took over the racing reins. We didn't go to quite as many meetings but it was good enough. The first one I remember us attending was at Nuthampstead in Hertfordshire. Dad spun off at the hairpin on every single lap yet still ended up coming third. I've got no idea how it happened. He tried to make out that it was all part of some grand strategy, but I think he was just as shocked as we were.

After that we went to a meeting at Rye House in Hertfordshire. These days they've got a very professional set-up there but back then it was just like all the others – basic. I remember Dad had been lapped in one of the heats and as he came down the straight another kart wanted to pass, but instead of just pulling to one side he went straight off the track, through some bales of hay, and almost slew the bloody starter. Dad had a ginger beard at the time, and when we eventually found him all we could see was hay, the ginger beard and some flags. I think the absolute world of my dad but when it came to racing he had no natural talent whatsoever. He was just awful!

A couple of weeks later, when Dad was racing at Tilbury, I decided to start smoking, only to stop smoking about ten minutes later. Because I wasn't racing I had quite a bit of time on my hands at meetings and when one of the other kids suggested a few of us try a smoke, I said OK. Once again this was the 1970s and back then smoking was not only common, it was cool. After sneaking into the greasy spoon we went round the tables, pinched all the dog ends out of the ashtrays (classy, eh?), then sneaked into the back of an empty truck in the adjoining scrapyard. Ah, the glamour of motorsport.

One of the boys I was with was obviously quite a seasoned puffer and kept on blowing the smoke out through his nose. I'd seen people do it on *The Sweeney* but never in real life.

'How do you do that?' I enquired.

'It's easy,' he said. 'You just suck on the end like this, breathe in, and then breathe out through your nose.'

'Right then, I'll give it a go.'

So I lit up a dog end, took a big suck, and breathed in. All going well so far. The trouble is I then forgot to breathe out and ended up swallowing it. According to a mate, within about five seconds my complexion went from a healthy reddish colour to yellow, and then finally to green, just like a traffic light. God only knows what my stomach thought but it wasn't at all happy. The taste was just hideous, and before you could say 'pass me a bucket' I vomited all over my brand-new trainers.

'That's not supposed to happen,' one of the boys said.

No shit, Sherlock!

As much as I regretted puking on my pumps, it was the entire incident that put me off smoking for life and even today the smell makes me heave a bit.

The one other event of note that happened during my enforced sabbatical was going to watch my first ever British Grand Prix in July 1976 at Brands Hatch. These days that particular track obviously evokes some pretty extreme emotions, but back then it was different. That was the day I got the F1 bug and decided that, come hell or high water – or, unbeknown to me at the time, my feet almost being ripped off – I would one day compete in Formula 1. It was real hair-on-the-back-of-your-neck stuff.

Until then the extent of my professional ambitions had been to work on a lathe or a milling machine: I was never what you'd call academically inclined and metalwork was the only thing I was any good at. Becoming an F1 driver just about nudged it into second place, though.

I don't remember a great deal about the race to be honest, save for the fact that James Hunt won the race, but was later disqualified by the FIA after an appeal by Ferrari. I remember him signing autographs both before and after the race – fag in gob of course, and flanked by a couple of models, holding a glass of bubbly in one hand and a pen in the other. How could you not become hooked after witnessing that? He really was living the dream, albeit an occasionally rude one.

Now I'd turned twelve I was allowed to compete again and by the time I got back in the kart I was champing at the proverbial bit. The only problem was the financial side of things. Competing in the Junior National Championship meant undertaking regular trips the length and breadth of the country, so as well as having to fork out for everything associated with the kart, my parents were also having to spend quite a bit of money on things like petrol, not to mention general maintenance on the family car. Prior to that we'd always got by on a shoestring with regard to the kart. Apart from sending it to Mick Fullerton, brother of the famous racer Terry, to get it tuned occasionally, we'd been able to cut all kinds of corners. Whenever we used to go testing, for example, Dad would go through the bins and pick out all the tyres people had thrown away. We might not have had much money but there were plenty of people in karting who did and as soon as the inside edge became a little bit worn, many of the drivers, or rather their well-heeled benefactors, would simply chuck the tyres away and put on a new set. All Dad did was mount them the other way round. It wasn't perfect by any means, but it was a great way of saving a few quid. Chains, too, would often be thrown away willy-nilly; Dad would gather them all up, take them to pieces, then link up all the best bits. Running a kart recreationally, however, is quite different to running one competitively, and with me now back and on the brink of achieving something, we could no longer afford to skimp. Dad's attitude was 'if you're going to compete, you have to do it properly', so we needed to get some help. (Having said that, the tyre–recycling operation did continue for some time. It was just too bloody tempting.)

While we were up at the Morecambe meeting Dad had been approached by a man called Bill Sisley who sold karts and parts out of a shop in Swanley in Kent. Bill had said to Dad that he thought I had quite a lot of potential, so when Dad decided that he could no longer afford to fund things on his own he tracked Bill down to his shop and paid him a visit. He took me along for the ride; I remember standing next to him at the counter. Being neither biased nor delusional, Dad proceeded to inform Bill that since Morecome I'd progressed so much that I was now the best driver in the country and that it was only a matter of time before I became world champion, if only he could find a backer. To be fair to Bill he managed to prevent his sides from splitting, and instead of laughing us out of the shop suggested a test over at Tilbury. 'Let's see the boy in action, then I'll make a decision,' he said, adding, 'He is a boy, isn't he?'

Well, you couldn't say fairer than that. Bill did all of his testing at Tilbury, and because I knew the track like the back of my hand I was sure I could impress him.

I think you can tell in about a minute whether somebody's any good or not, but what you can't make an immediate call on is whether they'll be able to make a career out of driving. Luckily for me, Bill thought I had potential, and because I was still young I hadn't picked up too many bad habits and could be easily moulded.

'Look,' he said to Dad, 'my brother-in-law, who used to be an engineer, wants to design a new kart and I've agreed to build it for him. We're going to need somebody to help develop this new kart and do all the testing, so that's my proposition. It won't cost you a penny because my brother-in-law and I will be funding the operation, and young John will get more kart-time than he could ever wish for.'

From then on I spent many of my waking hours at Bill's. When I wasn't working on the kart I'd help out in the shop a bit – not that I was any use. I didn't speak much in those days and apparently that's quite important when you're serving people. We used to get the likes of Riccardo Patrese and Andrea de Cesaris coming into the shop when they were racing at Brands Hatch. They were mad-keen karters in those days and would come to Bill's for spares to take back home with them. Andrea, who tragically died in a motorcycle accident in 2014, used to have a nervous facial twitch, and every so often his eyes would roll up until just the whites showed. Funnily enough, the twitch stopped when he gave up racing. It used to terrify me at the time and I don't remember ever saying a word to either him or Riccardo. I suppose I was a little bit star-struck, but I was also very shy. Instead of rubbing my hands together and saying, 'And what can I do for you two gentlemen?' I'd just stand there like a lemon with my mouth wide open and wait for Bill to come through.

The kart in question was christened the Tarantella (after an Italian dance, I'm told), but, despite being quite quick and us winning a few races with it, it had one fundamental flaw. Back then nearly all small kart chassis were straightforward ladder chassis which the kart's original inventor, Art Ingels, had designed back in 1956, but the tubing on the Tarantella came right into the middle of the chassis where it was welded on to a box before continuing out to the stub axles and the front wheels. The concept worked really well because it flexed, and we had a couple of struts, one either side, which gave it a bit of stiffness at the same time. The only weakness was where the tubing went into the box. It used to split around the weld during a race, and the Tarantella would sometimes become Tarantellas. Surbiton was the first track I remember it happening. I was going down the straight, and as I broke for the corner I felt the front of the kart begin to pull away from me. It was like some kind of clown's car. We persevered with it for a while but eventually Bill's brother-in-law began losing interest so we started looking at alternatives. Or rather Bill did.

Help came in the form of a friend of Bill's called Vic Gray. He was in engineering and had a little factory near Ashford that was sitting empty. 'I'll design them and then you make them and sell them' was, I think, what Vic suggested, so off we went again. The two karts we ended up producing were the Kestrel, which was 100cc, and the Cobra, which was 135cc. Both karts were big successes and very soon Bill was selling about five hundred a year of each. I say *me* ended up producing them because as soon as I could leave school I went to work for Bill as an apprentice engineer and started manufacturing components for the Kestrels and Cobras. Unfortunately, and despite my initial enthusiasm at school, I was about as much use on a lathe as my dad was in a kart, and after producing some stub axles with, shall we say, questionable shaft diameter I was put back in a kart and told never to darken the factory floor again.

Once again modesty should forbid me from even speculating about why those karts were so successful, but to save time let's just say that it was all down to my testing and development skills. Actually, that's not strictly true. Those karts were just very well designed and very well built; but because I'd been spending so much of my time in them I'd started to learn one or two tricks, the most famous of which was counter-balancing a kart on two wheels. We used to have some of those old-fashioned petrol pumps at the factory and after Bill had drawn a figure of eight through and around them I'd make my approach, tip the kart on two wheels and trace the figure of eight. According to Bill, the only other person he'd ever heard of who could do that was a driver called Roberto Moreno, who went on to drive for Benetton in 1991, in between my two stints there. Everybody used to stand back in amazement when I did that, but at the risk of sounding either big-headed or blasé it was all quite easy. There's no use pretending it wasn't.

I was getting noticed, and in 1978 I was selected to represent Great Britain at the Junior World Karting Championship in Luxembourg. None of the family had ever been abroad before, so instead of me going over there with somebody else we hitched up the old caravan to the back of the car and used it as an excuse to do a bit of globetrotting. Not that we saw a great deal of anything. It was the same as a normal weekend in the UK: you arrived, you practised, you raced, and then you made your way home. I should stress that Mum and Dad were still an integral part of what was going on, Dad especially. Although not a natural racer, he now knew his way round an engine and could mix it with the best of them. I said before that the vast majority of racing drivers are a product of either enthusiastic parents or former drivers. Well, even though my introduction to karting happened by accident, if it hadn't been for Mum, Dad and, to be fair, Uncle Pete, identifying my talent and then nurturing it I would never have ended up working with people like Damon. The blame has to lie somewhere, I'm afraid.

Competing in the world championship having only just turned fourteen was a real eye-opener, and I had an absolute bloody nightmare. It wasn't so much chalk and cheese as spaghetti and fish and chips. I'll explain. Back then, the Italians were probably the best in the world at karting and had been for a very long time. They had the best karts, the best drivers, everything. It may seem like I'm being a bit unfair on the British contingent, and we certainly had some big talents – people like Terry Fullerton and Mickey Allen – but the fact is that from a development point of view they were just a little bit more advanced than we were. That was in no small measure down to money. The Italians seemed to be dripping in it. When we discovered, when we eventually got to Luxembourg, that they even had different engines for qualifying we almost packed up and went home. Qualifying engines, for heaven's sake! That was just *so* Italian. From where we were standing their set-up was more akin to Formula 1 than karting, and I remember feeling just a little bit intimidated.

Dad, though, was in his element, and his frugality went into overdrive. In addition to engines, the Italians also had qualifying tyres – something even F1 didn't have then – and they were manufactured by companies like Dunlop and Bridgestone. Dad used to call them 'paper tyres' because they only seemed to use them for one lap. He was convinced that they were good for one or two more, so in an attempt to prove his theory he went off to liberate a few. Sure enough, he was absolutely right and the tyres were OK. In fact, compared to what we had they were a bloody revelation. The trouble was, the Italians also had the racing equivalent of this new generation of tyre and they were probably worth four or five seconds a lap to them. We'd never seen anything like it before. In the UK you had two choices: Carlisle, which were hard, cheap and generally not that quick, or Goodyear, which were more expensive but a little bit better. They were all so bloody hard, though; we could make a single set last at least a season. Personally I always had Carlisles on the

31

front and Goodyears on the back, but a few months after the junior world championship a man called Jim Cruttenden, the owner of Dartford Karting, gave me some of these new tyres, but only the rears. They had so much grip that with the rock-hard Carlisles on the front I could hardly bloody turn.

I eventually made it to the semi-final in Luxembourg but I was way back on the grid and certainly didn't trouble any of our Italian friends. It had been an experience, though, and one I was eager to repeat, just perhaps on a more equal footing. I didn't care what I drove, just so long as I was competitive.

In 1979 I won the junior national championship, but not before I endured yet more disappointment abroad. I'd have to wait a bit longer for that equal footing. This time I was selected to compete at the European Junior Championship which took place in September, and we had to travel to Fano in north-east Italy. I was rather hoping I could omit telling you where I finished in this final but in the interests of consistency I've been told I must. I came twenty-fifth. Do you mind if we move on now?

The following month we travelled up to Felton in Northumberland for the British Junior National Championship where, despite eventually winning the title, things were far from straightforward for me. Then again, things rarely are. My biggest rival at the time was a boy called Simon Sutton who was a decent driver, and we got on OK. I was the favourite, him second, and after making mincemeat of the rest of the field in the heats we easily bagged the front row for the final, with him on pole. Fortunately I managed to jump him at the start and by the halfway point I was well in control.

Then, just a few laps later, Simon decided that if he couldn't pass me using conventional means he'd have to try something more drastic, and just as I reached the hairpin, where the pits were, he nudged me and I spun off. Actually it was probably a bit more than a nudge, but the result was the same. Seeing red, I jumped out of the kart, took off my helmet and began berating him. 'You idiot! What a stupid thing to do!' Then I suddenly realized that (a) he couldn't hear me, and (b) as I was shouting the odds he was disappearing into the distance. Quick as a flash I got back in the kart, asked one of the dads to start me off again, and then proceeded to try and make my way back through the field. I rejoined the race in about sixth but before too long I was back up to second. I ran out of laps in the end but it was touch and go. Still fuming, I followed Simon back towards the pits, and when I saw he'd parked up I deliberately drove into the back of him. Cue lots of argy-bargy and a little bit more swearing.

In the end it went to the RAC, and this time, instead of banning me for twelve months they declared me the 1979 100cc Junior National Karting Champion. Simon's move had been deemed illegal, so that was that. I'd had things like this happen to me before, quite a few times, and I remember starting to get a bit fed up with it – hence my reaction when Simon took me off. He was the one who unleashed the beast, so to speak. I did attempt to give like-for-like on a few occasions but every time I did try to nudge somebody back I ended up going off with them. Rightly or wrongly, my decision to drive cleanly stayed with me throughout my career and I've got no regrets.

There will always be a debate as to whether that kind of thing has a place in racing, but in my opinion it does not. Winning at all costs is something we all have drummed into us but what differs from driver to driver is what constitutes that phrase 'at all costs'. I appreciate that people often do things in the heat of the moment so things aren't always clear cut. I get all that. Some actions, though, are impossible to dress up as anything other than gaining an unfair advantage and that's what I have a problem with. The stock-in-trade defence for drivers who take it too far is 'they wanted it more', but I'm afraid that's just drivel. If I won a race but knew I'd done so having gained an unfair advantage I'd feel like a fraud, not a winner. I've never put myself in that position, partly because I'm just no bloody good at it but mainly because it doesn't sit well with me, but I know plenty of drivers who have. What's more, those who do it rarely seem to have a problem with their actions. I find that very strange. Anyway, rant over. There'll be more on this later anyway.

It was in 1980 that I really started to come of age as a driver. This happened at the British Junior National Championship, and as I was the reigning champ, there were an awful lot of eyes on me. Not that I had any idea about that. I was still a pretty bashful young man and although I was never rude to people, if I didn't have to speak to them I wouldn't. I never read the press either so I was always oblivious to any outside opinions.

One of the turning points for me, even though I was still a junior, had been my introduction to something which, without any exaggeration, transformed my life – gears. The first thing I ever drove with a gearbox was a 125cc kart and that had taken place in late 1979 courtesy of a mate of Bill's. We were up at Fulbeck in Lincolnshire and this chap, who raced 125cc karts and was a big supporter of mine, called me over.

'Do you fancy a spin, John?' he said.

I didn't need asking twice.

Once again I had no instructions on how to drive a kart with gears, I just got in and worked it out for myself. What a feeling! It was a revelation, and not just from the point of view of speed. Gears gave you options, and discovering these for the first time was a thrill, a gift that kept on giving. Once I'd mastered the basics I began tearing up the track – I didn't even have to think about it. I managed to catch a glimpse of this friend of Bill's once or twice as I whizzed round – the grin he was wearing was almost as big as mine.

'The sooner you're a bloody senior the better,' he said when I finally got out.

Knowing now what was awaiting me, I couldn't have agreed more.

Anyway, back to Clay Pigeon Raceway in Dorset, the venue of the 1980 British Junior National Championship. There were three heats followed by a semi-final and then a final, and the field was massive, about forty karts. Things started going well for me right from the first heat where I finished in the late teens, and even though that's where I started, in the second heat I managed to finish a more than respectable second behind Kevin Warner.

The third heat was a disaster as I wasn't able to finish the race because of an engine malfunction, which meant I started the semi-final from close to the back of the grid. It was there that I first remember experiencing an almost overwhelming feeling of, for want of a better word, bravado. If I had to translate into words how I was feeling it would be something like this: 'Right, then, I'm going to have the lot of you.'

The thing is, I very nearly did. I was furious that the engine had failed but elated that I'd done so well, and it was a perfect combination. From the start I was like a man-child possessed. On the first lap alone I got myself into the mid-teens. Although I'd had that ruthless streak that a driver needs for a while now, I never really thought ahead in a race, which is one of the reasons why I'm saying this was where I started coming of age. The driving itself still required little in the way of thought but my head was now full of questions about how I was going to take the rest of the field. I started noticing the mistakes those in front of me were making as well as calculating their strengths and weaknesses. If somebody tended to brake early going into a corner, I'd pick up on it and think to myself, *That's where you can take him.* The performance of my kart, too, was something I was now constantly aware of. Before now I'd just driven hell for leather and the nuances of either a driver or a track meant little to me. I wasn't totally ignorant of them but they didn't feature highly on my cognitive radar. Having natural driving ability's all well and good but unless you possess a keen sense of awareness and can read a race as a whole, it's worth nothing. Master all three, however, and you've got a good chance of making it.

By the final lap I'd managed to get into second, and as I took the chequered flag I was probably only a tenth behind. What's more, the winner's kart broke down less than halfway through the slowing-down lap, so one more bloody lap and I'd have won. You see what I mean about coming of age? Everything had moved on a step. Don't ask me how it happened because I couldn't tell you. All I know is that my once fairly dormant brain was now, come race day, like a mini pit wall.

Incidentally, I can recall one driver in particular who was always meticulous when it came to details, and his name was John Weatherley. While everyone else was tucked up in bed he'd either be working on his kart or studying the track or some reports on the other drivers. This used to drive his girlfriend bananas, and it all came to a head one night prior to a meeting when we were seniors. John had been out tinkering with his kart but because he'd refused to come back and go to bed at a reasonable hour his girlfriend had locked the caravan. John, who was obviously perturbed by this course of action, decided to get in his Transit van and tow the caravan at full speed down a track near the site that was about as flat as the surface of the moon. Then, once he'd done that, he did it again. Until then I'd had no idea caravans had such terrific suspension. As well as what I assume were cups and plates smashing all over the place I could also hear these faint cries of 'John, you idiot, stop the van!' When he eventually returned to the pitch and did as he'd been asked to do, the caravan door opened and out fell his girlfriend followed by half the contents of the caravan, at which point John got in and locked the door behind him.

The most successful year I had in karting was 1982, and there were two particular events that made it one to remember. The first, which took place at Fulbeck, was the British Championship. This was one of my first big meetings as a senior and the only thing that made me nervous, although just slightly, was seeing and competing against legends such as Terry Fullerton and Mickey Allen. They were two of the best-known drivers in the world at the time, not just in Britain, and unbeknown to me they'd been paying me quite a bit of attention. In fact, according to Bill Sisley, Terry had been on the track timing me at one of my first ever senior meetings, and according to him he'd looked concerned.

There were obviously drivers who had talent in the juniors, but the difference between that and driving as a senior was, in every sense – mentally, physically and mechanically – men versus boys. I'd had a promising start to my senior career, however, and despite the big names and what was at stake nothing phased me. After a bit of a threat from Richard Weatherley and Terry Fullerton, I hung on to become what was then the youngest ever 135cc British champion in the International class. I was driving a Cobra, of course, as built by Sisley Karting. Bill was never what you'd call an emotional man, and like me he's quite shy, but on that day at Fulbeck I could have sworn I saw a corner of his mouth move north.

The second event took place at Kalmar in Sweden, where Ayrton Senna, who was then dominating the Formula Ford Championship before going on to dominate Formula 3 the following year, returned to karting one more time in an attempt to win just about the only title that ever eluded him, the world championship.

I remember starting that championship quite well in free practice and was eighteenth after the time trials. Once again, though, Sisley Karting was an independent outfit and our budget compared to the others' was minuscule. We turned up with three sets of tyres which had to see us through everything, from the time trials to the final. Fortunately Dad was only too happy to go on another liberation mission, and he didn't let us down.

I think I was twenty-fourth after the final heat, which was a miracle really as I'd had a collision late on with a Finnish driver called Ari Karhu that put me right at the back of the field. By the end of the semi-final I was up to eleventh, and with less than two laps to go of the final I sat a fairly astonishing seventh. I might well have made it into sixth had it not been for my chain snaking. That was a massive wrench as seventh for a young Brit with no money would have been a massive achievement. In the end I was classified eighteenth – still not bad given the circumstances. A British karting legend by the name of Mike Wilson, who ended up a six-time world champion, topped the podium.

The core skills karting teaches you, from basics such as learning racing lines through to the more complicated and involved skills I've mentioned, are as important as anything else you'll ever learn as a racing driver and have been the cornerstone to many an F1 world champion's career. Ayrton Senna, Alain Prost, Nigel Mansell, Michael Schumacher, Jenson Button, Lewis Hamilton, Sebastian Vettel – they all started off in karting. There are some exceptions, such as James Hunt and Niki Lauda, both of whom learned their craft racing Minis, and Damon Hill, who started off on motorbikes, but they're few and far between. Formula 1 owes karting a lot, and I for one will always have a profound respect for people like Bill Sisley – men and women who often stay in the sport for life and whose main ambition is to discover and nurture the next generation of drivers – because without them, not only would I not have had a career in motorsport, but we may never have witnessed some, or even any, of the aforementioned champions. Not a pleasant thought, is it?

Before we move on from my seven-year stint in karting to single-seater cars, I just want to tell you about an off-the-track incident that happened right at the end of my karting career. The reason I've decided to put it in is because it goes completely against my personality, and when it happened it was a big surprise to me.

We'd been to a meeting at a track called Wombwell, which is near Barnsley, and afterwards had decided to go to the local pub which was just over a nearby railway line. I was with six or seven fellow drivers including Lee Cranmer and Paul Dryden, and after we'd been there an hour or so a few of the locals came in. From then on the atmosphere began to change and what had started as a relaxing post-race drink was in danger of turning into something a little bit unsavoury.

We had two girls with us who were sisters of two of the drivers, and after a little bit of verbal jousting between us and the locals, one of them made a pass at one of the girls. From that point on it went nuclear.

Now, if somebody had asked me beforehand what I'd do in the event of a big punch-up, I'd probably have answered, 'Walk quietly away and let them get on with it.' What took place was diametrically opposed to this scenario. When the brawl began to unfold, instead of putting down my drink, shaking my head and making for the exit, I jumped on a table, assumed the position of a ninja warrior and began kicking and punching anyone I didn't immediately recognize. I even jumped on the back of somebody at one point. It was a side of me I hadn't known existed. I have to be pushed a very, very long way before I lose my temper. But if you ever do see me standing on a table somewhere, run like hell.

Three

AT THE RISK OF sounding like a popular 1970s bread commercial, my journey to and from Bill's factory each day, which I made by pushbike, was a sixty-mile round trip, and although I've been a keen cyclist since then I have to admit that at the time I got bloody fed up with it. You can have too much of a good thing, and my God, was I saddle sore. Incidentally, had I been a little bit more proactive about implementing any good ideas I had while cycling I could well be a billionaire today, as on the way to Bill's there was a recycling plant, but the only thing they processed was paper. Every morning I used to look at that place as I whizzed by and think, *Recycling . . . you get it for free and then make money out of it. Why don't we do it with everything?* Just imagine . . . I could have been as rich as Bernie Ecclestone.

What I needed at this point in my life was a car, and not just one for getting me to and from work. I was in my late teens and I'd won just about everything I reasonably could in a kart, so the time had come to move on. The question was, where? My parents didn't have any rich relatives on their deathbeds, and the extent of our ambitions in the sponsorship world, outside of Bill, had been blagging a caravan battery from a company in Dagenham. Not exactly a five-year deal with a blue-chip, is it?

One day Bill sat me down and outlined all the options in detail, and then suggested a possible way forward. He'd recently been made an offer on a unit he owned at Brands Hatch that was used for manufacturing karts, and the company that had made the offer had money behind them. The man who owned what would eventually be called Valour Racing had bought the unit because his daughter wanted to take up karting and he needed somebody to show her the ropes. 'Get in with him and that could be your answer' is what Bill was saying, and that's exactly what happened: I taught this man's daughter how to drive and he set me up in a Sparton Formula Ford 1600.

I did manage to get a test in a Formula Ford car just prior to working with Valour, but unlike my first experiences in a kart, which had all been positive, this had felt a little bit unnatural. I know it doesn't exactly scream *safety*, but one of the things I really liked about karts was the fact that you were completely unencumbered. Yes, you were open to the elements a bit and there were times when that could work against you, but to go from having complete and utter freedom to being surrounded by bodywork and mirrors was more than a little disconcerting and at first I was all for getting straight out again.

After being instructed to desist from behaving like (and I quote) a 'big girl's blouse', I took a deep breath, pulled myself together and started up the engine. This just made it worse. We used to have an old Transit van that was used for lugging the kart around the country, a real bone-shaker, and at first it felt just like that. It was awful. After enquiring as to why a car might feel like a £200 Transit van and being told once again, although with less patience, that I should pull myself together and start the bloody test, I put the car in gear, took another deep breath, and set off on my first ever lap in a single-seater.

The chaps running the test at Brands Hatch, which included Vic Gray, told me afterwards that as I'd driven off into the distance they'd tried to have a little wager on how many laps I might manage, but before they could place any money on the timing of my inevitable demise, I came off. I remember going into Paddock Hill Bend in fourth, but as I dipped the clutch and tried to put it into third I managed to lock up the wheels. One minute I'm an aspiring motor-racing driver with a half-share in a Transit and the next I'm, well, just a bit of an idiot. That's how I felt at least. This wasn't a learning curve, it was an almighty baptism of fire, hell, brimstone and just about anything else you can think of that isn't very pleasant. Until then I'd had it all my own way. For me, it was like going from wearing a nice pair of soft Italian shoes to an old pair of damp wellies. To use a technical term, I arsed it up like a good 'un.

These days, if you manage to graduate from karting there are all kinds of simulators and tools to help you on the way, but back then the only tool you had, apart from your skills as a driver, was trial and error. If you made a mistake, you put it right, but you had to *learn* from that experience and make sure it didn't happen again. That was the key because the faster you learned, the quicker you progressed. I know it all seems like blindingly obvious stuff, but without the benefit of either technology or tuition that was the extent of our schooling. You ask anyone from that generation or before and they'll tell you the same. I'm certainly not saying that the old way was better, by the way, but what I will say is that when you master something from a standing start using nothing but your intuition and some perseverance, it galvanizes you like nothing else.

Sitting there, stationary, just off the inside of the track at Paddock I certainly needed galvanizing, although my testing committee seemed to be far keener on pulverizing. 'Bit of wheel lock changing down, eh?' one of them said. 'I take it you haven't mastered heel-toe shifting yet?'

I was just about to say 'What's that?' when I realized how that might look. 'No, still working on it,' I said. 'I'll get it, though. Right, I'm off again.'

I ended up being about three or four seconds off the pace by the end of the test and although it wasn't what I'd either wanted or expected I was desperate to do it again. Sure, I'd found it bloody difficult, but that's what I mean about trial and error. Some progress, however inconsequential it may seem, is better than none at all, and you have to concentrate on the positives and work through negatives. When the next test at Brands came along I was just two seconds off the pace, and by the time I was ready to make my competitive debut, at the 1983 Formula Ford Festival, the gap was under a second.

The Formula Ford Festival, held every year at the end of the season at Brands Hatch, started in 1972 and was, until the 1990s at least, the highlight of the motorsport calendar. It used to be an absolute behemoth of a meeting, often featuring hundreds of entrants from all over the world. In addition to the main event you'd also have support races featuring hundreds more, so you can imagine the number of people it used to attract. I'm not sure exactly how many people Brands held back in those days but hundreds of thousands must have visited over the duration of the festival. More importantly though, for a driver at least, if you managed to do well or even win the Formula Ford Festival it could have a very positive effect on your career. I wasn't really aware of this at the time, having only recently entered the formula, and I'm actually quite glad of the fact as I might have found it a bit overwhelming.

My one abiding memory from that first festival, and one of the most vivid of my entire life, was hearing a V12 Ferrari going down the back straight into Westfield in one of the support races. All of a sudden there was this awesome scream. The pitch of the engine was just astonishing, and as daft as this might sound I'm pretty sure I welled up. It is to this day the purest and most perfect sound I have ever heard, and despite there having been many events and factors that have made motorsport special to me over the years, *that's* what locked me in. From an aspirational point of view, the British Grand Prix I'd attended back in 1976 was a bit like going to see *Star Wars* and then deciding you wanted to become Luke Skywalker. It was just a dream, the only thing backing it up a year or two of recreational karting. This, on the other hand, was almost an invitation. It was as if the V12 was saying to me, 'Come on then, Johnny. This is what's waiting for you if you get it right.' It encapsulated every dream or aspiration I'd ever had about the sport, or have done since. It was the Freddie Mercury of engines.

Now I'd love to be able to follow that story up with a nice win, but I'm afraid that without rewriting history that's simply not possible. In fact – and this is the first time I have ever owned up to this – about halfway through the quarter-final a seldom-seen but rather petulant version of me made a badly timed cameo appearance, one which won me the self-appointed title of 'Arse of the Festival'.

Allow me to explain. Although I bagged a fourth in one of the heats, I'd been an also-ran throughout most of the proceedings, and because I'd become so used to winning I didn't like this one little bit. Now some might say I simply had a winner's mentality, and had I just become angry and perhaps driven a little too aggressively for a while I dare say I could have been forgiven. But instead of this I'm afraid I got so worked up that I deliberately drove off at Clearways. 'Sod this,' I remember saying, 'I'm out.' And off I went. The really stupid part of this story is that I was running a more than respectable tenth at the time and the chances were I'd have made the semis, and even the final. In fact, who knows, I might even have won it. I told you – what a stupid arse. I just wasn't used to running tenth, I'm afraid, and that was my response. Throwing your toys out of the pram is one thing, but actually trying to break them is quite another. It's one of my few regrets from that period.

From a results point of view things did improve for me in Formula Ford, but I never really got used to it. I expected it to be the most demanding thing I'd ever done within the biggest grid on the planet, but I also expected it to be the most exhilarating. Instead, for me the experience was awkward, slow and uninteresting, and I never felt in control of things. Even when I did well at Formula Ford it was almost as if it were a means to an end as opposed to something I wanted to do.

On a more positive note, I do remember reading a very complimentary report in one of the motorsport magazines after the festival – probably the first time I ever took any notice of the press. It read something like this: 'Perhaps the most remarkable performance was the fourth position of karting graduate Johnny Herbert in a works Sparton who fought every inch to inflict defeat on the experienced Wil Arif, Allard Kalff and Peter Bell.'

Not bad, eh? If only somebody had told me then that they wouldn't always be quite so complimentary.

Nineteen eighty-four should have been my first full season in Formula Ford, but despite the opening race at Brands Hatch yielding me a very promising sixth I very nearly lost my genitals the following week. Yes, you read that correctly: I was almost parted from my twig and berries. I was part-way through a test at Oulton Park in Cheshire, and as I turned into Old Hall, which is a right-hander, I probably overdid it a bit and in an attempt to regain traction I kept my boot in. Unfortunately the traction was regained just a little bit late so instead of wrestling back control of the car and continuing, I flew headlong into the barrier. I remember feeling dazed after impact (nothing new there) and I had a warm feeling at the top of my right leg, but no pain.

Had I been less confident about my supreme bladder control I'd have said I might have wet myself. When I looked down my initial thought was that one of the suspension links had just ripped my race suit. It was only when the rescue team arrived and tried to move me that I realized the wishbone had gone clean through my leg and was about a millimetre away from my family jewels. Mark Blundell, Perry McCarthy and Jonathan Bancroft had also been testing that day and were kind enough to come and visit me in hospital that evening. Not that they asked me how I was or anything. They just wanted to take the piss out of somebody who'd almost had his manhood got at. Disgraceful, isn't it? That wishbone is still in my possession, by the way, and after the accident it spent years on the wall of the Valour Racing workshop, underneath a particularly rude caption.

By the way, did I tell you that the early part of my Formula Ford career was funded almost completely by drugs? It's absolutely true, I'm afraid. It turned out the chap who'd bought Bill's unit was importing cannabis by the ton, and without realizing I was doing it I'd been helping him. As well as teaching his daughter to drive a kart I used to help out in the Valour factory, like I did in Bill's shop, and looking back I can't believe I didn't twig because he used to have us doing some very strange jobs. One of these was done in stages. First of all, about nine o'clock at night, we'd drive down to a housing estate somewhere and eventually another car would turn up. After about five minutes the other car would start flashing its headlights, which was obviously the signal for this chap to go and get into the other car and have a chat with the flasher. Then, after about fifteen minutes, he'd get out of the flasher's car, and we'd drive home.

Nothing was ever said and I never asked any questions. I just did as I was told. I was the perfect accomplice if you think about it: silent, obedient and *very* naive.

The following morning I'd go to his house and he'd take these big bags out of his fridge (which I later learned were full of cash), and then off we'd go again to the housing estate. You'd think by this point I might just have twigged that he wasn't trying to purchase a couple of carburettors, especially as he was often sweating like Mark Blundell at an all-you-can-eat buffet, but it just never occurred to me. A few days after these 'drop-offs' took place a wagon would turn up with packs of laminate flooring in the back which would be stored in the factory for a few days before being collected. 'Laminate flooring?' I hear you cry. 'What's that got to do with either motorsport or drugs?' Well, laminate flooring, in and of itself, has clearly got nothing to do with either, but once the inside has been scraped out, replaced with drugs and then sold on, it can obviously fund a Formula Ford racing team pretty easily.

There you have it, then: drugs got me into racing.

When all this eventually came out and the chap was arrested I was living in a place called Windlesham in Surrey. One Saturday night at about 9.30 I heard a knock at the door. I never used to answer the door at night but when they knocked a second and then a third time I had a peek through the curtains. I saw two well-dressed gentlemen on the doorstep, looking rather impatient, and when I opened the door they handed me a summons instructing me to appear at the Old Bailey on such-and-such a date to act as a character witness for the man driving the laminate flooring lorry. The only thing I remember about being in the dock is being told off by the judge for not taking things seriously enough.

'I do wish you'd show the court a little more respect, Mr Herbert,' he said. He was very stern!

I can't remember what got me into trouble but I think I was so nervous that I just said whatever came into my head – and that, believe you me, almost always leads to trouble.

That Formula Ford class of '84 was jam-packed with talent: Damon Hill, Mark Blundell, Bertrand Gachot, Paulo Carcasci and Perry McCarthy, to name a few – there were at least five future F1 drivers. Mark Blundell was probably the front runner then. His dad had a bit of money, I think, and it didn't matter what time of year it was, come the weekend Mark would be racing. Do you remember the old Honda three-wheelers? Mark used to have one of those, and after a race weekend we'd set up a little track somewhere and have a competition. Despite being bloody death traps those things suited people of my height perfectly, so even though Mark usually used to win, I was always second. Poor old Damon didn't stand a chance, bless him. In fact, I think he'd have been better off with a penny-farthing. (Can you imagine Damon Hill on a penny-farthing, wearing a top hat? I can.)

My God, we were competitive, though. It didn't matter what we were doing – racing cars, three-wheel bikes or playing pool – nobody would ever give anybody else an inch. Saying that, we all got on really well, and we all had nicknames. I was Little 'Un, for obvious reasons, and Damon was Secret Squirrel, because he always played his cards very close to his chest. Mark Blundell was Mega, because he liked mega cars and mega bikes; Julian Bailey was Grumpy, because he was; Martin Donnelly was Yer Man, because that's what he used to prefix everybody's name with; and Perry McCarthy was Mad Dog, which was after a character from a cartoon strip in *Autosport*. At some point we were christened 'the Rat Pack' by a motorsport journalist and since then have been joined by the likes of Derek Warwick, Steve Soper, Martin Brundle and Jason Plato. We still meet for dinner every so often, although these days we're not so much the Rat Pack, more the cast of *Last of the Summer Wine*. Complan, anyone?

Of all the people I've ever driven against the most unlikely in terms of how you'd expect a racing driver to behave is Damon Hill. I wasn't convinced to start with, but he's been one of the most impressive. When he first appeared on the scene I, like many people, assumed he was only there because of who his father was and that he must have more money behind him than half the grid. Well, it just goes to show how wrong you can be, doesn't it? In terms of finance, Damon was probably in a similar position to me when he started, and he was given no preferential treatment whatsoever. It doesn't matter who your father is, if you're not good enough you'll get found out very quickly.

I'm not here to tell somebody else's story, but one of the things that impresses me most about Damon – and there are many of them, both as a driver and as a human being – is he's the same person today that he was when I first met him back in the early eighties, and bearing in mind what he's achieved I think that makes him pretty unique. He's certainly one of the most modest drivers I've ever met. Just the other day he told me that he won every race he ever finished on a motorbike, but followed it up with the caveat that his bike must have been better than everybody else's. Later on we got on to the F1 World Championship and he pretty much said the same thing. 'Oh, I was probably just lucky,' he claimed. Could it be false modesty? Of course not. That's just who Damon is.

With me it's slightly different. I've been accused of the same thing over the years, and although it's not in my nature to go boasting about my abilities or my achievements, the overtly self-effacing persona which I seem to have perfected (now I am bragging) was actually a bit of a defence mechanism, partly so that I didn't give anything away, but also in an attempt to lull people into a false sense of security. Just by listening to people like Damon and me you'd think we hadn't got it in us to compete as racing drivers, Damon being more like a bank manager and me a postman, or a miniature male model. It's always the quiet ones you've got to watch, though.

In total I was out of that 1984 season for nearly four

months after the wishbone-nearly-touching-the-willy accident.
By 1 July, my return to the track, I was driving a Van Diemen
RF84, and after a third, two fourths and two fifths, on
2 September I finally won my first race in Formula Ford. It took
place at Silverstone (a good omen?), and I've had to refer to an
old magazine to remind me of the details. Just after the start of
the race Mark Blundell, who was on pole, moved left, forcing
Andrew King into Jonathan Bancroft's Reynard, so even before
the first corner two of the favourites, Blundell and Bancroft,
were already on their way back to the pits. After picking my way
through a second incident which happened at Copse on lap 2, I
managed to establish myself at the front of the field alongside
a driver called Miles Johnston. So began a tactical battle that
would last until the final corner of the final lap. Time and time
again I led going on to the straight after Club, only for Johnston
to out-brake me going into the next corner, Abbey. The defining
moment came on the penultimate lap when Miles overshot his
turn-in point. I capitalized, but as Miles was later on the brakes
going into the very last corner we came out almost neck and
neck. I just managed to outdrag him to the line. The win itself
felt great of course, but to do so using race-craft, and in a car
that I wasn't particularly keen on, felt sweeter still. In fact it was
just what I needed.

My mechanic in those days was a German chap by the name
of Alex Oxlinger, or Herman the German as we used to call
him. He was kind of an accident-prone scruff-bag, the subject
of literally hundreds of stories. My personal favourite took place
at Cadwell Park in Lincolnshire. One of our cars arrived at the
paddock and without even thinking about it Herman opened
the back of the transporter and unstrapped the car. Not many
of you will be aware of this but the paddock at Cadwell is on a
slope, so a few seconds after Herman jumped out of the trailer,
the car followed him.

When we used to go to meetings together Herman and I would take this huge V6 van. It was like a big Transit and would fit Herman and me in the front and the car and all the spares and equipment in the back. While we were away, Herman and I used to sleep in the back of that van, me in between the front wheels and him the rear, whereas Mark 'Mega' Blundell used to have this bloody great Winnebago thing complete with beds, showers, toilets and a kitchen. (Do you know he never once invited me in, not even for a cup of tea?) I had to make do with a sleeping bag and a mad German who used to whiff a bit. Sometimes if I was busy I'd have to drive to meetings alone in my Mini 850, and because of my sensitive nose I'd often end up sleeping in there. Could you imagine that happening these days? No, neither can I.

Now you might be thinking that because we worked together, Herman's Formula Ford driver of choice would have been yours truly. Not a chance. In fact, although we got on well, I don't think Herman ever liked me as a driver. His favourite was always the aforementioned Mega Blundell. Why, I'm not sure, but it was confirmed to me directly after my win at Silverstone.

As I said before, Mark had only lasted a few hundred metres in that first race, a BP Super Fund FF1600, and was due to race again later in the meeting. On arriving back at the pits Herman had obviously taken pity on Mega, because when I returned victorious to the garage, as opposed to lifting me out of the car, holding me aloft and shouting 'VICTORY IS OURS!', he said, 'Vell done, Johnny,' ushered me out of the car, and then began stripping it down.

'What are you doing?' I asked him.

'Mark is in trouble,' he replied. 'I need to help him.'

With that, he continued stripping off what he needed and then started working on Mark's RF84.

What a bloody turncoat. But Herman was a fantastic mechanic.

The chances are he still is, although I've no idea where he lives these days. Probably in the back of a van somewhere, maybe stalking Mark.

I remember driving home from a meeting one day and for some reason we'd been hammering it. The van didn't seem to like this and we got as far as the Brentwood turn-off on the M25 when all of a sudden we heard this bang, which was followed by a big puff of steam rising from beneath the bonnet.

'*Scheisse!*' Herman hissed. 'Now vot?'

'Don't worry,' I said, 'there's a spares shop nearby. Let's have a look and if you think it can be mended I'll go and fetch what you need.'

Within about an hour he'd stripped the entire engine down, fixed whatever he had to, and we were on our way again. I didn't take in everything Herman did as a lot of the time I couldn't understand him, but over the years he taught me a lot.

In between the win at Silverstone and the Formula Ford Festival there were three races remaining in the 1984 BP Super Fund season, and the best result I managed was a third at Oulton Park. The highlight of this particular meeting was undoubtedly the team catering. At some point after I'd joined Quest my dad had given us the old caravan we used to stay in (we'd upgraded to a twelve-footer somewhere along the way), and that had become the Quest motorhome. All of us used to stay in it, so it won't surprise you to learn that in addition to getting a little bit messy from time to time it used to stink to high heaven. None of us was what you'd call a tidy individual so if you ever happened to walk in there by mistake you'd have been forgiven for thinking that you were on the set of a particularly nasty horror film.

We all had different jobs to do in the caravan, half of which were never done, and mine was cooking. I was head chef. The kitchen – or kitchenette, as it was – consisted of a Baby Belling, a frying pan and a tiny fridge, and that was it. Everything was cooked in either butter, lard or both and should probably have come with a government health warning. This was the 1980s, though, so cholesterol was still only something Terry Wogan mentioned in margarine adverts, and a furry artery sounded like some kind of cult American toy.

I used to enjoy knocking up breakfast for the boys, but on this particular morning at Oulton I was suffering from a bad cold. No matter though: the cars may run on petrol but a racing team runs only on its stomach, so after putting about half a pound of lard into the pan, I unloaded all the bacon. (The smell of frying bacon was always welcome as it used to drown out the smell of the mechanics' feet. Have you ever been at close quarters with the feet of a mechanic before? Well, my advice is, don't. They're a lot more dangerous than even the lardiest fried breakfast and don't smell anywhere near as nice.) Just as I was ready to serve up I shouted, 'Come and get it!' But before any of them could drag themselves out of their pits an almighty sneeze came upon me, and before I could turn my head the entire contents of my nose found their way – very quickly indeed I might add – into the frying pan. I'm not really sure how you translate the sound of sizzling snot on to paper, but this was the mother of all of them.

TSSSSSSSSSSSSSSSSSSSSSSSSSSSSSSSSSS it went (sorry, but that's the best I can do).

'Was that your sneeze sizzling there, Johnny?' came a voice from the other side.

'Noooooooooo!' I lied. 'Actually, yes, it was.'

Silence.

'Shall we go to the greasy spoon?' the voice said again.

'I think that's probably quite a good idea,' I replied. 'Unless you're all up for a bacon and snot sandwich?'

The festival, which featured entries from Roland Ratzenberger and a young Eddie Irvine, kind of summed up my season really.

I came second in the heats, holding off a late charge from Ruairi O'Coileain, and was third in the quarter-final. Then, in the semi-final, my throttle cable snapped and that was that. When I say the festival summed up my season I don't mean it in a negative way; it was just representative of the fact that it had a bit of everything. Fortunately there was no leg skewering at Brands Hatch but all the other ingredients were there. The main thing was I had a win under my belt. All I needed now was a car that was more suited to me.

Four

THE COMPANY THAT had sponsored the heats I drove in at the 1984 Formula Ford Festival was called Quest Racing. They manufactured parts for cars and had made the wishbone I'd impaled myself on. Even though it was the right wishbone that had gone through my leg, it was left wishbones that I actually went through like I did underpants. Damaging the front left was my Achilles heel back then, and because of this I got to know the people there quite well. The owner of Quest, a guy called Mike Thompson, decided one day to start a Formula Ford team using a new car they'd been developing called – and I can't for the life of me think where they got the name from – the Quest. Once again, in order to do that they were going to need a driver. Nobody with money would ever drive something without a proven track record, so because I didn't have any money but could drive, I was ideal.

The chap Mike hired to run the team was called Ian Blackman and we all got on like a house on fire. It was a fantastic opportunity. Because the Quest had quite a short wheelbase it drove far more like a kart than the Sparton or the Van Diemen. It was more zippy and responsive, and of course that suited me down to the ground. It still felt quite heavy, and because of the all-weather tyres we had to use it tended to slide around quite a lot, but for me it was a massive improvement.

Despite my not getting on with it, the Van Diemen RF85 was still by far the most popular car at the time and was probably driven by six or seven of the top ten drivers. The Quest, although competitive in the right hands, was, by comparison, an acquired taste; even though the team had three works cars I was the only driver who really took to it. They sold plenty though, so I wasn't completely on my own.

I contested two championships in 1985, the Esso and the RAC, and my main competitors were Bertrand Gachot, Mark Blundell, Damon Hill and Paulo Carcasci. By the middle of the season I'd had five or six second places between the two, a couple of thirds, and the rest had been retirements. This was to be expected as the car was still in development but it didn't stop the chaps from Van Diemen having a good laugh at our expense. We were probably their only real threat that year, and despite all the mickey-taking and bravado they were, for want of a better phrase, absolutely crapping themselves. The Quest had better grip than the RF85, and if you threw it over a kerb it remained stable. This was unheard of in Formula Ford so from the very start of the season there had been a lot of squeaky bottoms in the Van Diemen factory.

To counter the rather desperate taunts from Van Diemen, Mike Thompson began taking out a series of adverts in *Autosport*. These were to become a source of great embarrassment to the company and in my opinion are works of genius. The first one appeared after I'd managed to get pole position at Thruxton, despite being shunted by Carcasci who was driving a works Van Diemen.

GOT POLE POSITION BUT WAS ASSAULTED FROM
BEHIND BY A BRAZILIAN WITH V.D.

Ralph Firman, the boss at Van Diemen, was not at all pleased, but they had started it and Mike had no intention of letting up. My personal favourite read:

JOIN THE FIGHT AGAINST V.D.
BUY A QUEST!

The second half of the 1985 season yielded more of the same: apart from a win at Brands in a one-off appearance in the EDFA Euroseries, I was either retiring or coming second. I was therefore among the favourites for the Formula Ford Festival, and this was one of the first occasions I can remember being nervous. With the Quest being competitive but ultimately under-developed, the only way I was going to be able to salvage anything from the season was to win the big one, and because it took place at Brands, which is of course kerb heaven, I would certainly have an advantage.

It perhaps won't surprise you to learn that my greatest ever moment in Formula Ford, indeed one of the best of my entire career, started off in the worst possible way. It was the first lap of qualifying, and as I approached Paddock Hill Bend I remember thinking to myself, *Just bide your time*— But before I could finish the thought I'd spun off into the catch-fencing.

'That's it,' I said to myself. 'That's it, it's over. I've thrown it all away.'

The rule was that if you didn't complete a minimum of three laps during qualifying you had to start the race from the back of the grid *and* with a ten-second penalty. In other words, you were fucked.

The Van Diemen boys were wetting themselves when I walked past them on the way to the pits, and they had bloody good reason. With me out of the running they were all but guaranteed a winner. I didn't just feel bad for me. Mike, Ian and the team had worked tirelessly on the car and it was bloody quick, which is possibly something I'd underestimated. Anyway, we were where we were, and to be fair to Mike and the boys they didn't give me any stick. They just laughed and called me a twit. Fair enough.

As I lined up at the back of the grid for the first heat I thought back to that British Junior National Championship in 1980 when I came from the back but ran out of laps. I'd managed it then. Why couldn't I now? Since the qualifying debacle I'd forgotten that I was an extremely confident driver who had a lot of belief in his ability. The mistake had knocked me, but there was nothing I could do about it now. I still had a chance, however slim, and I wasn't going to balls it up a second time.

This newfound confidence stayed with me even as I sat out the penalty – the longest ten seconds of my life – at the end of which the entire field were completely out of sight. When the flag went and I eventually set off I must have been getting on for half a lap down on the front runners, and it was only an eight-lap race. By the second lap, going into Clearways, I began to reach the tail-enders, so I had six laps to get through. But nobody was really racing towards the back which meant they were holding each other up, so that made it even more difficult. By lap 6 I'd managed to worm my way up to tenth, which in a field of about thirty isn't bad, and by lap 7 I was eighth, just behind Kevin Gillen. He was a stubborn bugger and gave me no ground whatsoever. Even so, I managed to take him and Ted Whitbourn, which meant I finished the heat in sixth. It wasn't a bad drive, even if I do say so myself.

Finishing sixth meant I started the quarter-final in twelfth place, which was the middle of the fifth row. This might sound strange but they line up 3-2-3-2-3 in Formula Ford, so when we started there were ten cars in front of me. At the green I went straight on the outside and remained there up to Druids, by which time I was in ninth place. Taking Eric van de Poele on the second lap got me up to sixth, and by the end of lap 4 I was fifth. Next was Andy King, whom I took on lap 6, and as I passed Allan Seedhouse for third, I broke the lap record. All this meant I'd start the semi-final from the middle of the third row. This was now looking good as out of a field of twenty-six the first thirteen would make the final.

The semi-final started off with a big accident. Gachot was touched, he somersaulted and, after taking out Paulo Carcasci, took out a further four cars. No bad injuries, thank God. At the restart I once again took the outside line around Druids which gave me the inside line for the next corner. I was running fourth now and was once again having my view spoiled by Seedhouse. Fortunately, after some persistent pressure Allan cracked and I managed to take him on the inside. From now on I only had Ruairi O'Coileain and Jonathan Bancroft in front, and to announce my intention to take them I did another 48-second lap. At Paddock I tried to take O'Coileain on the outside, and although he resisted we were now running side by side. Even so, I'd have to wait until lap 11 before I got another chance. It was an easy one, though, because as we went into Surtees, which is an uphill left that leads out into the country, O'Coileain went off on to the grass and I was through. There was only Bancroft now, but he was a very good driver. Once again, as with Seedhouse in the quarter-final, I managed to apply enough pressure on Jonathan to be able to sneak a dead heat.

Damon Hill won the other semi-final, which meant that me, him and Bancroft would start on the front row for the final. Luckily for me I had the left-hand position which, after a good start, gave me the lead going into Paddock, with Jonathan second and Damon third.

I'm sorry if I sound like a bit of an arrogant bugger, but I knew the moment I reached Paddock that I'd won the festival.

Jonathan came close once or twice but that was only because I let my concentration slip. Once I knew he was there I just accelerated and that was it. After everything I'd been through there was no way I was going to give it up, and as I went through the chequered flag and began to slow down I suddenly became aware of the crowd. They were going bonkers. It was a popular win, I think. Real David and Goliath stuff.

People always ask me how I reacted to the victory, expecting me to say that I drank champagne for a week and went a bit mad, but when I tell them the truth they're usually a bit disappointed. At the risk of sounding arrogant again, or perhaps a bit blasé, I just took it all in my stride. There was certainly no whooping or throwing my hands in the air. Why? Because I always expected to win races, and if I did, job done – now move on and try and win the next. I was simply going about my business.

I've since learned that one of the people who was most impressed by my even-tempered, business-like attitude was Peter Collins, who was to become team manager at the Benetton Formula 1 team. As far as I know, this was the first time I registered on Peter's radar, and thank God I made a good impression because without him I'd never have made it into an F1 car.

What gave me the most pleasure that day were the actual races. To be in a good car at a legendary track and at an event featuring a big field and some bloody good drivers was manna from heaven for me, to win it the icing on the cake. You offer any racing driver that situation and they'll snap your hand off. Then again, if somebody had asked me prior to qualifying whether I thought it was possible to win the Formula Ford Festival from the back of the grid and with a ten-second penalty I'd have laughed them into Paddock. I suppose it's one of those things that seem impossible when you first think about it but then in reality aren't – like walking on the moon or making a racing driver buy a drink. I was the first person to achieve that particular feat (win from the back of the grid, that is), and since then only two other drivers, Dave Coyne in 1990 and Jan Magnussen in 1992, have managed to do the same.

Incidentally, the line-up on that final front row was Quest–Van Diemen–Van Diemen, so as I walked back to the pits I received some dark looks from the 'V.D.' boys. My quirky Quest and I had been a thorn in their side all season long. Had they been able to acquire a handful of Johnny Herbert dolls I have a feeling they'd have been reaching for the pins. Did any gloating take place? Yes, of course it did, but not by me. That was never my style. The fact that Van Diemen, the most successful car manufacturer ever in Formula Ford, saw me and the Quest as a threat I took as a massive compliment.

The other enjoyable aspect to winning the Formula Ford Festival, or winning any race for that matter, is seeing the effect it has on those around you. I remember a sponsor of ours – Pete King, who used to co-own Ronnie Scott's Jazz Club – running down the pit lane after the race. He was a big supporter of mine and seemed to be over the moon. As Pete approached the garage, Mike, who was also in buoyant mood to say the least, decided to play an awful trick on him. Mike had already been to see the scrutineer after the race and the car had been passed, but as Pete ran towards the garage like some kind of demented lottery winner, Mike saw the scrutineer walking not far from us so ran up to him in full view of Pete, shook his head and shouted, 'You mean we've lost because of two pounds of weight? I don't believe it!' You should have seen the look on poor Pete's face. It was one of pure, unadulterated horror. If Mike hadn't put him right he might have pulled out a saxophone and clubbed the scrutineer to death. As it was I think he was all for clubbing Mike.

I forget what the financial reward was for winning the festival (it wasn't much), but what I remember very clearly is that in addition to bagging a few quid I was also given the chance to test a Formula 3 car on the club circuit at Silverstone. That was a bit more like it! The test had been awarded to the winner by a Formula 3 team owned by Graham de Zille called Pegasus who were also one of the festival sponsors, and I covered about 130 laps in all, wet tyres in the morning when it was damp and slicks in the afternoon. What's more, I took to the car like a duck to water; my best time of 54.2s would have put me on the front row for the Marlboro British F3 round that had taken place that August. The main difference between this and everything else I'd driven was the sensitivity of the car, for instance, if you were losing time at Becketts, with understeer, you could just put a pencil line of front wing on. That would give you more downforce and so more grip, yet you still wouldn't lose any of your breaking stability. I can't recall how many times I came in altogether, but to say that I took advantage of the car's adaptability would perhaps be a bit of an understatement. Trevor Foster was the head of the Pegasus team, and we'd go on to work together at Lotus, and also when I drove at Spa in one of Zac Brown's Audi R8s.

'Stowe's not too smooth, Trevor,' I'd say. 'Anything you can do?'

'Give it here. Let's have a look.'

I was like a boy with a new toy, and once again I felt spurred. For a start it was great to be back on slicks again – something I hadn't had since the back end of my karting days – but apart from the fantastic grip I was also able to judge the car's limits much more easily, and once I got used to the braking, which was also incredible compared to anything I'd driven in Formula Ford, I found I could turn into corners and get back on the power again straight away. Driving something with gears had been a revelation, as had learning a bit about aerodynamics; but driving that Pegasus Formula 3 car was like getting a little glimpse of my future. Or at least the future I was hoping to have.

I'm not sure if I fully realized it at the time (I think I probably did), but there was a fundamental difference between Formula Ford and Formula 3, one that made me want to make the step up even more. Although people often progressed through Formula Ford there were a lot more who stayed in it for good, and so it had its own identity. If you were using it as a stepping stone, fine, but its existence did not rely on Formula 1; in fact, if anything the drivers used to turn their noses up at it. Formula 3, on the other hand, was far more synonymous with Formula 1, and although you got a few drivers who stayed long-term, the majority had at least one eye on bagging a drive in F1.

The question was, would this desired future come to pass for me, and if so, when? Mike Thompson and the boys were planning to launch the first Quest Formula Ford 2000 chassis at the London Racing Car Show in January 1986, and I was down to drive it. Unless somebody from F3 came in for me quickly I'd have to wait perhaps another year, or maybe more.

Alas, come the new year there were no offers on the table, so it was all systems go with the new Quest. I suppose I was a little bit disappointed, but at the end of the day I had a drive and was lucky enough to be working with a great team of people.

However, I knew from the moment the wheels started turning that 1986 was going to be a problematic year. The only saving grace was that it was purely down to the car, so it didn't tarnish my reputation as an up-and-coming driver. Despite the festival win, sponsorship had been hard to come by, which meant that unlike the factory boys, who were always able to hit the track running, we were at best underprepared and at worst just pissing into the wind. We'd made a step up, now competing in the Formula Ford 2000 Championship, but apart from sticking a 2000cc engine and an inch-spacer on the back of the old car it was a bit hit-and-hope. We found some wings in a storeroom somewhere and tried them, but they weren't any good. Then we tried putting a Formula 3 wing on, but that was just a disaster. As for wind tunnels, well, our car never even got a sniff of one, whereas the Van Diemens and the Reynards probably did. As I said, we were just playing hit-and-hope. It was nobody's fault, we were simply working within our parameters. It wasn't a matter of want of effort: Mike and the team worked their arses off. But making a silk purse out of this particular sow's ear was a step too far, even for them.

That lack of aerodynamic work cost us, and I felt it most keenly at tracks like Silverstone. Basically the car used to create a massive tunnel of air which every other car behind could take advantage of. Efficient it was not. The Van Diemens, on the other hand, were quite slick, and I remember finding it almost impossible to slipstream them. Even in a tow I was still creating this mess behind me. It was hopeless. My best result that season was a third at Brands, and I think overall I finished fifteenth. There'd been so much good press and so many positive remarks after the 1985 festival that I'd forgotten about things like finance and development. What did they matter? I'd won the Formula Ford Festival *and* had a test in a Formula 3 car. When it came to reconvening, then, and starting work on the new car it was a bit of a wake-up call.

Do you remember that old saying our parents and grandparents used to come out with when we weren't allowed to watch TV? 'We used to have to make our own entertainment when we were young.' Well, in the absence of a competitive car that's exactly what I and two of the other drivers did. The chaps in question were a Swedish driver called Jo Lindstrom, who I knew from my karting days, and a Canadian called Paul Tracy, who went on to have a lot of success in IndyCar, and because we were all driving pigs we decided that if we couldn't compete at the front of the grid we'd try and make it more interesting by competing against each other at the back. The fact that we were also-rans was irrelevant because not only were we racing and having some proper wheel-to-wheel battles, we were also having fun.

If I remember rightly, Mr Lindstrom used to enjoy life off the track even more than he did on it. There were several occasions when he started a race without having had a wink of sleep. He was like a Swedish James Hunt in a way, and even drove like him. Paul, on the other hand, reminded me a bit of Mr Mansell. He was unassuming and looked more like a lorry driver than a racing driver, but unlike Nigel he was quite thick-set. Get him behind a wheel, though, and the similarities returned because he too was a menace who had balls of steel. I remember seeing him not long after I'd finished driving in Formula 1. I was in Michigan attending an IndyCar race, and as I sat there watching them all flying round at 220mph, bombing along right at the top of the oval was Paul, and he wasn't taking any prisoners. It was an awe-inspiring sight. That was him, though. He pushed everything to the limit.

The person who I think took the failure of the new Quest most to heart was Mike Thompson. He had so much faith in me as a driver and was as determined as I was to get me into Formula 1. A few months into the campaign he decided that instead of waiting for the season to end before trying to find me an F3 drive, he'd try and find some money right away so as not to let my momentum slip. And find some cash he did – about £25,000 from Steve Sydenham at Racing for Britain. Envelope in hand, he approached an existing Formula 3 team called Mike Rowe Racing about getting me a drive. And so, on 20 July 1986, at Donington in the heart of England, I made my competitive debut in a Formula 3 car.

The team was probably mid-table at the time so even though it was a good car – certainly the best thing I'd ever driven – it wasn't what you'd call a contender. Even so, I managed to qualify seventh for the race which, as well as putting a smile on my face, not to mention those of Mikes Rowe and Thompson, impressed a representative from *Autosport*, who said I'd been 'sensational' and that I had 'attacked both circuit and challenge with gusto and considerable skill from the outset. Quickest of all in the early minutes, Johnny wound up fifth at the break, having nudged the nose-cone at McLean's.'

Fifth was where I remained for the rest of the race. Not a bad start, was it? I know it might seem a little bit big-headed including such a complimentary quote but Donington was a proud moment for me and I was desperate to justify Mike's faith in me, not to mention the money he put up. Trevor Foster, who had now moved to another Formula 3 team called Swallow Racing, apparently had a bet with his new team owner about where I'd qualify and the owner, not knowing me from Adam, said I'd be down the order.

'I'm going for the top eight,' Trevor had announced.

'Really?' said the owner. 'Do you know something I don't?'

I'm not sure whether Trevor let on that he'd seen me test for Pegasus but I know he won at least a shilling or two.

I managed to compete in another six races after Donington but because we eventually ran out of money, the last couple were for a team called Intersport, for whom Damon and Martin Donnelly would race the following year. James Hunt's brother David was the other driver at Intersport and I'm pretty sure the car was a Ralt, as was the one I drove for Mike Rowe. I still had the same people with me though so it wasn't too much of an upheaval. Despite the toing and froing, I managed to rack up some decent results in those races after Donington, including a third at Brands Hatch, a fourth and a fifth at Silverstone, and in

Belgium an eighth at Spa and a tenth at Zolder. We certainly put the wind up the establishment, and it provided me with a terrific shop window.

Five

By the end of 1986 everybody assumed that because I'd acquitted myself well in the races for Mike Rowe and for Intersport I'd be a shoo-in for a drive the following season, but that wasn't the case. Talent alone wasn't enough. Unless you had a benefactor who was prepared to undergo open-wallet surgery you really didn't stand a chance. It had been the same since Formula Ford 1600 so it wasn't any big surprise. I did have a meeting or two with Swallow Racing but for some reason Trevor Foster was unable to persuade his boss, Tim Stakes, to stump up the cash. I had a little bit of money behind me at that point but it was nowhere near enough, so eventually we just left it.

And I'm very glad we did, because not long after that I got wind from Mike Thompson that Eddie Jordan was interested in signing me. Eddie, in addition to being one of the true legends of modern motorsport, is one of the nicest guys you could ever wish to meet and, together with Bill Sisley, Mike Thompson and one or two others you'll hear about later, he had a very positive effect on my career. You see, as well as being a good egg and a bloody good team owner, Eddie also had a big talent for nurturing young drivers, and because he'd raced to a fairly high standard himself and knew his way round an engine, he understood every aspect of the sport.

He'd formed his first racing team back in 1980, not long after he retired as a driver, and in the early days the head office was just a lock-up garage in Silverstone. Since then he'd made great strides in Formula 3, finishing runner-up in 1983, 1984 and 1986. That was a pretty meteoric rise all things considered, so by the time I first met Eddie, which would have been some time during the 1986 season, he was making a real name for himself. The first time I spoke properly to him was at the 1986 Formula 3 End of Season Dinner which took place at the Grosvenor House Hotel in London. He seemed more surprised than anyone that I hadn't been offered a drive.

'It's money, Eddie,' I told him. 'I don't have that much behind me so nobody wants to know. I honestly don't know what I'm going to do next.'

'How about driving for me?' he said.

'Really? But aren't you sorted for next year?'

'Not yet. But I hope to be soon.'

By the end of the evening we'd written out an agreement, quite literally on the back of a napkin. It was linen, too, so that could be deemed vandalism. In total Eddie had to find about £150,000 to run the car, which to me was just a telephone number. He was as good as his word though, so even before the end of the year I was confirmed as Eddie Jordan's first signing for 1987.

Apart from enjoying a fairly unique perspective on motorsport, which is due partly to the diversity of his experiences but also his great age, Eddie Jordan is without doubt one of the world's finest man-managers, which made my time at Eddie Jordan Racing both successful and enjoyable. I was still quite shy at the time and had never come into contact with anybody quite so flamboyant, certainly not in motorsport. In my experience people in this industry were usually quite reserved, unless they'd had a few, but Eddie completely broke the mould. He was like some kind of mercurial whirling dervish, and if you were lucky enough to be part of what he was trying to achieve, you just knew that, win or lose, it was never going to be boring. Right from the very beginning Eddie went out of his way to make me feel part of the family – his family: I must have spent more time at his house than I did my own. Was it premeditated? Perhaps a little bit, but it was a very effective way of building a team ethic and making everybody feel special. It was genuine, too, which is the main thing, and that's what made it work. What you see is what you get with Eddie. He's always been the same.

Eddie's ambitions within motorsport pretty much mirrored my own in that ultimately we both wanted to get into Formula 1. The public found out how good a driver he is when the new incarnation of *Top Gear* began (appalling), and during the 1970s he'd come pretty close to making it and had driven in both the Formula Ford and the Formula 3 Championship. When the dream of making it into F1 behind the wheel began to fade for Eddie, instead of just giving up he simply shifted his ambition sideways and became an owner/manager. Where did it all go wrong, Mr Jordan?

What he and I had in common was an understanding that in order to achieve our ambition of entering Formula 1 we would have to win the Formula 3 Championship, so that was a good basis for our relationship. Eddie had come close on three occasions so by now knew exactly what was required. I was far less experienced of course, but I was considered to be one of the best young drivers in the country at the time, was very willing to learn, and could be moulded. On paper it was pretty much a marriage made in heaven. All we needed to complete the package was a competitive car.

The engine Eddie sorted out for the 1987 season was a development-tuned Volkswagen Spiess. Nobody had really heard of them in the UK but they'd been very successful in Germany. Toyota TOM's, which is Toyota's tuning arm, had just brought out a brand-new sixteen-valve Formula 3 engine which was being used by Damon and Martin Donnelly at Intersport. Ours was only eight-valve and was coming to the end of its shelf life, but it was still just about good enough.

When it came to testing, I got into Eddie's good books almost immediately because the way I liked to do things, although a little unorthodox, could be very easy on the wallet. It all changed when I went into Formula 1 of course, but back then, if I thought a car felt right for the race I'd stop, say, 'That's it, we're there,' and jump out of the car. This could be after five laps or it could be after fifty laps. Either way it was the opposite of what used to happen in Formula 3 testing: regardless of how the car felt drivers would usually just go round all day and then put their lap times in at the end. My way of doing things used to save Eddie an absolute bloody fortune, so with money being as tight as it was he always appreciated the way I managed to meld intuition with laziness.

In all seriousness, one of the main reasons I never utilized my laps with the Jordan in testing is because the car was just so good. One of the very first tests we did was at Snetterton in Norfolk, and because it went so well we decided to knock it on the head after just five laps – partly because the car felt brilliant but also because we didn't want to give anything away. Everybody knew that Eddie would be going all-out to win the championship in 1987, and although signing me had been a statement of his intentions, the less people knew about the car the better.

My co-driver at Jordan, for the first three or four races at least, was an American chap who I think had been bought the drive by his father. This happens quite a lot in motorsport and has always been a bit of a bone of contention. Like it or not, it can often prevent teams from going under, although I don't think this was the case with Eddie. He wasn't awash with money by any stretch of the imagination but I think that if he'd had to choose between taking on a good driver with no money or a bad driver who was loaded he'd rather take the cash and put all of his competitive eggs into one basket – in this case a short blond basket from Romford. I must admit I rather liked having all the focus on me, so from my perspective it was the right move.

This particular driver was bad, though. He used to play this hugely irresponsible game where he'd drive from London to Silverstone and see how many red lights he could jump. Now don't get me wrong, I'm certainly no slouch when it comes to a bit of tomfoolery, but I always try to keep it on the racetrack. He, however, thought this was great fun and used to brag about it when he got to the garage. 'Guess what, guys. I managed to jump a hundred and fifty reds. Hey, how about that?'

I used to think to myself, *You absolute dickhead. You could have killed somebody.*

One morning he didn't make it as far as Silverstone so that was the end of that. Nobody was killed, thank God, but I'm pretty sure he had both his legs broken. Idiot.

The only time I ever really had any trouble with Eddie was when I wanted something new. This was understandable to a point, for reasons I've just mentioned, but even so his reaction whenever I suggested that he might have to spend a few quid was priceless. Just say I asked him for a new set of tyres. First his face would scrunch up a bit and then he'd start stuttering a bit. 'Well, well, well, well, well, well, you know what it's like, Johnny. You know what it's like. Money's awful tight just at the moment and they're not in the budget.' To be fair to Eddie he always made sure I had enough to do the job, but only just. That's the sign of a good team owner, I suppose, being able to control a budget and remain successful. Some of the faces he used to pull, though. As I said, priceless!

*

Driver-wise, the 1987 Formula 3 Championship was very strong, one of the strongest ever in fact, featuring the likes of Damon Hill, Martin Donnelly, Thomas Danielsson, Gary Brabham, Perry McCarthy, Roland Ratzenberger, Mark Blundell, Peter Kox, Jean-Denis Délétraz and Bertrand Gachot. I didn't know it at the time but Bertrand would turn out to be my big rival that year; he, along with Martin, gave me a real run for my money. Bertrand was the opposite of me in that he was always very out-going so sponsorship was never really a problem for him. He was like a European Derek Trotter in a way. But as well as being quite proficient at talking himself into the money he also had a fabulous knack of talking himself into trouble. A 'gob on a stick' is how I often referred to him.

Once, racing at Castle Combe in Formula Ford 1600, Bertrand had his nose put out of joint by something Mark Blundell did during the race – I forget the exact details – and by the end the Frenchman was apoplectic. Instead of waiting to remonstrate with Mark in the paddock somewhere, Bertrand stormed into the scrutineer's office where Mark was and began taking him to task. Whenever Bertrand got angry he'd get right in your face, and Mark didn't like this one little bit. A lot of pushing and shoving took place, and in the end a mate of Mark's who was about six foot ten waded in to try and stop the fight but ended up punching Bertrand and knocking him spark out. He could be his own worst enemy in that respect, but once again, as with so many drivers, it was all or nothing. Waiting his turn and then asking politely for a quick chat in the garage was never going to be an option with Mr Gachot. He wanted a fight there and then, and unfortunately for him that day he got one.

But in addition to being a little bit loud and erratic, Bertrand could also be quite cunning. I wouldn't have trusted him an inch back then, nor him me. Things would change by the time we were racing together at Le Mans, but in 1987 there was always an air of suspicion surrounding us. It all stemmed from something that, again, had happened in our Formula Ford 1600 days.

We were at a meeting at Silverstone, and the catalyst for what was becoming a series of unfortunate events for Bertrand was who else but Mark Blundell. He'd been quickest in qualifying by quite a margin, and this had obviously got Bertrand thinking (or rather scheming) as to how we could stop him.

'Johnny,' he said to me outside the Quest garage. 'Mark is faster than us, yes?'

'Well, his car is.'

'Look,' Bertrand said, 'why don't we agree to slipstream each other, that way we'll have a better chance of keeping up and even passing him. It'll be quite easy to arrange.'

I wish we'd had some kind of machine that could have read our thoughts at the time, because although I said to him, 'Yeah, OK, Bertrand, that's not a bad idea,' all I was thinking was, *Right then, how can I turn this to my advantage?*, and I guarantee he was thinking exactly the same thing. Treacherous bastards, us racing drivers!

As the race approached all I could think about was how I could get one over on Bertrand and make this skulduggery work for me and me alone, because I just knew that he'd be up to something. In the end I decided that whatever Bertrand was planning he'd be playing the long game so whatever I was going to do I'd have to do it early doors.

After the start of the race Bertrand was in front, so as quick as I could manage it I got into position, made sure he knew I was there, and then slipstreamed him. No problems there, thank God. Two laps later, just as we were coming up to the Hangar Straight – we must have been doing about 130mph – I saw Bertrand in my mirror getting ready to slipstream me, but just as he began to pull out and make the move I went over to the left slightly which forced him on to the grass. I knew from personal experience that this particular stretch was like a Highland moor, and sure enough a second or so later Bertrand was about six feet in the air and on his way to the back of the field. I, on the other hand, was now a few places up, minus one of my fiercest rivals.

I had to be the one to do it first because, believe you me, Bertrand would have done exactly the same. Sure enough, not long after the race had finished he came up to me in the garage.

'You're a tough bastard,' he said, laughing. 'You trusted me even less than I trusted you!'

There was no honour among these particular thieves, but although we were always a bit wary of each other after that there was a lot of mutual respect. Most importantly, Bertrand's a good bloke. He was a damn good driver, too, and I'm pleased that he also made it into F1 and ended up having an excellent career.

The first race of the 1987 Formula 3 season took place at Thruxton on 15 March and we couldn't have wished for a better start, taking pole position by well over a second. The race itself, or rather the start of it, was slightly less straightforward as I was overtaken by Bertrand and, I think, three other drivers before the first corner. That was my only weakness at the time, but I did manage to sort it out pretty quickly. Within a lap or so I'd managed to pass the other three and then took back the lead, and from then on it was plain sailing. Bertrand said in an interview afterwards that the speed at which I'd caught him had scared him half to death, so instead of trying to block me he'd been happy to let me go.

What was our secret? Well, at that particular track, in addition to a good car and a fantastic driver, we were also using a spool differential, something we'd first tried at the Snetterton test. That was the reason why we'd packed up after five laps. Nobody else was using one and when we realized the difference it made we just upped and left. I also took a slightly different line at Thruxton which gave me an advantage. It was on a quick corner coming out of the back, and as everybody went to the left and then round the corner I just went straight and overtook them all. We raced at Thruxton three times that season and to this day I'm at a loss as to why nobody copied me. I'm grateful, though. Maybe the spool differential helped, I don't know.

I'm going to go into this in more detail later on, but after that first race at Thruxton I began to develop a feeling of – and there's no other way of describing it – invincibility. It's strange when you read it on paper as it just seems like I'm saying I had my head up my arse, but in fact it was a culmination of things, the result of everything finally coming together. First there were the two karting championships, then the Formula Ford Festival, and now the Formula 3 Championship, which was going like a dream. This time, though, *everything* was in place. The chassis – a Reynard, which had won the 1986 championship – was tremendous, and the engine, as I've already said, was tried, tested and reliable. Eddie had been fabulous, the perfect mentor, and I was to all intents and purposes his sole driver. He and his team, and also his family, was the final piece of the jigsaw. As the season progressed this sense of being unbeatable became more intense. I didn't win every single race of course, not even Ayrton did that – and later in the year when those sixteen-valve engines began to dig a bit, I started to become slightly less competitive – but I always knew we had enough to win the championship and that's all that mattered.

The only slight downside to this newfound impregnability was that it did result in me doing some slightly hare-brained things on occasion, much to the exasperation of my flamboyant but frugal team owner. Rightly or wrongly I used to get bored from time to time so to liven things up a little bit I'd often let some of the other drivers catch me so that I could then race them. Eddie used to go absolutely fucking ballistic with me when I did this, and he was well within his rights to do so. That belief that I would always ultimately triumph was sometimes a little bit overwhelming for me and I couldn't help myself. The only time I'd ever experienced such a feeling before was in the final race of the Formula Ford Festival; but the difference now was that it felt like it was here for good. It would stay with me until 21 August 1988.

By Monaco, the traditional support race for the Grand Prix, I'd won four out of the first seven races, and although this one had no bearing on the overall championship I was still keen to put on a good show. All the Formula 1 bigwigs would be in attendance so it was yet another shop window – the biggest and most terrifying of them all. Do well and you never know what might happen. Make a mess, though, and you could damage your prospects for good. They were all there: Enzo Ferrari, Frank Williams, Ken Tyrrell, Ron Dennis, Bernie Ecclestone too, managing the Brabham team. I'd never been to Monaco before so the moment we all arrived I decided to walk the track a few times before going back to my hotel room, lying on my bed and then trying to visualize it all so I could have a kind of 'virtual practice'. Believe it or not, this cognitive PlayStation of mine actually worked, and when I got on the track the following morning I was pretty much au fait with every part of it.

Unfortunately, some idiot then came up with the extremely bright idea of putting the spool differential back on, which was an absolute disaster. That idiot was me I'm afraid, but because I hadn't yet experienced any understeer with it on I was convinced that it would work. I remember suggesting it to my engineer, Dave Bembo, and then him looking at me like I'd just grown a second head or something. I still go red thinking about it.

Fortunately we managed to get the spool differential out before second qualifying, and after starting the race fourth on the grid, which wasn't at all bad, I finished on the podium behind Jean Alesi and Didier Artzet. That was the best finish by a Briton since James Weaver back in 1984, and the only reason we got a chance to take part in the first place was because Eddie had managed to snaffle a bit of cash out of a company called Rider Jeans. Thank God he did, because in addition to getting myself on the podium at my Monaco debut I was also invited to do a test at Brands Hatch for the Benetton Formula 1 team. I can't tell you exactly what I said when I found out, but this particular turn of events, unlike the Formula Ford Festival, was impossible simply to 'take in my stride'. In fact I may even have said a rude word.

Peter Collins had been the Benetton team manager for a couple of years by this point, and before that had been the boss at Lotus and then Williams. God only knows what he must have thought when he called me because the quiet, almost nonchalant attitude to success which had first impressed him at the Formula Ford Festival had been replaced by something slightly more audible.

I later found out that Peter wasn't the only interested party at Monaco, but while the rest of them simply pondered the idea of either talking to me or giving me a test, Peter picked up the phone, chased me down and put me in a car – and that would be the trend from then on really, or at least until the mid-1990s. He was like a dog with a bone as far as me and F1 were concerned. He even refused to let little things like my not being able to walk and having one foot hanging off get in the way of breaking into the sport. Not a bad chap to have backing you, then.

The test for Benetton was to take place on the shorter Indy Circuit at Brands Hatch, and despite how sure of myself I was when racing I was acutely aware as I arrived at the track that there were a lot of people good enough to drive in Formula 1 who never got the chance. This was usually just down to lack of opportunity, which is why the Bertrand Gachots of this world often did OK. The trick was, if you could manage it, to get a Formula 1 sponsor behind you while you were racing either in Formula 3 or Formula 2 (which was about to be rebranded F3000) and keep them on board until you were deemed ready. These days the path to F1 is quite structured and formulaic, but back then you often had drivers – Ayrton Senna, for instance – making the jump from F3 straight to F1 and winning almost straight away. Young Max Verstappen, who has recently won his first Grand Prix after replacing Daniil Kvyat in the Red Bull, is the latest driver to skip a formula, but it doesn't happen much these days. Gachot, like me, had to go the scenic route and raced in F3000, but ever since his Formula 3 days he had been sponsored by Marlboro who were heavily involved in Formula 1. This provided Bertrand with a tunnel into the sport, and he took full advantage of it. Yes, he had the necessary talent, but without the Marlboro connection it might never have happened for him. Being a bit of a shrinking violet and having no commercial savvy whatsoever meant I was never likely to have that kind of backing, so to be courted by the manager of an existing Formula 1 team while still in Formula 3 and with no contacts in F1 was as rare as rocking-horse . . . manure.

The next thing that struck me as I arrived at the track was that I was about to drive a car with slightly more horsepower than I was used to – about 850 more to be precise. It would be a turbo, too, the last of a dying breed. Did this make me nervous? What do you bloody think! The previous year I'd seen Nigel Mansell win his first British Grand Prix in a Williams Honda at this very track, and here I was about to drive something very similar. Now it was all starting to hit home.

This was nothing compared with what greeted me at the

paddock, though. The one thing I hadn't reckoned on when Peter Collins invited me to test for Benetton was that I might have a bit of company on the track. When I realized that what I was actually taking part in was a normal F1 testing day featuring just about every team and every driver on the grid, I experienced more feelings and emotions in that one moment than I'd had in my entire life. I was terrified, anxious, nervous, excited, bilious, enthused, star-struck (if you can call that an emotion), surprised, impressed – you name it, I had it jumping up and down in my body.

The mood in each of the garages seemed to tally with many of the drivers' reputations. Derek Warwick was always meant to be a bit of a joker, and as I walked past the Arrows garage I could hear a lot of laughing. Then, as I reached Lotus, the mood was quite serious and pensive, as was Ayrton Senna. Nigel's garage was just very laid-back; in fact, everyone there seemed to be in a state of recline.

One of my other abiding memories from that day, prior to the drive, is all the drivers and mechanics staring at me once I'd got my race suit and helmet on.

'Who the bloody hell's that?' they were all saying.

'That's Johnny Herbert.'

'Johnny who?'

The next firm memory I have is of sitting in the car for the very first time. Once the mechanics had shown me the controls (they weren't that different to an F3 car, apart from things like fuel boost), I tried to get myself comfortable. Thierry Boutsen and Teo Fabi were Benetton's regular drivers that season, and it was Thierry's car I was about to test; he'd already completed his laps, his best time being 36.4s. Because Thierry's quite a bit taller than me they had to go to the Benetton motorhome, which was run by the legendary Di and Stuart Spires who went on to become godparents to my daughters, and pinch a load of cushions which they then had to stuff down my back to help me reach the pedals (story of my bloody life. Incidentally, everybody who'd had an influence on my career to this point was present that day, including Mum and Dad, Bill Sisley, Mike Thompson and Ian Blackman, so I was very well supported. Better than the seat, anyway.).

The last person to speak to me before the engine was switched on was a guy from Cosworth, and once he'd finished instructing me and I was ready to go I held up my hand. I remember being amazed at how high-pitched the starter motor was – much higher than an F3 car; but when the motor itself kicked in it was a whole different kettle of fish, much deeper this time round with far more vibration. You just knew that what it represented was a calm before a very noisy and powerful storm. The actual noise it made was a kind of 'wom wom wom wom wom wom wom wom wom wom', and the anticipation it generated was just incredible.

Right, into first we go, I thought.

Wom wom wom wom wom wom wom wom wom WAP—

Stalled it. I was too embarrassed to say anything so just sat there.

'Shall we go again?' someone eventually said.

So they rolled me back in and we tried again.

Wom wom wom wom wom wom wom wom wom WAP—
Oh, shit.

This time I managed a sorry.

'Don't worry. Right, wheel him back in, lads.'

At this point they must have thought they'd invited Johnny Morris not Johnny Herbert. In the end I managed to stall it four or five times before lift-off – and I use the word lift-off advisedly.

On track, I remained in first as I approached the first brow. As I got to the second brow I shifted up to third. What was it Terry Wogan said on *Top Gear*? 'Slow and steady wins the race.'

It was all a little bit *Driving Miss Daisy* so far. I think I was still in second by the time I went into Paddock Hill Bend. It was as I came out of it I remember thinking to myself, *Right then, let's see what this thing can do.*

There's a bit of a dip straight after Paddock before Hailwoods Hill, and after changing up into third and putting my foot on the throttle there was a pause. *Nothing's happening*, I thought. I looked to the top of Hailwoods Hill as it goes into Druids, and just as my eyes started to adjust to the view I heard the turbo kick in, and then the boost.

Shh–shh–shh–shh–shh–shh–shh–shh–shh–shh–shh–*shhhhhhhhhhhhhhhhhhhhhhhh* . . .

What the hell's going— but before I could finish the thought, I swear to God I was at the top of the hill turning into Druids, exactly where I'd just been looking, at least six hundred yards from the end of Paddock. I don't remember anything about Hailwoods, that completely passed me by. What a bloody thrill, though. None of that linear acceleration you get these days. It was and still is the most exhilarating driving experience of my entire life. The grin I was sporting almost cracked my bloody helmet. I felt totally at home and didn't want to get out. *I don't care if I piss my pants and end up starving to death, just don't make me get out of this bloody car!*

The next thing I noticed, on the following lap, were the brakes on the car, and once again they were diametrically different to anything I'd ever experienced. Their sensitivity and power were truly incredible. Instead of simply slowing down as I approached the next corner, Surtees, I almost came to a complete standstill. I could have stopped that car on a sixpence.

Subliminally I'd always had this wish that eventually I'd drive a car that had all the grip that a kart had, just with a lot more power, and although the Formula 3000 car I drove the following year would come closest to that – certainly with regard to power-to-weight ratio – this was like something from a different universe. It was the first time I'd ever driven a car that I felt wouldn't limit me. Once again there's a potential bighead alert here, but everything I'd driven prior to that car had only been able to fulfil part of what I felt I was capable of achieving, whereas the Benetton B187, powered by a turbocharged Cosworth V6 yielding about 1000bhp, was more than a match for anything I'd ever be able to do. It's hard to describe the freedom it gives you, but it must be like discovering a gold mine: you just don't know where to start.

Controlling the power was probably the biggest challenge I had. With Formula 3 and Formula Ford cars you'd always shift down, turn into a corner, then floor it when you came out, but you couldn't do that in a turbocharged F1 car. You'd still brake, shift and turn, but because of the turbo you couldn't floor it coming out. I remember being in second going into Clearways and then I'd go short-shift third, short-shift fourth, short-shift fifth, get on to the pit straight, and *then* I'd be able to floor it. Try doing it before that and it'd just chew you up and spit you out into a barrier somewhere. It was such an effective weapon, and you had to carry the power with you and use it very, very carefully.

I still lament the passing of those turbocharged engines. I was only in my early twenties so I must be one of the youngest people on the planet to have driven one in anger. Lucky old me, eh? It's very hard to explain to somebody what they were like to drive because when you watched them on TV they tended to look a bit tame and a bit sluggish, and you can understand why: they had fat tyres, no power steering, the suspension was nice and wide, and they clearly had a lot of grip and a lot of downforce. But with all that power, though! The car I drove had about 2.5 bar but some of the previous cars, the ones with about 1500 horsepower, had 5 bar, which is just ridiculous. They were absolute animals to drive, but wonderful animals. In my opinion the ultimate driving machines.

So why did they go out of circulation, then? I think that, like Concorde, it was something they couldn't develop any further, which kind of made them obsolete – a victim of their own success. On top of that you also had the cost element. Burning hundreds of gallons of rocket fuel every week is an expensive business, and at the time a lot of teams were feeling the pinch.

Anyway, back to Brands.

Because of the stark difference in performance between the cars I'd driven and the car I was driving now, my body wasn't used to the pressure so after about fifteen laps I decided to call it a day before my head fell off. I think it would have as well. What a lesson that was. From now on I'd have to think about doing a few exercises every now and then if I wanted to make it in F1. Ability's obviously a prerequisite, but without physical strength it's worth bugger all. *No more winging it*, I thought. *You're going to have to get yourself to the bloody gym.*

Thierry Boutsen's time of 36.4s was pretty good, and despite being super-confident because it was my first time out, I never thought for a moment I'd get anywhere near it. Not crashing had been my biggest ambition, so returning the car unscathed was a cause for celebration.

'I've got some good news for you,' said Peter when I got out of the car.

'Really? Are you offering me a seat for next season?'

'Not a chance. You beat Thierry's time, though.'

'Seriously? What was my best time?'

'Thirty-six point one. That's pretty good, Johnny, especially for a rookie driving somebody else's car.'

My next question was bold to say the least, but I couldn't help myself.

'How far off Senna and Mansell was I?'

Peter smiled, as if to say, 'you cocky little git'.

'Point two off Senna's best and half a second off Nigel.'

'Really?'

If I'd managed to puff my chest out any further, I'd have needed a bra.

I later heard that when Nigel found out how fast I'd been his reaction was fairly typical. 'Half a second off? That would have been at least a second on the Grand Prix track.' That's Nigel, though. If there's a threat coming along, especially a British one, stamp on it.

As far as Peter Collins was concerned, this didn't just rubber-stamp his faith in me as a future F1 driver, it jumped up and down on it, rolled it around and then fired it out of a bloody cannon. There were certainly no high-fives – we didn't do things like that in those days, thank you very much – but I remember seeing the smile on his face when I arrived back at the garage, which was when I knew I couldn't have done too badly.

'Do you fancy testing again, Johnny?' he asked before I left.

'I dare say I might be persuaded,' I replied.

'We've got one coming up in Jerez before the Spanish Grand Prix. Let me speak to Eddie and make sure it's OK.'

As excited as I was about getting back in the B187 again, there was still the small matter of the Formula 3 Championship to think about and I was aware that I could secure the title at Spa on 13 September, just a couple of weeks before Jerez. Bertrand Gachot was going to be just as determined. Even though he had a French passport, he drove with a licence that had been granted to him by the Belgian FIA so professionally he'd be racing on home ground. In addition to that he was just a few points behind me, so the title was still wide open. Once again these new sixteen-valve engines were producing just that little bit more top-end power so Bertrand, with his Alfa Romeo-powered Ralt, was on pole, and I was alongside him in second. If I won the race, or neither Bertrand nor I finished in the points, I'd win the championship – Eddie had been reminding me of that for days – so bearing in mind my lack of valves the latter was probably the best I could wish for.

It's different now, but in the eighties the start at Spa was on the way down to Eau Rouge. As we approached the first left, I was side by side with Bertrand, me on the left and him on the right. Then, as we went into the chicane, I had one of those invariably doomed notions where I decide to be a little bit cunning. Once again it's different today, but back then a public road used to cross the track at Spa and where the two joined there was a mighty drop. Almost a hole, really. It was only at one section of the join, but if you hit it at speed you'd be in trouble. 'I know,' I thought to myself, 'I'll drive Bertrand on to the hole!'

If any further proof were needed that words like 'wily', 'shrewd', 'cunning' and 'sly' should have been removed from my vocabulary, the whole thing backfired disastrously. I executed the move without any trouble, forcing Bertrand on to the drop, but instead of getting a repeat of what happened on the grass where he bounced a few times and rejoined at the back of the field, he launched into the air, bounced one way, flicked another, and then hit me. Bertrand's rear diffuser shot up into the air, and after breaking away and then colliding again I cannoned hard into the barrier on the right before hurtling back across the track, right in front of the following pack, into the opposite barrier. Nice one, Johnny. I ran back to the garage to see if anything could be done for the restart but it was hopeless. Bertrand, on the other hand, had suffered far less damage than me and was on pole. I remember watching the restart thinking, *What a bloody stupid thing to do. That's it, from now on, no more scheming.*

Fortunately for me the starting grid was facing downhill – something else that's now changed – and by the start of the parade lap Bertrand had allowed his brakes to get hot which had resulted in them locking. It was a schoolboy error: what he should have done was keep it in gear and hold off the brakes. When Bertrand eventually got off the mark he had a lap in which to decide what to do: either start from the back of the grid like he was supposed to or weave his way to the front and suffer a penalty. Bertrand chose the latter, and despite starting from pole and finishing first he incurred a one-minute penalty which meant he only finished nineteenth. Damon won in the end, which was his second win of the year. I did feel for Bertrand a little bit because he drove a brilliant race – after I'd tried to kill him, of course – and had it not been for that braking error he'd have taken it to the final race of the season.

My sympathy for him did eventually subside, after a minute or two, and by the time Eddie and his assistant, 'Bosco' Quinn, saw me in the garage and told me I'd won the championship, I'd forgotten all about . . . what was his name again? It had gone up to the stewards after the race and because we had no idea what penalty they were going to dish out it was all a little bit tense. I was just sitting there with Dave Bembo, my engineer, and then Eddie and Bosco walked in grinning like idiots. Personally I'd have tried to pretend it had all gone horribly wrong, so they missed a trick there. It was a perfect end to an imperfect but eventful season, and it had been a tremendous team effort.

The last time I heard from Dave he was working on the touring-car circuit in Germany. He was a fantastic engineer and a very jolly character, great company. Bosco Quinn unfortunately died in a car crash in 1991. He'd been Eddie's right-hand man since about 1983 and must have done the work of three men. He never stopped. Eddie was always very good at delegating, which is the mark of a good manager apparently, and if you ever asked him a question he wasn't overly comfortable with he'd always reply, 'I think you need to speak to Bosco about that.'

Ever since Eddie and I had had that initial chat at the awards ceremony everything had felt good, and I think it's what he'd achieved prior to that which really made the difference. The team he'd created were dedicated, knowledgeable and welcoming, which enabled you as a driver to concentrate on the job in hand. Take my word for it, just being allowed to get on with your job is a rare commodity in motorsport, and Eddie and the team made sure there were no distractions. That chassis which had won the previous year's championship with Andy Wallace (the Madgwick Reynard 863) was still only two years old; Eddie, who can be quite persuasive when he wants to be, had actually talked Adrian Reynard into *giving* him a car, which meant all he had to do was find the right engine. From the moment we first hit the track that car was nigh on perfect so every single element, whether human or mechanical, was quality – even the driver. The absence of a second car for much of the season was just the icing on the cake. Yes, I still had to drive the thing, but although it's always possible to overachieve you're never going to win a championship in a crap car. Thanks to Eddie and his team, that was something I never had to worry about.

Now that I'd secured the Formula 3 Championship, all I could think about was getting back in the Benetton again. So when Peter Collins called me to confirm the test at Jerez I was cock-a-hoop. You may have noticed by now – I might even have mentioned it already – but the road to success (or even failure, for that matter) is very rarely without incident when I'm on it. So, instead of winning the championship and then flying straight over to Jerez and wowing Senna, Prost, Mansell and Piquet with my astonishing speed and ability, I first got into an arm-wrestling contest with a mechanic in the back of Eddie Jordan's motorhome.

I forget whereabouts in the country we were, it could have been Snetterton, but as I said, I was in the back of this motorhome with a couple of Eddie's mechanics and one of them suggested that we have an arm-wrestling competition. I was quite strong in those days and despite these mechanics having arms like tree trunks I fancied my chances, so without further ado I pulled down the table from the wall and asked who was going first.

'I'll go first,' said one of them.

Brilliant, I thought. *He's only about my height. I should be able to do him easily.*

'Take the strain,' said the other chap. 'Aaaaaaaand, go!'

To try and conserve some energy for the forthcoming rounds I decided to go for the early win, and right from the off I gave it beans.

HRRRRRRRRRRRRRRRRRRRRRRRRRRRRRRRRRRRR!

My opponent didn't move a millimetre, nor did he make any stupid straining noises like me. He just sat there like a statue. A very strong statue.

Right, you bastard, I thought. *I'll have another go.*

HRRRRRRRRRRRRRRRRRRRRRRRRRRRRRRRRRRRR!

Once again, not a move did this superman make, nor a sound emanate from his lips. I wasn't even sure he was breathing.

My next (and final) attempt was so Herculean that my rival had to try a little bit, which resulted in the table coming off the wall. Eddie was none too happy about this. Another result was me pulling a nerve in my shoulder. At first I thought it was nothing, but the following morning I was in agony. These days you get F1 drivers doing all kinds of silly things – Max Verstappen driving the Red Bull RB7 down the Streif ski course in Kitzbühel in Austria springs to mind – but I'm afraid that arm-wrestling mechanics in the back of motorhomes belonging to Irish team owners with a propensity to get angry over the smallest thing is quite possibly the silliest of all, and it's something I'd advise the likes of Toto Wolff, Ron Dennis and Christian Horner to do everything in their power to prevent.

The test in Jerez, while not a complete disaster, did not live up to its original billing of 'the second coming of the next big thing', and because things like changing gear and even steering were so bloody uncomfortable, I didn't exactly set the world alight. It was a lesson learned, and fortunately for me Peter was fairly understanding. In fact he was more incredulous than anything.

'You got injured doing what?'

'Arm-wrestling in a motorhome.'

'Bloody hell!'

The final test of the year for Benetton took place in December at Imola and featured me, Stefano Modena and Alessandro Nannini. There was nothing at all routine about this session, however, as it had been staged specifically to help Benetton decide who would partner their number-one driver, Thierry Boutsen, the following season. Peter had had to fight tooth and nail just to get me on the test as Luciano Benetton wanted an Italian driver in the team. That was understandable, I suppose, but even though I knew I was going to be at a disadvantage it was still a massive opportunity for me. 'Push, push, push,' Peter told me. 'You're a better driver than either of these two and if you manage to outperform them, Luciano's going to find it very difficult to say no.'

I'd never driven at Imola before, but instead of me having to set up my cognitive PlayStation like I had at Monaco they allowed me two or three laps in a road car the day before. This was certainly useful, but there was no way in the world I could familiarize myself with Imola's quirks and permutations in just a couple of laps. There was a lot at stake, though, and when I went out on my installation lap the following morning I had no choice but to, as Peter had suggested, 'push, push, push'.

I remember that lap with frightening clarity. As I came down to Acque Minerali, which is a small chicane at the halfway point, I hit a kerb that must have been about the height of a medium-sized dog. It was pretty wet that day and the pre-heated slicks I had on must have gone cold, which resulted in my losing grip. I hadn't noticed the kerb the day before and at the time I was pretty angry with myself, especially given the prize on offer. Because of the importance of the occasion, instead of pitting I just kept on driving. When I eventually did make it back to the garage I was told by one of the mechanics that I'd bent the bloody suspension.

'Didn't you notice anything?' he asked. 'Any bumps at all?'

'Erm, well, I might have hit a kerb going through Acque Minerali,' I whispered gingerly.

'What, the high one?'

'Possibly.'

He gave me a kind of 'you bloody pillock' look and told me to get out of the way. 'I think we'll be able to fix it,' he muttered.

Fortunately they did, so off I went again, but although I gave a good account of myself I was nervous and even a little bit anxious – two emotions I wasn't all that familiar with. I was also still on a very big learning curve (even bigger than the kerb that did my suspension) and it certainly became a day for firsts: my first time at Imola, my first time in the wet in an F1 car, and my first time driving for an F1 seat. The entire driving experience had also been edgier and far more dangerous than anything I'd ever been through.

By the end of the test I was a few tenths quicker than Stefano but about a tenth slower than Alessandro, so despite my best efforts I hadn't managed to give Luciano Benetton any difficult decisions to make. Not yet, anyway. Peter was pleased, though, and before I left for home he took me to one side and assured me that, come hell or high water, he would get me into Formula 1.

I know it's just a turn of phrase, but pretty soon the words he used would become frighteningly prophetic. There might not have been a great deal of water involved, high or otherwise, but there was about to be a colossal amount of hell.

Six

WHEN I ARRIVED back at Eddie Jordan Racing preparations were already underway for the following season, and as I hadn't got the drive at Benetton, my and the team's immediate ambitions had realigned once again. While I'd been busy trying to skip a formula, with Eddie's help and blessing I might add, he and the team had been hard at work preparing a Jordan entry for the 1988 Formula 3000 Championship, the precursor to GP2. Once again money, or lack of it, was hampering Eddie's efforts, and although it probably didn't touch the sides with regard to the overall budget, Peter Collins came up with an idea that would (a) serve his and my future ambitions at Benetton, and (b) put some much-needed cash into the Jordan coffers, while at the same time helping Eddie's search for a new engine.

I don't know what the exact details were, but in a nutshell Jordan would become a kind of feeder team for what became the Benetton junior team, and as well as having an option on me for the following season Peter also assured me that he'd get me involved in some more testing. I suppose it was like a part-time apprenticeship in a way, and it did wonders for my confidence. These days a lot of Formula 1 teams work with drivers from a very young age, McLaren and Lewis Hamilton being one of the better-known examples, but in the late eighties things were not only far less structured, but a driver was almost expected to bring some sponsorship or money to the table. To have a recognized F1 team effectively bringing through a financially embarrassed driver was almost unheard of.

Alex Hawkridge, who was a mate of Peter's from his Toleman days, was now at a company called Zytec, and after a bit of gentle persuasion from Peter and Eddie he eventually offered to supply the engines. The Jordan chassis would once again be provided by Reynard, although at first Eddie was far from keen. Whatever the reasons, he didn't think Adrian Reynard was ready to make the first step up to Formula 3000 and thought we should be using a March. Adrian managed to persuade him in the end (probably by offering him a couple of free cars), so apart from the engines it was an almost identical package to the previous year. The only main addition personnel-wise was Trevor Foster, whom Eddie had poached from Swallow Racing.

Come the start of the season the car was still pure white and we didn't have a single sponsor on board, but it wasn't through want of trying. Eddie Jordan is a genius when it comes to persuading people to part with their cash – forget ice to the Eskimos, he could sell smiles to Jean Todt. This was one hell of a tough sell, though: we were new to the formula, had an untried and untested chassis, and a driver who, despite having a bit of F1 experience, was a total novice to F3000. It doesn't exactly scream 'Buy me, buy me!' does it? On top of all that the first round of the F3000 season was at Jerez, and apart from the test I was a novice there too.

'Nobody wants to know, Johnny,' Eddie said to me, 'and between you and me I can barely afford to get us over there. I feel like I'm letting you down.'

Even though Eddie and I shared the same ambition, he knew that as things stood I'd probably get to Formula 1 before he did – not because of talent but because there's a lot more to prepare and consider when you're a team owner – but that never stopped him from pushing me and promoting me. He was like Peter in that sense, except at the time he couldn't offer me a drive in the top tier. I wish we could have gone into F1 together, Eddie and I, but such is life. He's done OK and so have I, and I'll always be very grateful to him. As a boss he inspires confidence; as a friend he just inspires, full stop. He's got very nice hair, too. And so versatile.

He and his wife Marie have a beautiful villa in a place called Sotogrande in southern Spain, and just before the race in Jerez Eddie flew us out there for a few days. It was a really nice gesture, and I'm afraid that I repaid his kindness by going out and getting drunk for two days with a shark fisherman.

Mr Jordan was not at all happy, and if ever I either annoyed or worried him he'd always say, in a very schoolmasterly way, 'Johnnyyyyyyyyyyyyy, Johnnyyyyyyyyyyyyy!'

'Johnnyyyyyyyyyyyyy! Johnnyyyyyyyyyyyyyyyyyyyyyyyy!' Eddie said when I sloped back. 'Where the bloody hell have you been? I've been worried sick. We're supposed to be driving down to Jerez in a few hours!'

'I'm sorry, Eddie, but I got talking to this fisherman.'

'For two bloody days?' Eddie spluttered.

He was a victim of his own success, I'm afraid. I was far too relaxed and happy to care about anything.

Before we get back to Jerez, I just want to tell you about a mystery that was solved on the flight out to Sotogrande. Eddie will probably want to murder me, but I'm sure he'll forgive me. Ever since the 1970s Eddie has sported a toupee, something he's always been very open about. I too have suffered from hair loss but instead of investing in a wig I chose instead to go for a weave, which I think looks very fetching. Anyway, back then we obviously all knew that Eddie wore a wig but nobody could work out how he stopped it blowing off his head and so in the end we decided to open an

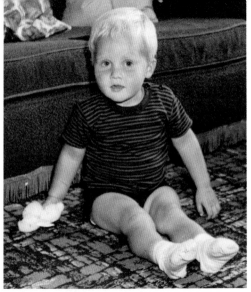

The young John Paul Herbert (**left**), ready to take his first steps in the motor racing world. A family holiday to Cornwall and my uncle Pete were the catalysts to taking up karting (**below**), and the number 69 was soon to become a feared sight around Britain as I moved up through the age groups.

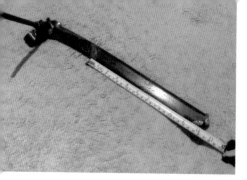

Left: Being impaled through the groin by this wishbone almost did for me in 1984, before I won my first Formula Ford race at Silverstone in September of that year (**below**), then the Formula Ford Festival itself in 1985 at Brands Hatch – my big breakthrough.

Bottom: With Eddie Jordan's team, I felt unbeatable in the Formula 3 Championship in 1987. Here I celebrate victory at Silverstone ahead of Gary Brabham (*left*) and Damon Hill, who clearly can't bear to look.

Above: Brands Hatch, 21 August 1988. The wreckage at the top left belongs to me, while the aftermath (**right**) was not for the squeamish.

Below: Back on track with Lotus at Spa in 1991. Who is that behind me? Oh, it's Michael Schumacher, making his Formula 1 debut.

Unbridled joy in winning the British Grand Prix at Silverstone in July 1995, with my wife Rebecca (**bottom left**) joining me for the celebrations before my musical talent was unleashed on an unsuspecting public.

I repeated the trick at Monza two months later, cutting a few corners (**top**), with Mika Häkkinen and Heinz-Harald Frentzen (**above**) replacing Jean Alesi and David Coulthard on the podium this time, although I seemed to be left alone for the victory jig (**right**). Still, finishing fourth overall in a Formula 1 Championship, and as a disabled driver, still seems like a pretty decent result to me, and Benetton beat the Williams of Hill and Coulthard to the Constructors' Championship.

Flavio Briatore and I (**above left**) did not, shall we say, see eye to eye, but for all the lack of teamwork at Benetton, and my differences with Michael Schumacher, there was still mutual respect between drivers, and we finished that 1995 season both on the podium in Japan (**below**).

Above: By then, the world of motor racing was a much poorer place after the tragic deaths of Ayrton Senna and Roland Ratzenberger in 1994. This is one of my favourite photos, taken at a karting event at Paris Bercy the previous year, with Senna (*far left*) joined amongst others by Alain Prost, in blue to my right, in his last year driving in Formula 1.

Below: The best of British. *From left*: Yours truly, Damon Hill, Derek Warwick, Martin Brundle and Mark Blundell.

Above: Hobnobbing with the reigning world champion before the opening race of the 1997 Formula 1 season in Australia. Damon may have had problems with his Arrows but it would be amiss of me not to point out that I finished two places above him in the drivers' standings come the end of the year ...

Below: 'Half a second off? That would be at least a second on the Grand Prix track.' Watching Nigel Mansell win his first British Grand Prix in 1986 was a big inspiration for me and even though I impressed him at a test the following year he wasn't giving anything away.

internal investigation. We'd been waiting ages for an opportunity to look, so when Eddie dozed off about halfway through the flight, we took our chance. Once he'd started snoring and the drool was beginning to appear, I crept over to him and pulled up the fringe a little bit à la Morecambe and Wise.

'It's stuck on with glue!' I whispered excitedly to my mechanic, Bruce Stewart. 'He should get UHU on as a sponsor?'

The last time I attempted to enquire after it, we were standing in a lift.

'So Eddie, how's your wi—'

'Johnnyyyyyyyyyyyyy! JOHNNYYYYYYYYYYYYYYYY-YYYYYY!'

Actually, we should maybe do a compare and contrast at some point.

By the time we got to Jerez for testing nothing had changed – no sponsor, no money, nada. The race was being televised, too, so we couldn't understand why nobody would give us a chance. Perhaps if we did well in qualifying?

Now I might well have been a novice in the eyes of a potential sponsor but I'd remembered a thing or two about the Jerez circuit, and despite all the money worries I was still able to put that to good use. For a start I knew it was a difficult place to set a car up for because the surface was coarse and abrasive and the rear tyres tended to go off quickly, resulting in brutal oversteer. Driving at Jerez also requires a tremendous amount of concentration because there are so many corners. The only way you can really make up time to any significant degree is by under-braking and then getting traction out of those corners. In a race, overtaking was almost impossible, or so I'd been told, except at the hairpin, where you could make a run down the inside and still find good grip. A flyer out of the chicane might also work, but at the majority of the corners attempts to pass would mess up your exit speeds and you'd probably lose out.

A little bit of knowledge can go a long way, so they say, and after averaging 100mph on my hot lap I qualified on pole, in the cleanest, whitest car the world had ever seen. Perfect for an Essex boy in the 1980s. Quick as a flash, Eddie was on to Duncan Lee at Camel Cigarettes and God knows who else about a deal, and by the time I lined up for the race the car was yellow and had been plastered with logos for Camel and Avon Tyres. Now all I had to do was win the race. 'They've only agreed to the one race, Johnny,' said our sales svengali. 'But if you do well we could be set up for the season.'

At the green light I made a good start, and as the power came on the car slid slightly. Once again, as with the previous season, everything felt good, and after the first two laps I already had a good lead. The only thing that surprised me a little bit was that at the start nobody came with me, but that made my job easier as I was able to pace myself early doors. Mega Blundell put in a couple of fast laps but I was watching the boards and I was sure he couldn't keep it up. There was one moment of alarm. I was lapping Andy Wallace at the hairpin, and because I made the move a little bit late Andy had already committed to turning in. We must have missed each other by millimetres. I wish I could have seen Eddie's face. He later said that the last lap of that race at Jerez felt like the longest and slowest in the history of motorsport.

We'd only managed about twenty laps in testing, so when I went through the chequered flag to win, that was the first time I'd ever done a race distance in an F3000 car. We should have left it white because we were all F3000 virgins, Adrian Reynard, Eddie, Trevor and me. I do remember Mr Jordan becoming rather excitable after the race (that happens occasionally), but it didn't take him long to get back into business mode. 'I think I'll be paying Mr Camel and Mr Avon a visit next week, Johnny.'

A race win couldn't have come at a better time.

The second race of the 1988 Formula 3000 Championship, which took place at Vallelunga just north of Rome, is memorable to me for one monumental reason: it was the first time I came into contact with a young Swiss driver named Gregor Foitek. I suppose he became my arch nemesis in a sense, the same way Blofeld became James Bond's. Gregor spent many years as the Herbert family's public enemy number one. That said, I would hardly have described him as an evil genius; more an overly aggressive, erratic and occasionally dangerous racing driver. But only in my opinion, of course. I think he must have modelled himself on Nigel Mansell, but what use is aggression if you don't have the finesse and judgement needed to turn it into a successful style of driving? Nigel had both of those prerequisites in spades, which is why he became one of the greats. Gregor, on the other hand, while managing to forge a decent career for himself, was sadly lacking in either, and left in his wake a string of furious drivers. In my case, on the receiving end of his 'over-exuberance' on more than one occasion, I was usually too badly injured to be furious with him. Although the second of these incidents would undoubtedly be the 'main event', so to speak, the first, which happened at Vallelunga, didn't do my season, or my head, any good at all.

How I got to Vallelunga in the first place is completely beyond me. For some reason I'd been unable to travel with the rest of the team so I arrived at Aeroporto di Fiumicino with just a map, a suitcase, details of my hire car company and no sense of direction. Actually that's not strictly true, I have a fairly decent sense of direction, but in the 1980s Italian road signs rarely corresponded to what was written on a map (or that's how it seemed to me), so when I left the airport, instead of driving straight on for a bit and then bearing north towards Vallelunga, I went straight on and then south towards Latina. Every time I realized I was travelling either south, east or west – i.e. in the wrong direction, and there were quite a few moments like that – I'd stop, get the map out and make a decision; and every single bloody time I made the wrong one. Toll road after toll road I went through. The first time I saw a sign for Rome I almost wept, but not for the reason you might think. I wept because I was driving in the opposite direction.

Eventually I noticed that every so often a gap occurred in the barriers on the autostrada, and in a fit of sheer desperation I prepared to make an emergency U-turn. Getting through this gap was like going through the Fairmont Hairpin at Monaco, except that instead of those around you also slowing down to about 30mph, everyone else carried on as normal, and it has to be said that the Italian idea of what is normal is quite different to our own. Fortunately there was nobody too close behind me – if there had been I wouldn't have made the move – but I do remember hearing quite a few horns after exiting the Rome-bound lane, not to mention seeing at least six of the top ten rude Italian hand gestures. They're such an expressive nation.

The next problem happened when I got to the first toll booth, by which time it was getting dark. I had a ticket to travel in the opposite direction, of course, so when I handed it to the gentleman in the booth he looked at me like I'd just arrived from another planet. In fact I'd arrived from Latina, just on the wrong side of the road. At first he didn't say anything, he just kept looking at the ticket, and then at me. Then, after a minute or two, he tried talking to me.

'*Come?*' he said, which is Italian for 'How?'

Not being that fluent in the language I gave him a Gallic shrug and uttered the words '*No entiendo*'. It was a very international conversation.

He went off to fetch a stern-looking man who I assume was his supervisor, as well as one or two of his colleagues, and again they started looking at the ticket and then at me. They were out of earshot at the time so all I could offer them were more Gallic shrugs. After about forty-five minutes of just looking and wondering, they decided to consign my case to the 'I really haven't the foggiest idea, let the little weirdo go' file. As I drove away I remember seeing them in my mirror, all lined up, staring at the car in wonder. I've never thought of myself as being particularly 'mysterious' before, but I suppose at that moment I was.

I got to Vallelunga at about eleven p.m., and fortunately the hotel we were staying in was right next to the track. The following morning, after regaling the team with my exploits on the road, we all walked down to the paddock to begin the test. Now that the finances were healthier, the mood in the garage was better than it had ever been, and as if to drive home the fact that we were making so much progress, we had a fantastic session on the track, the best yet in F3000. What I think was so important to me at the time was feeling like I was part of a family – and, as I said earlier, Eddie was very good at making that happen. In order for me to overcome my natural shyness and be open with people, which was pretty important, I had to feel completely comfortable. I'd have been a less effective operator had I been stuck in my shell so at the time that 'pastoral care', if you like, was as important to me as my driving skills. I loved to feel wanted, and the happier and more relaxed I was the better I drove.

My mechanics, Bruce and Malik, were both very laid-back but also highly experienced and they always went out of their way to put me at ease. By the same turn I think they were happy working with a driver who not only appreciated their efforts but who might actually achieve something, and at the beginning of that 1988 International F3000 season we were all very close. Practical jokes were an important factor in those relationships. Bruce in particular was an absolute bugger for them. First he started putting oil on the inside of my helmet and on the chin strap, which meant that when I took it off I looked like a mini Abraham Lincoln. I would counter this by going into the kitchen and putting things like washers in their food. Many's the time I sat watching Bruce and Malik tucking into their sausage sandwiches and biting down on something not very sausagey. You can't put a price on that kind of fun – or on dental surgery, for that matter.

Because the test went well, qualifying couldn't come soon enough for us. But once we were back out on the track we very quickly changed our minds. If memory serves me correctly, we started suffering some kind of engine problem which resulted in losing a bit of speed somewhere, so in order to qualify well I really had to push hard. This is where the Reynard chassis came into its own. Had I been driving either a March or a Ralt with the same problem I think I'd have been in trouble. The front end of the Reynard in particular was exceptional, giving you the ability to carry speed into a corner. That's what I mean about it being the closest thing I ever drove to a kart: you could use the front of the car almost as a brake, and the comfort factor was nigh on perfect. There was a tiny little chicane near the pits at Vallelunga and I was able to drive through that flat out at about 150mph. It was just incredible.

Despite the slight loss of speed, we still managed to qualify on the second row in fourth. By lap 45 of the race I was up into third. The man in front of me at this point was the aforementioned Flying Foitek, who on lap 46, just as we were coming out of the hairpin at the back of the pits, made a mistake and went on to the kerb. This now left a gap for me to come up on the inside, but just as I was taking advantage, Gregor then came back off the kerb, hit me sideways on, and sent me crashing into the barrier opposite. The next thing I remember is being in the medical centre, trying to give a urine sample (although I can't be sure if anyone actually asked for one); the crash itself is a blank.

According to one journalist, 'the savage impact tore through the sidepod, bursting a radiator, and Johnny's helmet took a heavy knock, probably from the cockpit surround. He sat stunned and was helped out suffering whiplash and bruising.'

It was a little bit more serious than that. By the time the medical team arrived I was unconscious. Once they got me to the medical centre I eventually came round, but according to Trevor I wasn't right at all and was rambling quite a bit. Some would say that's quite normal for me, but after a quick consultation, he, Eddie, Peter and Alex Hawkridge from Zytec decided to send me to see Professor Sid Watkins, the in-house F1 doctor. He ran some tests, and after eventually finding my brain he announced that although he didn't think I was 100 per cent I should be OK to drive again.

A few days later I started having one or two bad headaches, so a return visit to Sid Watkins followed, who diagnosed a slight swelling of the brain and recommended at least ten days' rest. Not having had a great deal of schooling I suppose I should have been grateful that my brain was getting a little bit bigger, but at the time I remember being quite put out. The next race was at Pau in France, and because that can be quite a dangerous circuit the decision was made to take the professor's advice and leave me out. I was furious at the time, which I suppose is under-standable, though not nearly as understandable as the call to make me rest.

I was out for about a month in all, but thankfully I only missed the one race. The week before that race Eddie had arranged for me to have a test at Silverstone with some sports cars, and even though the test went well I had a bit of a shunt at Copse Corner and so the session was cut short. This, understandably, went down like a lead balloon with all the other drivers and there might even have been a bit of handbags involved. That was water off a duck's back to Eddie, though, and so we walked away unscathed.

When I came back in at Silverstone for round four I felt like my old self again. If only I could have said the same about the car. We were still having problems but after qualifying mid-grid, which was more than respectable, I managed to trump that by finishing seventh. Yes, I was frustrated, as I knew exactly what the car was capable of, but it was a good drive.

Next stop was Monza, and once again we were struggling for speed. We'd mulled this problem over for weeks on end but whatever Trevor and the boys tried it just didn't feel right. It was like the car was holding something back; I only felt able to access about 80 to 85 per cent of what the V8 had to offer. It was infuriating knowing it was there but for the life of me not being able to bloody find it. No matter, we were where we were. With a following wind and a good drive, we might be OK.

I qualified on the third (or maybe fourth) row, which was an improvement on Silverstone, and going into the second chicane I overtook Cor Euser, who was driving a Madgwick, before setting my sights on Mark Blundell. Mark was in a works Lola, and as far as I could see he was having engine problems; but before I got an opportunity to take him, a crash occurred and they red-flagged the race. A restart wasn't ideal as I'd been going so well but at least it would close the gap between me and the front runners. Well, that was the idea. This was me, though, remember?

Unfortunately the flaming starter failed at the restart and instead of the marshals allowing us to push-start the car for the parade lap, they made us take it back to the pit lane. Cue quite a lot of rude words aimed at said marshals, not to mention a gesture or two. Once back in the pits they unjammed the starter and off I went, in last place. With the car feeling a little bit more responsive, and with nothing really to lose, I decided to give it beans, and the Italian crowd went absolutely wild. This time I was going in the *right* direction and I loved every single second of it. Somewhere along the way I managed to smash the lap record and was tearing up the track and overtaking everything and everyone in sight. The journalists, too, were impressed. One quote in particular from that day makes me grin like a Cheshire cat: 'Time and time again the yellow car arrived at the first chicane, its braking left to the last moment, millimetre perfect. Then it was over the kerb, stab, stab, stab on the power, and he was away, up the gearbox, deft flicks of opposite lock balancing the tail all the while. The crowd loved it, going wild every time he appeared.'

The reason I've included that paragraph isn't just because I'm an egotistical idiot – and believe me, I've had my fair share of bad press over the years – it's because it sums up that race and how I feel about Monza so well. I'd be back there in just a few weeks to test alongside a three-time world champion, but I didn't know that at the time.

After driving what had undoubtedly been the race of my life I finished third. Had I had the luxury of just a couple more laps, I'd have nailed it. The car still wasn't perfect but it felt like we were getting there.

After Monza came Enna, which in addition to being a power circuit is unique in that it circles the only natural lake in Sicily. This was a race to forget, as I spun off quite early on (it's the dust, you see). One thing I do remember clearly is being told before the race that if I happened to come off I should stay in the car.

'Why's that?' I'd asked.

'Simple. You're liable to get bitten by snakes.'

'Really? I'll stay where I am then.'

It wasn't one of the problems we were used to encountering but at least it made things interesting.

Next stop for the EJR F3000 team was supposed to be a test at Donington, followed by round seven of the championship, which would take place at Brands Hatch – or so I thought. A few days after returning from Enna I received a telephone call from Peter Warr, who at the time was the team manager at Lotus. 'We're running a two-day test at Monza, Johnny, and we'd like you to take part. I've already spoken to Eddie and Peter and they're happy to release you. It'll be good experience.'

Oh, all right then, if I must.

The test was due to take place about halfway through that Senna/Prost-dominated F1 season of 1988, in between the Hungarian and Belgian Grands Prix, and I'd be testing along-side Lotus's two main drivers: Satoru Nakajima and the current world champion, Nelson Piquet. Nelson was from the highest echelons of motor-racing society and in 1988 was the most decorated and experienced driver on the F1 grid. He may not have had the fastest car that season but he certainly commanded a huge amount of respect in the paddock, so just being in the same garage as him was going to be a thrill. I wasn't going to tell him that, though.

Funnily enough, one of the first people I encountered when I got to the Lotus garage was Nelson, and it was a wonderfully competitive yet ultimately comic encounter. Nakajima, whose car I'd be using, had just finished a few laps and was leaving the garage, so once he'd gone I introduced myself to the mechanics and then started having a good look at the car. That's when Nelson arrived. He sidled up, trying to look cool, said 'hi' to the mechanics, and then looked at me like I was some-thing he'd found on the bottom of his shoe after a night out on Copacabana.

'Who are you?' he asked, looking at me suspiciously, his chin in the air.

I drew myself up to my full height of five feet five and three-quarter inches and puffed out my chest. 'I don't know. Who are you?'

He raised an eyebrow, à la Roger Moore. 'That's none of your business. Now, come on, young man. Who are you?'

'I'm not telling you who I am until you tell me who you are,' I responded. 'Who are you?'

'Why should I tell you who I am before you tell me who you are?' Nelson snorted. 'You're the impostor, not me.'

And so it went on. The only thing we didn't do was challenge each other to a duel.

Nelson tried his best to be serious and authoritative but once we got started it was futile. That's him all over, though. He can be very severe when he wants to be, and is of course a tremendously competitive and successful man, but his sense of humour still gets the better of him occasionally.

The next person I came into contact with was Peter Warr, who used to run Lotus with the team's founder, Colin Chapman. Peter, like Peter Collins at Benetton, was a big admirer of mine and by his own admission had been looking for an excuse to get me into a Lotus for quite a while.

The test itself, for me at least, lasted just a day and a bit and I was there primarily to help with some aerodynamics work. Adrian Newey had just completed the March 881, which was the first car he ever designed for Formula 1, and it was causing quite a stir. He'd included two extra-long endplates on the March that sent the air past the inside of the tyres and this had been making a massive difference to the performance on the track. We're talking seconds here. Lotus, not to mention the majority of the other teams, had picked up on this and wanted to try and emulate the advance as soon as was humanly possible. I'd been going round in the late 1m 20s prior to them introducing the change, but once the plates were on the difference was immediate and gave me about a second a lap. Nelson had gone out in the other car before I'd started testing so had been given his plates sooner, so to speak, yet even prior to me getting the plates I was still either matching him or outpacing him. We were doing race simulations for most of the day and I managed to outpace him on every lap and in every situation. He might have been having an off day of course, and in my modesty the conditions may have differed slightly when he was out, but as far as I was concerned I'd just outpaced a three-time world champion. What a huge confidence booster.

There was one incident that day which I think demonstrates the mindset of a racing driver and what makes us different from normal, sensible people. I forget where it happened, but at one point during the test I lost control momentarily, travelling at about 150mph, and after missing the barrier by inches I went straight back to the garage and relayed the incident in detail. The point is that I'd continued to think logically during the incident and despite the dangers had remained focused on the test. This isn't a brag, by the way, and many would argue that my only concern at that point should have been my safety, but a combination of faith in my ability as well as an acceptance of what can happen on the track always kept that secondary, and I think you'll find that nearly all Formula 1 drivers are the same. If I take somebody out on a track for five minutes I can guarantee that by the end of it they'll be a gibbering wreck, and why wouldn't they be? It's a normal human reaction to feel fear when your life is in danger – and with me driving, it is! We don't feel any of that fear, though, or at least not much of it; just the adrenalin and the exhilaration. Racing drivers are weird.

Just about every team on the grid was out testing that day at Monza, including the mighty Ferrari, and as I was leaving the garage for the airport at the end of the session I was stopped by the assistant to the Ferrari team boss Marco Puccini. 'I've got a message from Marco,' he said. 'He's been talking to Enzo about you and they've agreed that you and Marco should have a chat about next season. Do you think you might be available for a meeting?'

Now this was just getting ridiculous. Benetton had an option on me for 1989 and I knew that Lotus were also very keen – even more so after the test, I later found out. But Scuderia Ferrari? The Prancing Horse? This happened very shortly before the great Enzo Ferrari passed away so I couldn't possibly say how much he'd had to do with the decision to meet me, but I didn't need a plane to take me back to England that afternoon, I could have floated. I'm not sure if it's quite the same these days – I'm afraid it probably isn't – but in those days every racing driver, regardless of nationality or ability, aspired to drive for Ferrari, and I was certainly no different. Gilles Villeneuve, who has always been my all-time favourite F1 driver, was a Ferrari legend – in my opinion the greatest of them all – and as Marco's assistant talked to me that was all I could think about. *I could be the new Gilles!* It was genuine boyhood-ambition stuff, like wanting to be an astronaut when you're six. The difference is, I was in my mid-twenties. I gave the guy my number, he said he'd call me once he'd had a look at the team boss's diary, and off I went to the airport. Not a bad day then, all things considered.

The first person who called me when I arrived back in the UK was Peter Collins.

'How did it go?' he said.

'Good, thanks. I don't think I disgraced myself.'

'No, you didn't. I spoke to Peter Warr earlier and he was very impressed. Looks like we might have some competition – should we decide to take up the option, of course.'

He was obviously joking, but I could tell by the tone of Peter's voice that he wished he hadn't let Lotus use me for the test. I therefore decided it was probably best not to tell him about Ferrari, who in fact called me later that day and left a message about setting up a meeting.

While of course being flattered by all this attention, I was conscious of the fact that Peter Collins was more than just an interested party. He was my mentor, and because of that I felt a certain amount of loyalty – not towards Benetton, as such, but him as a person. It was symptomatic of our relationship: you've looked after me and so I'll look after you. But unbeknown to anybody at the time that loyalty would one day cost me a drive with one of the true giants of the sport and consign me to a living hell.

By the time we completed the pre-Brands test at Donington, Trevor and the boys had managed to solve the speed problem once and for all, so to all intents and purposes the next round would be like starting the season from scratch again, just with the benefit of a little bit more knowledge and experience. Despite missing Pau and spinning off at Enna I was still only a few points behind the current F3000 leader, Roberto Moreno, and was confident, nay adamant, that we'd be back winning races soon.

Which just goes to show how wrong you can be, doesn't it?

Seven

WHEN I ARRIVED at Brands Hatch in mid-August for the next F3000 race, the entire paddock was talking about my test; news had even filtered out to the stands. Once again, without wanting to sound like a braggart, at the time I was quite possibly the hottest prospect in motor racing, and the fact that I seemed to be on the verge of making it into Formula 1 was causing a real buzz about the place. Everywhere I walked people just looked at me, smiled, then moved aside. I was like a mini motor-racing Moses!

The last person I spoke to before we began qualifying at Brands was Frank Williams. I'd picked up a whisper he was interested in me for the 1989 season but so far hadn't heard anything concrete. 'I heard about your test with Lotus, Johnny,' he said, half smiling at me. 'The moment you finish this race, would you come and see me? I've a proposition for you.'

If my motorsport cake needed any more icing, that was most certainly it. Enzo Ferrari was associated as much with road cars as he was Formula 1, but Frank Williams had only one association, and that was with F1. It was his life and, what's more, he was bloody good at it. He'd been in Formula 1 since the early 1970s and had a fantastic reputation, especially with young drivers. I figured there and then that I might stand a very good chance of finding out why.

For qualifying we were split into two groups. I was in one and Martin Donnelly, my new team-mate at Jordan and a very good driver, was in the other. He went out first and did well. In fact he was over a second quicker than anyone else. Then I went out in the second group and knocked a further six-tenths off Martin's time, which gave me pole. I was dripping with confidence: it felt like nobody could touch me. Martin had been brought in as a replacement for the Swedish driver Thomas Danielsson, who had been forced to retire from the team because of an eye problem. I knew Martin was going to be a threat but that was exactly what I needed to keep me on my toes, and providing I did so I knew I could beat him. Being the team's main focus had been great in F3 but now I needed to be pushed. There would be no more letting other drivers catch up with me just so I could have a bit of a race.

When I speak to people who were at that meeting at Brands Hatch, an awful lot of them claim that despite the buzz surrounding me and my promising career there was a sense of foreboding around the track. You get it sometimes, a feeling of uneasiness; I've experienced it myself once or twice. It doesn't happen often but when it does it envelops you and can create quite a disturbing atmosphere. Three very famous examples: Spa in 1960, where the F1 drivers Chris Bristow and Alan Stacey were both killed; Indianapolis in 1973, where during practice and in the race itself, three drivers and a pit crew member lost their lives; and of course Imola in 1994, where Ayrton Senna and Roland Ratzenberger were killed in separate accidents. If things start off well the mood can often lift, just like that, but if a meeting starts off badly things can grow deathly quiet. The spectators are almost expecting an accident to happen, and that's not healthy. Unbeknown to me, that was exactly what was happening at Brands that weekend.

It had started as early as Friday, during free practice, when the Italian driver Enrico Bertaggia had gone into the tyre-wall at Paddock Hill Bend. The accident looked so serious that everyone present thought Enrico had been killed, so they were astonished, and of course relieved, when he walked away with only minor injuries. It was an inauspicious start to the meeting, exactly the sort of thing people dread. From then on the mood just got darker.

Later that day, once again in free practice, the very promising French driver Michel Trollé lost control of his Lola going into Dingle Dell Corner and, like Enrico, ended up in the tyre-wall. Michel wasn't quite as lucky as Enrico and ended up sustaining some pretty horrific injuries to both his knees and ankles.

So, two serious accidents on the first day of the meeting – the atmosphere couldn't have been blacker.

It had already been a bad season for F3000 in terms of accidents: two broken ankles for Steve Kempton at Jerez, severe leg injuries for Fabien Giroix at Monza, and, at the same meeting, a cartwheel into the advertising hoardings and then into the trees at the first Lesmo corner for Massimo Monti. It really was a miracle nobody had been killed. Then there was my ever-expanding brain, of course, courtesy of that run-in with Gregor Foitek. It didn't strike me at the time, but looking back, it had been a bit of a shocker.

As with qualifying, the start of the race couldn't have gone any better for me and by the end of lap 20 I had a lead of almost twelve seconds, going into the second session with an almost unassailable lead.

Less than two laps later – midway through lap 22, to be exact – I saw a red flag being waved, signalling a restart. What an absolute disaster. A twelve-second lead gone, just like that. I found out before the start of the restart that the accident had been caused by Gregor Foitek. Who else? Roberto Moreno had apparently slammed hard into the Paddock tyre-wall while going wheel to wheel with an overly defensive Foitek. Moreno, who as I said was leading the F3000 championship at the time after wins at Pau, Silverstone and Monza, was furious and went on to say one or two rather uncomplimentary things about Foitek over the public address system as he walked back to the pits. *Quite a nice touch*, I thought.

That incident turned the entire day on its head for me, although as far as the meeting itself was concerned it simply brought it in line with the previous two days. From there, everything just started to go wrong. At the restart I made the stupid mistake of not parking the car straight in relation to the gradient of the track, so when the flag went and I put my foot on the throttle I started going sideways. I managed to pull it back but it was still a bloody awful start. In fact, not only was I third going into the first corner, behind Martin Donnelly and Pierluigi Martini, I was also side by side with Foitek, and, Foitek being Foitek, he moved across immediately and began trying to intimidate me as we went into Paddock. We banged wheels, which seemed to be Gregor's calling card, but I managed to stay ahead of him up into Druids. I'm sure Gregor's actually a nice guy, he might even be kind to animals, but at the time I'd had enough of him and just wished he'd piss off.

As we went through Graham Hill Bend towards Surtees I was in front of Foitek by about a second so I started thinking about an attack on Martini; but before I could get my head in gear, Gregor was on my tail again, so I had to give him my full attention. As we came out of Surtees he had a slightly better exit than I did going towards Pilgrims Drop.

For all his faults Gregor was a very quick driver and, as I looked in the mirror to see where he was, I knew that if he had the room he would almost certainly make a run at me going down into Hawthorns. When I looked again I decided that the gap was probably too narrow for him to pass, left or right, so, providing I held my line, I should be OK. A second or so later

I looked in my right mirror and just as I did, Gregor moved into view. From a spectator's point of view you'd have wondered what he was doing there as even if he'd managed to pass me he'd have been on the wrong side going into Hawthorns.

As he tried to pass me on the left he made contact with my rear left tyre. I knew there wasn't enough room. What the bloody hell was he doing? He should have realized there and then and just backed off. Even though you can't hear each other, drivers often shout the odds during races and, although I didn't do it much, I was starting to get annoyed.

'What the bloody hell are you doing, you idiot? There's no room!'

I was heading for the bridge towards the top of Pilgrims Drop with Gregor literally millimetres behind me. *He's got to pull back*, I thought to myself. This was just stupid.

It was too late, though.

Once again, Foitek decided to have a go down the left and, like before, he made contact, except this time it was far more than just a touch, and before I could do anything about it my car swung violently to the left, along with his. Unluckily for me, rather than heading for the barrier, which is what would have happened had Gregor hit me even a thousandth of a second later, I was heading straight for the steel girder at the base of the bridge, at around 160mph. It was at this point that I realized I was in a massive amount of trouble, and although it all happened in a fraction of a second I distinctly remember sensing death. It sounds a bit stupid when I read it back but that's the only way I can describe how I felt as I crashed into the girder.

The impact came about half a second after the shunt. When I realized I was heading for the girder and not the softer barrier I remember starting to say 'Oh shit', but I only got as far as the 'Oh'.

After that it was just complete and utter mayhem.

What amazed me most was the energy I felt going towards the girder. It was as though God himself had picked up the car, taken a huge run-up and then chucked it straight at the bridge. Just before impact, my head was going forward and down so fast that I thought it was going to come away from my body. The noise, too, was deafening. When the memory of it comes back to me, which thankfully isn't very often, it reminds me of the end of the world – a kind of hideous apocalyptic explosion that you feel as well as hear. I've spoken to dozens of spectators who were standing along Pilgrims Drop that day and they often describe it as some kind of thunderclap. It terrified them.

To my surprise, the initial impact didn't feel as bad as I'd feared it would, although it did rip the front of my car clean off, which meant that my legs and feet were now completely exposed. You can see this on the footage, and it's bloody frightening. There's no protection whatsoever. Had this happened towards the end of the accident I might well have been OK but this was right at the beginning, when I was still moving at about 140mph. After hitting the girder, the car spun round again and I began flying across the track towards the barrier on the other side. Olivier Grouillard's Lola, which was probably a second or so behind Gregor and me at the first shunt, came through the bridge just as we began ricocheting back across the track. And that's when things started getting really interesting.

The three cars all but disintegrated on impact, which meant that as we headed towards the barrier the entire area was now awash with wheels, smoke, components and literally millions of pieces of carbon fibre and aluminium. When people watch the footage it's at this point they usually say, 'How the hell did nobody die?' I still can't believe it myself.

As I went into the barrier I once again had one of my 'Oh shit' moments, except this time I also closed my eyes. I figured that if I was going to die I didn't want to see it happen.

After the second impact I remember being thrown back out on to the track, spinning round a few times and then eventually coming to a halt somewhere near the side of the track. Then, once all the tail-enders had passed carefully through, silence fell. It was so quiet that for a few seconds I thought I must have died, but then slowly I started hearing noises again. First I heard some quite terrifying screams, which must have been coming from the spectators, and then I started hearing a few voices. Not in my head – that would come later, when they put me on morphine. What I heard were people shouting, and I remember at least one was sobbing. It must have been the race marshals. The cars were in such a horrific mess that everyone must have thought we were dead, so God knows what they were expecting to find in the wreckage.

According to Mark Blundell, who was one of only nine drivers to make it through the destruction unscathed, the Italian driver Paolo Barilla cried like a baby when he got back to the garage as he was convinced there had been at least one fatality. He had also been one of the lucky nine, and when he glanced in his mirrors as he passed the carnage he completely lost it. Mark also told me that James Hunt, who was at Brands Hatch working as a driving adviser to Jean Alesi and Volker Weidler, ran up to inspect the cars as they were salvaged from the crash scene and returned shaking his head, his face as white as a sheet. He too was expecting at least one fatality. On a lighter note (well, kind of), after the crash Mark ended up with one of my boots in the sidepod of his radiator and at first thought it was one of my feet! You have to laugh, don't you.

Footage of the crash is freely available on the internet, but for those of you who are a bit squeamish, I'll just finish off describing it.

Gregor had followed me from the bridge girder into Olivier and then on to the barrier. From there he'd literally barrel-rolled right along the top of the barrier all the way down to Hawthorns. Olivier, on making impact with Gregor and me, had hit the barrier too before coming to a halt about ten metres south of me. Five or six other cars were caught up in it, either crashing into me, Olivier, a passing wheel or piece of carbon fibre, but fortunately the impacts were minor. Funnily enough, both Olivier's and Gregor's crashes look just as spectacular as mine, yet I was the only one who sustained any serious injuries.

When I eventually opened my eyes all I could see in front of me were trees and grass. As I already said, the front of my car had been completely ripped away and most of the monocoque with it. Then I saw my knees, but nothing behind or below them. I remember thinking, *Well, that's it, then. They've gone wherever the front of the car has gone.*

Just then a marshal stuck his head into the cockpit, or what was left of it, and asked me if I was OK. Then another marshal turned up, looked down towards where my feet might or might not have been, and vomited. I thought about trying to make a joke out of this but for the life of me I couldn't think of anything. I know I often try to make light of the crash, and I'll explain why in a moment, but it was a catastrophic end to what had been a pretty awful weekend, and that bubble of success and confidence I'd been living in had now been well and truly burst.

A minute or so later I had quite a crowd of people round me. As more and more of them began to react to what had happened beneath my knees, the more I started to worry. In the end I just kept asking them to knock me out. I wasn't in any pain, I just couldn't cope with the enormity of losing my feet or even my legs, which is what I thought had happened. Some people find it hard to believe when I say that I felt no pain, but that's God's honest truth. I was later told by one of the doctors treating me that after very severe injuries the body often produces a kind of natural morphine. It's something to do with a chemical called tetrahydropapaveroline (try saying that after a few); as long as you try not to move, it can last quite a while. Luckily for me I had an ambulance crew with me within minutes and they were armed with a huge canister of a very strong painkilling gas called Entonox. Once they put the mask on me I was told to take some deep breaths, and as I did so I could feel my head start to spin. After about ten breaths I was absolutely flying.

It's strange. I'm relating this as one continuous playback, but in fact I only remember certain bits about the crash at certain times. Sometimes I don't remember a damn thing, and then suddenly, for no reason whatsoever, I'll see the vomiting marshal and it all comes flooding back.

The next people to put their heads in the cockpit were Trevor Foster, my engineer, and Adrian Reynard, the car's designer. They looked even more shaken up than the marshals. 'Would you mind getting the spare car ready?' I asked, and then I grinned at them. They just looked at me in horror.

And that, ladies and gentlemen, is where Johnny Herbert the joker was born.

Until then I'd liked a laugh as much as the next diminutive racing driver, and there was definitely a kind of 'naughty schoolboy' element to my personality, but only if I felt comfortable with people. I used to enjoy getting up to mischief occasionally and if it made people laugh, then all the better. This was different, though. It was the first time I'd ever been seriously injured and therefore the first time I'd ever seen anybody react to me being seriously injured, and this was my way of coping. Yes, I was off my box on Entonox and my own brand of morphine, but I was so taken aback by their reactions that I just had to do something. The look on their faces was one of pure devastation and terror, as though they'd just been given some appalling news, and even though I was right in the middle of it all, I felt an overwhelming compulsion to try to soften the blow.

After that it just became the norm, and it's now as much a part of my personality as all the charm, warmth and generosity I'm famous for. But to begin with it was used purely as a coping mechanism: firstly to try to stop people worrying about me, and then to deflect attention from any pain I was experiencing. Without it, especially with the pain I would experience over the coming months and years, I'd have gone completely mad, and there's no way I'd ever have raced again. It hasn't always served me well, because a lot of people, especially team managers, have mistaken the humour for unprofessionalism. It's cost me a drive or two over the years, the biggest of them McLaren, which I'll talk about later. But that's the only downside. Along with the Brands Hatch crash and my wins at Le Mans and at the British Grand Prix, it's probably what I'm best known for. A shunt, a few wins, and a bit of a giggle. I think I'll settle for that.

Not long after speaking to Trevor and Adrian I must have blacked out, because the next thing I remember is waking up in the hospital the following day. I've since learned what happened in between, and, as I'm sure you can imagine, it was a pretty grim state of affairs. Mum and Dad were at the circuit, and after getting wind of the accident they were approached by Bertrand Gachot who told them I was OK. After that they went to the medical centre where they thought I'd be. I'd been stabilized there prior to going to hospital, but by the time they got there I was already on my way. After being brought up to speed by one of the St John Ambulance people, Mum and Dad managed to get a lift to the hospital, and were joined there by my wife, Rebecca (who was then my girlfriend), Eddie, Trevor, Ian Blackman and Mike Thompson.

I don't remember a thing about the journey to Queen Mary's Hospital in Sidcup, but according to Neil Harper, who was lucky enough to be looking after me, I was quite entertaining, although a bit of a pain in the arse. One of the things he had to be careful about was not letting any of the drips that were attached to me fall out and this required quite a bit of concentration on his part. I, on the other hand, was to all intents and purposes as pissed as a rat (or at least that's how I acted), so while he was busy trying to keep me alive, I just wanted to chat.

'How many times have I been world champion?' I apparently asked.

He ignored me at first but I'm afraid I was insistent.

'Come on! How many times have I been world champion?'

'Once. You've been world champion once.'

'YAAAAHOOOOOOOOO!'

Two minutes later I asked again: 'How many times have I been world champion?'

'Three times.'

'Really? That's the same as Jackie Stewart. Do you know Jackie Stewart?'

'No, I don't.'

'Do I know Jackie Stewart?'

This poor man. It must have been a bloody nightmare for him.

Once I'd been deposited safely at Queen Mary's the first thing they did was remove my T-shirt. I'm told I was devastated.

'NOT MY TEEEEEEEEEE SHIIIIIIIIIIRT! NO, YOU CAN'T HAVE IT!'

'Come along now, Mr Herbert, it's for your own good.'

'Do you know Jackie Stewart?'

Because everybody had seen that my left foot was hanging off by a bit of skin they were terrified that when I got to hospital an immediate attempt would be made to amputate. So when the doctors started appearing, Trevor and Mike took them all to one side and said, 'Whatever you do, please don't take his foot off. He's a racing driver so you *have* to save his foot.' The doctors told them they'd do their best. Then they and the rest of my family and friends began speculating about how bad the damage was. The general consensus, despite pleading with the doctors to save the foot, was that my driving days were over and that I'd probably never walk again.

A few minutes later the doctors brought out a disclaimer for my parents to sign.

'I'm afraid there's every chance we will have to amputate Johnny's foot so we need you to sign this,' they said.

Mum and Dad were in a complete daze but they signed the form, which meant the doctors could go ahead and operate.

Trevor Foster maintains that if it had been a member of the public who'd sustained the same injuries in a road accident, they'd have amputated straight away. When the surgeon eventually came out and said he'd managed to save my foot, he followed it up with the words 'but I'm afraid his sporting days are over'.

About half an hour after the operation everyone was allowed in to see me, but I was on so much morphine that I didn't recognize anybody. Mum told me Michel Trollé was behind some screens on the other side of the room. Everyone had been desperately worried about Michel since his accident, and even though I was still completely off my box I tried to attract his attention. First I tried to sit up in bed but that was never going to work, so once I'd got my breath back I tried whistling for him and calling out his name. This would probably have worked quite well had I been compos mentis, but because I was under the influence I couldn't quite remember how to whistle. What's more, when I called out Michel's name, I did it in a French accent. Morphine certainly takes away the pain but it can also make you act like a bit of a tit if you're not careful.

'Michel, Michel! *Répondez s'il vous plaît!*'

Fortunately for Michel he was out for the count at the time, otherwise it could have been a very interesting exchange which may well have involved my asking him whether he knew Jackie

Stewart. Later, the surgeon who had operated on me showed Mike and Trevor Michel's X-rays. His leg was so badly crushed that it was a fraction of its original size. He raced again, though, and went on to compete at Le Mans.

Talking of morphine, because of the amount they'd had to give me, I began having the most bizarre dreams. There was one in particular that used to scare the living daylights out of me. This is the first time I've ever talked about it, and if my wife Becky had her way I wouldn't be doing so now, but it's just so weird and incredible that I have to share it.

It started off underneath a waterfall on some beautiful island somewhere, and Becky and I were having a bit of a kiss and cuddle. Not a bad dream so far. Idyllic, in fact, and a little bit saucy. Then, all of a sudden, we both began to turn into huge scaly monsters, complete with large pointy ears, claws and enormous bloody teeth. Straight after that, our skin began falling off like banana peel, after which I'd then eat Becky. Once I'd finished devouring my girlfriend and wife-to-be, some more monsters would turn up and I'd start eating them, and then them me. It was without doubt the most hideously entertaining thing I've ever experienced in my life, and I can recall it as clear as day.

Whenever I opened my eyes the dream would stop, but then as soon as I closed them again it would start. You know when you're having a wonderful dream and you wake up in the middle of it? You always hope that when you go back to sleep you'll start the dream again, but it never happens. Well with this dream that's exactly what I could do – in fact I had no choice. I can laugh about it now but at the time it was very unpleasant. In the end I had to plead with the doctors to start weaning me off the drug. It was all getting a little bit too 'I Am The Walrus' for me. I decided to choose severe physical pain, tempered by a little bit of humour, over watching myself consume the woman I loved, six or seven times a day.

Weaning me off the morphine certainly did the trick – within a few days the dreams had all but disappeared – but because I was now properly 'conscious' for the first time since the accident and no longer under any kind of influence, I quickly began to appreciate the extent of what had happened to me, in terms not only of the injuries I'd suffered but their consequences, which led quickly to the realization that all my dreams and aspirations, everything I'd worked towards since the age of ten, had just disappeared. Just a week earlier I'd been the Crown Prince of Motorsport, according to many journalists, and Jackie Stewart, the most exciting prospect since Jim Clark. Jim Clark, for heaven's sake!

I know this habit of comparing emerging talent with actual legends is quite often a dangerous game but I flatter myself that much of what had been written about me thus far was justified. Bearing testament to that is the fact that I had four of the biggest names in Formula 1 wanting to sign me. Emphasize the word *had*. Those contracts would be safely back in somebody's inside pocket by now, I realized. And who was I now? A recently retired racing driver with feet and ankles that were about as much use as a chocolate chassis.

This was my feeling-sorry-for-myself phase, by the way, in case you hadn't noticed. I felt so empty. Yes, I still had Becky and my friends and family, but all my interests, both professional and otherwise, revolved around motorsport. With that gone I'd have to start completely from scratch, and I wasn't sure if I could. The only job I'd ever had that wasn't either racing karts, cars or making a mess of manufacturing components – apart from standing in Bill's shop and staring at people – was driving a van for Mike while I was at Quest. Testing, racing and developing the car took up the majority of my time but I also drove the van and used to go and collect the tyres from Dunlop, the brakes from AP in Leamington Spa and the engines from a company called Nelson based somewhere near Hungerford.

The van in question was white, by the way, but even though I was without doubt a white-van driver, my shyness would always preclude me from indulging in any of the usual stereotypical escapades. This didn't stop me from getting up to mischief, though. My co-driver Gary Ayles and I used to change places while driving hell for leather down the motorway. Why? Well, for a start we were too lazy to stop, but also because it was just a fun thing to do.

That was it, then. If I had to give up motorsport, I'd become a van driver.

Things reached their bleakest point the day after I came off the morphine. I was lying in bed one morning when all of a sudden I noticed my feet. They and my ankles were heavily bandaged, but the thing that made me panic was that the bandages were quite red in parts so I was clearly still bleeding. I knew very little about what had happened, so when Becky arrived at around lunchtime I asked her to start filling me in on exactly what had happened since the crash. I could tell she felt uneasy about it, but I had to know.

'You've had five operations so far,' she told me, 'and you may need more. Your left foot was so badly damaged that the doctors spoke to your parents and me about amputating. It was what they recommended at one point but your dad told them that they weren't to do so unless it was absolutely necessary.'

I'm not afraid to admit that I was terrified listening to her. It felt like the beginning of the end of the world.

'And will it be necessary?' I asked.

'They still don't know. It's OK for now, but you've been very ill, Johnny.'

Trevor Foster later told me that I looked like a starving child when he saw me after the first operation. 'You'd lost such a lot of weight,' he said to me. 'I thought you were dying.'

When Becky had finished telling me about the operations she

stood up, sat down on the edge of my bed, and started to cry.

'There's something else,' she said. 'But to be honest I'm not sure I can tell you.'

I kind of knew what she was about to say. We'd covered all the immediate stuff, the operations, et cetera. This was about my future.

'I won't be able to race again, will I?'

She slowly shook her head. 'Not according to one of the doctors.'

'Will I walk again?'

'He says you should be able to. But with a stick.'

'A walking stick?'

'Yes.'

'But I'm twenty-four!'

'I know.'

It was then that I started to panic.

'Becky, I'm only twenty-four years old! What the bloody hell am I going to do?'

'I don't know, Johnny. Let's just see what the doctors say, shall we? That was only one opinion.'

I lay back on the bed and closed my eyes. I'm certainly no quitter, but at that very moment in time – just for a moment, though – all I wanted to do was go to sleep and never wake up again.

Eight

IN ADDITION TO my parents, Rebecca and everyone I mentioned earlier popping in to see me, day in, day out, I had a steady stream of other visitors, and between them all they didn't allow me to become either depressed or despondent for too long. Perry McCarthy, who is one of my oldest mates, in that he is no longer young, must have turned up every other day to start with. He's great to have around in a crisis because it doesn't matter how bad life becomes or how desperate things get, a quick look at Perry will always make you feel better about yourself. We've always made each other laugh. I'll never forget him picking up one of my leg X-rays and saying to the doctor, 'Bloody hell, doc, it looks like a map of the Caribbean.' Talk of things like amputations and 'tragically curtailed careers' was treated with a mixture of humour and disdain, and literally minutes after feeling like the world was coming to an end I'd be back fighting again. Every time I felt myself getting a bit down I'd picture Eddie saying, 'Johnnyyyyyyyyyy! Johnnyyyyyyyyyy! Pull yourself together!'

I remember one time the suggestion of amputation coming up while we were talking to one of the doctors and I said, 'Fine! If they cut my foot off, I'll have a stump. I don't need a foot to work a clutch. A stump will work just as well. What do I need a foot for?' You should have seen the look on my poor mum's face.

She didn't know whether to laugh, cry or give me a rollocking. It was gallows humour, I suppose, but I was serious all the same. As long as I could drive I didn't care what I had below my knees: stumps, feet or pieces of bloody cheese. Just put me in a car!

Even though Becky and my parents had been told I would never race again, that was only the opinion of one doctor, and after everything I'd been through trying to get to a position where I could race cars for a living, I was damned if I was going to give it all up. Not without a bloody big fight, anyway.

This bravado of mine may seem quite impressive to some but, once again, it was only with the help of those around me that I was able to convert it into something other than words and feelings. Peter Collins never believed for a moment that I wouldn't race again (or if he did he hid it very well). Every day he'd call me and ask how the feet were. 'How are they today, Johnny? Looking any better? How's the feeling on the left?' Mike Thompson was exactly the same. Their faith in my ability was just astounding. It seemed to know no bounds. I could have lost both arms and both legs and I'm sure they'd still have worked out how to get me into a car. What a lucky guy, eh? Peter even told me his intention was still to get me in a Benetton for the following season. I was dumbfounded.

'My feet are suspended two feet above the bed and they're covered in bloodied bandages,' I said.

'So what?' he replied. 'It's early September now and there's a test in three months' time. That should be long enough. A lot can happen in three months, Johnny.'

I simply wasn't allowed to fail.

To demonstrate how much things did indeed progress in a short space of time, almost a month after the accident, in mid-September, I remember seeing my left foot move for the first time and then telling Peter about it. It was less than three months to the test at this point, and it only moved a few millimetres, but it was a massive step – or rather a step towards taking a step. If you'd heard me talking to Peter on the phone you'd have thought I'd won the world championship.

'It's moved, Peter! My left foot has just moved!'

'That's fantastic, Johnny. You see, I told you it would happen. How far did it move?'

'A few millimetres.'

'Brilliant!'

Not long after this I received a call from Peter telling me that Benetton had decided to take up the option on me for 1989. It was one of those moments in life that you remember for ever. I can tell you when it was, where I was, and even what I was wearing and what I was doing. I won't bother with the sartorial details but it was the day of the 1988 Spanish Grand Prix, 2 October, and I was at home in a wheelchair with my left foot resting on a table in front of me. I was in bloody agony at the time and when the phone went I may well have been less than conversational.

'Yes? Who is it?'

'It's Peter. I'm in Jerez.'

'Good for you. I'm in Surrey.'

'I just thought I'd let you know that we're taking up the option on you, Johnny. It's all been agreed with Luciano and as long as you pass the required fitness tests and don't make a mess of the tests, you'll be on the grid in Rio next March.'

I felt like such a prat, although a very happy prat. I just couldn't believe it. One minute I'm a grumpy little git in a wheelchair who can barely walk, and the next I'm a bloody Formula 1 driver. You couldn't make it up, could you?

After over a month of watching things like *The Flying Doctors*, *Neighbours*, *Home and Away* and *Rainbow*, Peter suggested I go and see a specialist he knew in Austria called Toni Mathis;

Benetton would, pardon the pun, foot the bill for the treatment. Toni had treated all kinds of sportspeople, including Nigel Mansell and Keke Rosberg.

When I first arrived at the clinic I couldn't walk at all, and because the bone in my left ankle was effectively like plasticine I couldn't put any pressure on it whatsoever. I was OK putting pressure on the right foot, providing the surface was flat (although the heel and toes were extremely painful), but that was about it, so for the first couple of weeks there I spent most of my time in a wheelchair. Gradually, though, Toni started working on me. I don't remember receiving much in the way of physiotherapy while I was there but he certainly got me on my feet again; it was all to do with circulation at first, as well as a bit of massage and manipulation.

By the end of October I was ready to take my first steps using crutches. The pain I experienced was unbelievable. When I put my left foot on the ground for the first time it throbbed so much that I genuinely thought it was going to explode. It was terrifying. In fact I wish it had exploded, then it would have stopped throbbing. It was still so raw – it is a bit to this day, unfortunately – which made the pain even more excruciating.

I managed about two steps that first time, and just to do that required every bit of mental and physical strength I had in my body. I was exhausted afterwards. After that it was just relentless. As I stood there, trying not to faint, Toni would wave this metal rod over me and then plug in all kinds of electrodes. He used to call it 'mountain power', which might have had something to do with the fact that his clinic is based in the mountains, but wherever the power came from, it certainly speeded up the healing process. Once I was able to walk a few more steps he got me doing a bit of swimming. He even got me on an exercise bike. The swimming especially must have been something to behold. When I entered the water it was with all the grace and poise of an inebriated water buffalo. Neither foot was what you'd call normal, in fact the left one felt like a lump of steel, and was just as supple. This meant that instead of acting like flippers, my feet just impeded me. It did wonders for my core and upper-body strength, though, so despite it not being pleasant to watch, the benefits were undeniable.

Toni used to offer all kinds of treatments and courses at his clinic. I recall some drivers from the Mercedes DTM team, including, I think, Bernd Schneider, arriving not long after me to do a fitness course. I ended up chatting to them over dinner one evening and they asked me if I'd like to go into Feldkirch, the nearest town, with them for a drink. 'I'd be delighted,' I said. 'Thanks very much.' I remember making it there OK, but in town we came across not one flight of steps but about six, and there must have been a hundred steps on each flight. The German boys took them all in their stride and were atop Mount Feldkirch within a couple of minutes. I, on the other hand – old Hopalong Herbert – hadn't yet had to deal with such things and so I had to duck out. Even to this day my left foot doesn't bend backwards at all, so when I'm tackling things like steps I have to bend my hip out and do all sorts of other things. It's just as unsightly as the swimming but a damn sight more uncomfortable.

Unbeknown to me, Toni had already decided that this kind of exercise was the way forward, so after walking into town he had me scaling these steps, time after time, up and down. I forget how many times I had to do it but I came close to vomiting at least three times. After that we went into the nearest forest and once again a hill was found which I had to walk up and down ad nauseam. My entire left ankle was red raw. It felt like walking on the open wound once somebody had chopped off your foot. Then, when all I wanted to do was lean on the other foot to lessen the pain, that foot had had the heel bent round so badly that the ligaments had been torn, which meant the toes were pointing downwards like talons, making each and every one of them a hypersensitive portal to the purest pain, especially when walking on a step or, worse still, either up or down a hill. Every footstep I took – and this was just with the right foot – felt like I was smashing several fractured bones against a brick wall. There was nobody to moan to either, so it didn't matter how bad it all got, I just carried on doing it, crying constantly. And I mean constantly.

Crying because you're in pain is slightly different to crying because you're sad, and it's that difference that makes the former a great deal worse. Crying when you're sad usually results in feeling slightly better afterwards – you know what they say, 'Have a good cry and you'll feel better' – whereas crying because you're in pain doesn't, it's just something you do because you're at the end of your tether. Neither is particularly nice but the pain version is far more concentrated and one-dimensional.

I used to have one day off a week, and during that day I'd try to pull myself together and psych myself up for the next six days. I knew what was going to happen and I knew how much it would hurt. It used to take me every second of that twenty-four hours I had off to prepare myself. Once a month for exactly one day it would all become too much for me and I'd suffer a short but severe bout of depression. A voice in my head would just keep repeating, 'I can't do this any more, I can't do this any more, I shouldn't be doing this.' I'd fight it at first but after a while I'd realize that was futile and, regardless of how unpleasant and overwhelming it was, I should let it take its course. Sure enough, the following morning I'd wake up and it'd be gone, so I'd just get on with it. It never lasted more than a day and as horrible as it undoubtedly was it was something I knew had to happen, like a kind of release.

Although the pain was at its most severe when I was scaling

those steps and hills it was always there, twenty-four hours a day, seven days a week – totally relentless. There was no respite, not even for a minute. It would be the best part of two years before I could honestly declare myself pain-free at any time during waking hours, and even then it was only for very short periods. The relief I felt when the pain disappeared was dramatic to say the least and I'd often cry, mostly because it had gone, but partly because I knew it would come back.

Although I'd continue going back to Austria for regular bouts of torture right up until March the following year, I also had to, prior to the test, re-familiarize myself not only with driving a car, but an F1 car, so in mid-October, a good week before I'd even taken my first steps in Austria, I returned to England and went to stay at Mike Thompson's place in Maidstone. By the time I got there he'd already obtained a kart and after I'd settled in we took it up to Buckmore Park, where Bill Sisley was now based. The helmet Mike gave me had lead weights stuck to it in order to help build up my neck muscles – everything we did was geared towards the test in December. I was in a wheelchair, and although I only had bandages on my feet and legs (I'd had a plaster on when I first left hospital), my feet and ankles were, as you know, in a hell of a mess. The left in particular was in need of extra protection and was honestly the size of a large melon. We tried all sorts of things and eventually settled on some foam, wrapped around my leg and ankle, and a huge motocross boot to protect my foot. I must have looked like a part-built mini Terminator, but it did the trick.

I went out on the track about two or three times while I was there and spent the majority of the time doing 360-degree spins as it was wet. Then, after the extraordinary delights of forest hill climbing and step training in Austria, I came back to England again, just prior to the test, which is when Peter started getting involved again. This time the team sent over a monocoque from the previous season's Benetton, the B188, which he'd had fitted with a seat, pedals and gear change; but to make it more authentic and to enable me to continue to build up my strength he made sure everything was spring-loaded. I must sound like a broken record by now, but that too was utter purgatory. I remember sitting there, day after day, just bawling my bloody eyes out. As with the bouts of 'mountain depression', as I used to call it, this was simply a release, and once it had subsided the upside to what I was doing made it easy to carry on: I was among people I knew, liked and trusted, and because I was familiarizing myself with an F1 car again, I could see that there was light at the end of the tunnel. It was something to aim for.

People who've labelled me unlucky over the years tend to forget that according to one or two doctors I should never have been driving again, let alone competitively in an F1 car, and had it not been for one or two tenacious individuals – namely Peter Collins and Mike Thompson – I'd most likely have disappeared into obscurity. In my eyes, even then, that made me one of the luckiest men alive, and maintaining that disposition and concentrating purely on the positives was a big help. With some people it's all about 'what might have been', and although that's suggested throughout in this book, it only tells one side of the story.

Luck notwithstanding, the legacy of the crash at Brands went far beyond the injuries I sustained on the day and the effect they had on me physically; but it was only when I got back into a car again that I began to discover the true extent of the damage. For a start, I would now be seen as damaged goods, not only by the likes of Luciano Benetton but by every team manager and team owner I would ever come into contact with as a driver. I still limp a bit even today, and when I was racing this was understandably seen as a flaw and a weakness. F1 drivers are supposed to represent the peak of physical fitness, so if you saw one walking down the paddock with his bum sticking out and looking like he'd just been kicked in the nuts you'd probably question his ability on the track. I know I would. Even worse than this was the effect it had on a fundamental part of my racing ability, something that doesn't really have a name, yet was one of the main reasons why the likes of Bill Sisley, Peter Collins, Mike Thompson, Frank Williams and whoever it was at Ferrari were interested in me.

I remember qualifying for a Formula 3 race once and for some reason I just couldn't place the car properly and everything felt just a little bit disjointed. It used to happen in karting on occasion, and what I'd do – which is what I did at the F3 race – was park up and go and grab five minutes somewhere. Then, when I got back in the car or kart, everything clicked back into place again. It was like pressing a reset button. Until the accident I'd only ever had to do it once in a blue moon; after it, everything reversed and that feeling of slight disjointedness became the norm, but I only ever managed to press the reset button and regain equanimity once more in my entire career. The work I had to put in trying to compensate for this loss was draining to say the least, and although I just about managed it, nothing would ever be the same again, apart from on that one occasion. I still had the ability, somewhere, but I had to fight bloody hard for it, and the fact that it was no longer natural took away much of its shine and effect.

This assault on my ability as a racing driver would turn out to be three-pronged, and the last element to succumb was my feeling of invincibility. It just evaporated after the crash, and regardless of what I achieved it never came close to returning. Prior to Brands I always said I could beat anyone, anywhere, on any track and in any conditions, and I believed it. What's more, so did many of my opponents, and that gave me a huge advantage. Of course it didn't work every time, but if I ever lost, it was almost always down to something like human error or a technical fault, as opposed to my being out-raced. That unshakeable belief that I was unbeatable as a racer had been incredibly empowering and, together with my natural ability, just gave me a kind of aura. Some people mistook this for arrogance, but it wasn't. I was just in a very good place. When I arrived at Brands Hatch on that fateful day in August 1988 I was like King Midas on wheels. Now, as the week of the Benetton test finally arrived, in addition to having two very badly damaged feet, I was minus the two qualities that had set me apart from the rest of the field.

In mid-December 1988 I was like a caged animal but with very visible wounds. My judgement going awry was a blow and would plague me for the rest of my career, but then so would my physical injuries. Peter Collins still reckoned that 80 per cent of Johnny Herbert was worth a punt so that was all that was on my mind. I wasn't sure what would happen – nobody was – but I was going to give it my all, and if it did go belly up it wouldn't be for want of trying.

On 14 December, the day before the actual test, I took a B188 out on Enstone Airfield, just to prepare for the following day, and from the moment I ditched my crutches and started to manoeuvre myself into the cockpit I began to feel at home again. It had been a hard road and the majority of it had been uphill, both literally and metaphorically, but I was still alive, and what's more I was on the brink of becoming an F1 driver. A journalist from *Motorsport* magazine was at Enstone that day, and later he described my run-out as being like 'a fish put back in the sea after months in a tank', and that's a pretty good description, I think.

Within minutes of setting off I was moving through the gears as freely as ever and when I got to either end of the runway I performed a 180-degree turn, and even spun it on the straight once or twice. It was a celebration, I suppose, a reward for enduring four months of agony. I was looking forward to the test, but that was going to be different. That was work, and I'd be there doing a job for Benetton. This was just a track day, but my God, it felt good. Pure bloody ecstasy!

The weather at Silverstone the following day was foggy and cold which meant I was never going to be able to get the tyres to the optimum temperature. Again, I'd be driving last season's car, the B188, and the corresponding qualifying times at the previous season's British Grand Prix for the Benetton drivers had been 1m 12.737s for Sandro Nannini and 1m 12.960s for Thierry Boutsen.

'If you can get to one minute seventeen I'd be a very happy man,' said Peter.

'Leave it with me,' I replied. 'I'll see what I can do.'

On my first trip out I started at about 1m 22s, and by the end had got down to 1m 17s. That was OK, but I knew I'd do better the next time round – not that I was going to tell Peter that. With hindsight it was probably a bit cruel of me, but when I came in after my first session I just sat there looking crestfallen.

'I can't do it, Peter,' I whimpered. 'I can't go any faster. Nothing feels right so I don't think I'll be able to do it.'

You should have seen the look on his face. He went completely white.

'What?' he said. 'You've got to be joking, Johnny. You've got to keep trying.'

'But I don't know if I can, Peter,' I pleaded, trying to look like I was on the verge of tears. 'I'll go out again just in case, but I think it's hopeless.'

Within about three laps I'd put in a time of 1m 14s, which would have put me eighteenth on the grid at the previous year's British Grand Prix, and when I got back into the garage I took off my helmet, looked at Peter with a huge smile and said, 'Gotcha! You fell for that one.' I couldn't possibly tell you what Peter said in return but there was an 'off' in there somewhere, as well as a reference to my height, and I do believe he even questioned my parentage. It was a cruel trick, I admit that, but what a fantastic way to end the test. It felt like we were definitely in business.

After a second test at Paul Ricard in the south of France in early 1989 we went to Jerez, and if there were any questions about the efficacy of my legs at the time, these were about to be usurped by some different questions regarding my hands. On the first lap I came out of the third corner and as I went to change from third to fourth I got second instead and over-revved the engine. There was a threshold, I think it was about 13,800 revs, where it was OK to take the Cosworth and I had taken it to about 15,500 revs, which was way over the 'it's OK' bit. Saying that, Cosworths were always very sensitive, and even unto this day that's my excuse. Back to the garage I went, and after plugging in the computer I was told to get out. 'You may as well get a drink,' they told me. 'The engine's been over-revved and it's going to take at least an hour to change it.'

A new engine, I thought. *Oh, shit!*

An hour and fifteen minutes later I set off again, and coming out of the twelfth corner I did exactly the same thing – went for fourth, got second instead, and over-revved the engine. Back I went again, although slightly slower this time, as I was not looking forward to the reception.

'Right, out you get,' said the mechanic. 'See you in an hour.'

By this time I was feeling a little bit foolish, but that was nothing compared to how I felt when I brought the car back in for a third time having done the same thing again.

'You are joking, aren't you?' said the mechanic. 'Three engines in three laps? That's got to be a record. Luciano's going to love you.'

After covering myself in all kinds of glory in Jerez we were all set for Rio, where we'd test first, and then race about a month later. Flavio Briatore had been brought into the team by this point, and according to Peter he had been against my appointment from the off, favouring instead an Italian driver – or should I say *any* Italian driver – and preferably one without any injuries. He started making his presence felt almost immediately. When I arrived at Heathrow for the flight to Rio I was told by him that I was not, under any circumstances, to be seen using either sticks or crutches. Actually, that's not strictly true. I was told by one of Flavio's secretaries that I couldn't use sticks or crutches. He was a marvellous delegator, Flavio, one of the true greats, especially when it came to having to communicate with people he either didn't rate or hadn't recruited himself, and unfortunately for me I fell into both those categories. To be fair to him I can understand why he didn't think I was the right man for the job, and as an undoubtedly ambitious individual who must have had his eyes on Peter's job he perhaps saw my potential failure as a route to getting where he wanted to be.

After checking in I went to see which gate I'd have to get to. When I looked at the departures board it said gate 74.

'How far is gate seventy-four?' I asked somebody on the information desk.

'Ooh, about a fifteen-minute walk. Just under a mile as the crow flies.'

'Really?' I said. This was not good news. Although the ongoing pain had begun to subside slightly and my core fitness was excellent, I was not good at walking long distances; in fact, the furthest I'd walked since the crash – bar what went on in Austria – was probably just a few yards. I'd had no reason to do any more than that. I did see a few buggies flying around, carrying older people to and from the gates but I figured that if Flavio didn't want me to be seen using either sticks or crutches he'd go mad if I, a Formula 1 driver, was spotted being given a lift on a vehicle designed for the infirm. I didn't want to give him any ammunition so with a heavy heart and even heavier feet, I set off for gate 74.

By the time I boarded the plane I was in agony, but at least I'd done it. *How about that then, Flav*, I thought to myself. What I didn't consider at the time, though, was the fact that we had to change in Phoenix, Arizona. When I got to the transfer desk there and asked which was the gate for Rio, I almost died.

'Gate one hundred and seventeen, sir,' said the woman. 'About a half-hour walk.'

'You're joking,' I said. 'Half an hour?'

'That's right, sir. I could always try and arrange a lift for you if you feel you can't make it.'

'No, no, don't you worry about me. I'll be fine.'

In the end it took me an hour to get to the gate, so bearing in mind I walked like a constipated Transformer I actually made good time. *Two-nil to Mr Herbert!*

This was far from over, though. When we arrived in Rio we parked at gate 48, which, according to one of the stewards, left us with about a fifteen-minute walk.

'You have got to be joking,' I spluttered. 'I've already done about three bloody miles.'

'I'm sorry, sir,' he said.

'Don't be,' I replied. 'It's not your fault. I blame my Italian friend.'

He looked at me quizzically but I couldn't manage any more chit-chat. I had to get to passport control, and after that find my way out of the airport.

By the time I got to the hotel I was, for want of a less crude term, absolutely shagged out. But the final leg of my tri-continental walking holiday was yet to be announced.

'OK, sir,' said the receptionist, 'you're in room eight-one-two, which is on the eighth floor, but it's at the far end of the building so you've got a bit of a hike ahead of you.'

'Really,' I replied, 'you don't say. And let me guess, will it take me about fifteen minutes?'

She looked at me like the air steward had done.

'Forget it,' I said, and then went on my merry way.

It's a good job Flavio wasn't there because I swear to you I'd have flattened him, probably using a stick, a crutch and at least one gammy foot.

I arrived in Rio about four weeks before the Grand Prix, and as I said was supposed to be testing in the meantime. I'm not sure why but the fuel didn't make it through Customs, or at least not immediately, so for the first five or six days we were left twiddling our thumbs. The hotel we were staying in was on a far corner of Copacabana Beach, so while we were waiting for the fuel to arrive, the mechanics would take me down to a local bar. Well, I say a local bar; in fact it was at the other end of Copacabana which involved a walk of – yes, you've guessed it – about fifteen sodding minutes. I remember eyeing the mechanics suspiciously and thinking, *Has Flavio put you up to this?* Naaaah, he couldn't have. Could he? I was becoming paranoid. Then I realized that the mechanics running the test were independent; the Benetton guys were due to arrive later.

This didn't stop them taking the mickey, though, and because I wasn't too quick on my feet they spent the entire week trying to buy me a skateboard from a peanut seller with no legs. Every bloody day we'd go to this bar and every day this poor chap would turn up on his skateboard. Then, after selling the mechanics a bag or two of nuts, they'd start trying to negotiate a price for this man's only means of transport. I'm not sure what the peanut vendor said to these mechanics because it was in Portuguese, but I'm pretty sure it was something along the lines of 'If I sell this to you, how the bloody hell am I supposed to get home?'

It should have been a great way to spend a week, lazing around on Copacabana, but instead of devoting the rest of my time to lounging on the beach like the mechanics, I just hobbled back to the hotel. Sand and dicky legs do not mix, so to a certain extent I felt a little bit alienated, not to mention very bored.

The test itself lasted a total of four days. Even though the previous tests had gone well, there were still a lot of rumours going round that I wouldn't be race fit. This was understandable as I was obviously still hobbling, but now even the race officials had got involved and this was making everybody nervous, not least Luciano Benetton and Flavio Briatore. The main concern the officials had was whether I could remove myself from the cockpit within seven seconds, which was the maximum time allowed, and until I proved to them that I could do this they were threatening to ban me from the race. My best time was six seconds, so in the end they went away happy.

The primary concern from Peter's point of view – and the reason for this became clear very quickly – was whether or not I could last a full race distance, so during race week he arranged for me to do just that. Until then the most I'd done in a stretch was about twelve laps, which was well below what would be expected. I wasn't sure at the time whether it had slipped his mind or if he had some other reason, but when he told me it was going to happen there was a definite sense of worry in the air, almost as if he and the rest of the team were afraid I was going to fail. I later found out that the moment I left the garage some of the mechanics started having bets on how long I'd last, as the others had at my Formula Ford test, and the most anyone had suggested was twenty laps. And I was supposed to be their new driver! I knew people had doubts but I had no idea this stretched to my own crew.

An hour and a half later, when the car had run out of fuel, they were all having a coffee outside and had completely forgotten about me. I could tell they were relieved though, and, despite my feet being extremely sore, I was glad I'd ticked the box. The last thing you need as a new driver is a team that doesn't think you're up to it. I was happy to do whatever it took to put their minds at rest.

There were still at least two more minds within the Benetton team yet to be convinced, and after successfully completing the race distance Peter asked if he could have a word.

'Luciano's in town,' he said. 'He and Flavio would like to see us.'

I knew what was coming. Sure enough, when we arrived at Luciano's hotel room it was immediately suggested that I wasn't capable of doing the job. It was the first time I'd ever met Flavio and he greeted me like you would a bowl of cold rice pudding.

'We don't think you can do this, Johnny,' he said to me.

'Based on what?' I asked. 'I've more than held my own in testing and, I don't know if you're aware, I've just completed a full race distance.'

They weren't aware, and what's more, they didn't welcome the news, telling me it hadn't been done under race conditions.

'Makes no difference,' I replied. 'In fact, if anything that would simply make it more interesting.'

I didn't know it at the time, but as Peter and I were fending off the Italian inquisition, a driver called Emanuele Pirro was standing by at Rome airport, waiting for a call from Flavio, so that tête-à-tête in Luciano's hotel room was supposed to have been my leaving party. If Peter hadn't asked me to do that race distance I don't think we'd have been able to persuade them to let me race, but with all likely scenarios having now been rehearsed, they didn't really have a leg to stand on – even with sticks or crutches. In addition, Peter can be a very persuasive man when he wants to be, and as close as Flavio clearly was to Luciano, Peter's argument was convincing to say the least – thank God.

The following day a spokesman for the Benetton team said, 'There are a lot of jealous drivers, particularly in Italy, who are wondering why Johnny is in the car and they are not. Johnny has withstood this pressure and so has the team.' It was a bizarre thing to say, but it was as close to a vote of confidence as I was ever likely to get.

I have to stress once again that although I might question some of their methods, I can completely see things from Benetton's point of view: not the bit about wanting to get another Italian driver on board, but the fact that I was damaged goods and not what a Formula 1 driver was supposed to look like. Formula 1 is a sport built on confidence and perfection. That has to come from all sides – the designers, the mechanics, the management, even the sponsors – but the ones who sit at the very top of this tree are the drivers, and if it's lacking at all there and you're stumping up millions of pounds of your own money, the chances are you're going to have the occasional doubt.

Come the morning of the race I felt fantastic. Qualifying had gone well. In addition to beating my new team-mate, Alessandro Nannini, by two-tenths of a second and lining up tenth on the grid, I would also be next to my old testing buddy, Mr Nelson Piquet. That's not bad, is it, starting your first F1 race alongside a three-time world champion? The only downside to the day came right at the start when I arrived at the drivers' briefing. I was one of the last to make it in there, and because I was a rookie, one of the stewards introduced me. And who was the first driver to hold out his hand? Gregor Foitek. He was also making his Formula 1 debut, with the short-lived and uncompetitive EuroBrun team, and unfortunately I didn't notice him until it was too late. Rightly or wrongly I would never have shaken his hand had I been given a choice because in my opinion – and I mean my opinion – he was the reason for all my woes. As I looked into his eyes, for just a few seconds it all came flooding back to me: the accident – or at least bits of it – and then all the agony I'd experienced in Austria. He just smiled, as if it were the first time he'd ever met me.

Jean Alesi, who has a very cheeky sense of humour, pretty much like my own, always says to me when we meet, 'Johnny, you know who my favourite driver of all time is?

Gregor Foitek. What a wonderful man he is. Such a splendid driver.'

As it was the Brazilian Grand Prix, with Ayrton Senna on pole, the crowd for the race was enormous – well over two hundred thousand apparently – and as we set off on the parade lap all I could hear above the sound of the slumbering engines was this wall of noise coming from the stands; it was only when we got into position on the grid and began revving the engines that Ayrton's adoring public were eventually drowned out. Experiencing a stadium full of Brazilians reacting to their national football team is impressive, but seeing nearly a quarter of a million of them cheering on one man is something completely different. Football may well be the national sport in Brazil but at the time Senna was the national hero. Seeing such a passionate country united like that was just breathtaking.

Although I'd out-qualified Nannini, he got away better than me and even cut across my bow heading down the straight. This turned out to be a blessing in disguise, as just a few yards later Gerhard Berger, Riccardo Patrese and Senna went wide into the first turn, resulting in a shunt which left Senna without his front wing and Berger getting turned sideways, although only temporarily. Patrese was the only one of the three to come out of the turn unscathed, and as Senna made his way carefully back to the pits for a new nose, Patrese charged on into the lead with me and the rest of the field running safely behind.

By the end of the first lap Berger had retired, Williams were running one-two, and I was back in eighth, having completed my maiden Grand Prix lap in 1m 45.968s. By lap 4 Thierry Boutsen, who was driving one of the Williams, had retired with an engine problem, which lifted me up to seventh. The lead for the race was becoming a two-way battle between Nigel Mansell and Alain Prost, and the fight going on between us Benetton boys was just as fierce. Nannini led throughout the early part of the race, but I stuck to him like a tube of Eddie's hair glue. When he was ready to go in for his first pit stop I was so far up his rear end that I could tell what kind of aftershave he was wearing (Old Spice, I think), and when he reappeared I'd made up enough time to ensure that he was behind me after my first pit stop.

By lap 17 I was up to sixth, and after both Derek Warwick and then Maurício Gugelmin pitted I was fourth. Fourth! This was bloody madness. On lap 25 Riccardo Patrese pitted, which meant I was now on course for a podium finish, but just before I went in for my second pit stop I ran wide, which allowed Warwick to re-take me. It would all change again though, and by the end of the second round of stops, of which I'd been one of the first, I was running fifth behind Patrese, Gugelmin, Prost and Mansell. Two laps later Patrese's engine failed which put me fourth, and there I would stay for the rest of the race.

From a pain point of view, both qualifying and the race itself were horrendous. There seemed to be more bumps at the Autódromo de Jacarepaguá than on any other track I'd ever been to. This probably wasn't the case at all, but it felt like I was racing on a bloody grouse moor, and every time I hit something I was in agony. The worst of these 'death bumps' was situated going out of the right-hander, then left on to the back straight. Every time I hit the thing my left foot would smash against the inside of the monocoque. I tried holding it away from the side of the monocoque but the forces were far too strong so the moment I made contact with the bump – WHAM! Every time it happened the pain, which was beyond excruciating, would shock me each time to the point where I felt slightly faint and also sick.

Halfway through qualifying I came to the conclusion that I wasn't going to be able to take it lap after lap and decided to take some pretty drastic action. As opposed to tightening my leg and resisting when I approached the bump, I just let it flop. This meant that it hit the monocoque even harder than usual but eventually that took me over the pain threshold which meant it no longer bothered me quite as much. It was still unbelievably painful, and I can recall crying in the car several times over the weekend, but something hideous yet constant was preferable to something intermittent and unbearable. It was like getting your foot out and then continuously smashing it against the ground, I suppose, but at least it worked. You see what I mean now about distractions? Driving the car was only one of a number of things I had to deal with.

Nannini did everything he could to prove he was Benetton's number-one driver (this was his fourth season in F1), and as well as posting a fastest lap during the race he threw everything he had at Derek Warwick, the man separating us. Unfortunately for Alessandro this was all to no avail, and as I went through the chequered flag in fourth I did so safe in the knowledge that, as well as outdriving him, I'd done a bloody good job for the team.

Incidentally, at the start of what was in fact the final lap I'd seen my pit board reading 'two laps to go'. So I didn't know it was the final lap, and thinking I had two left I started to make a move on Gugelmin, who was in third. Because I had slightly more speed than he did in a straight line I thought I might be able to make it and figured that if I got into the right position now I'd have at least two chances to overtake before the end. When I saw the chequered flag being waved about half a lap later I was gutted, but only for a split second. I'd just finished fourth in the 1989 Brazilian Grand Prix – my F1 debut – and in addition to beating my team-mate by about eight seconds, not to mention being just two seconds behind Prost in second and about a second behind Gugelmin in third, I'd earned three championship points for the team. Not bad for a disabled driver.

I was disabled, and what's more I'm proud of that fact. I honestly have no idea how many Formula 1 drivers have started a race in the position I was in, but I doubt there are many. I had no sponsors, no history in Formula 1, no money, and feet that looked like something you'd see on a butcher's floor. But what I did have was a smidgen of talent, a lot of self-belief, and a small but dedicated band of people who saw beyond my physical imperfections (slight understatement there) and had enough faith in me to make me believe I could build a scale model of the Taj Mahal single-handedly with no cement. This was pure unadulterated 'people power', and despite it turning out to be a bit of a false dawn (sorry for the spoiler there), it was a towering achievement for all concerned. I was the first F1 driver to score points on his debut since Alain Prost back in 1980 and that in itself was a testament to the efforts of everyone concerned – including, by the way, Luciano Benetton and Flavio Briatore. They may not have been complicit in my long-term ambitions – in fact, as you're about to find out, this too was not part of the plan – but without their go-ahead I'd never have started the race so for that I will always be grateful.

When I got back to the garage and saw Becky and Peter waiting for me, the waterworks started pretty much straight away. I'd gone through a lot over the past seven months, and so had they. For a start, they'd had to put up with me. At that moment I think we were all reliving our experiences. It was just an outpouring of emotions. I can only begin to imagine the kind of pressure Peter had been under, and I'd seen first-hand the effect my injuries had had on Becky. Like me, they'd had to deal with the majority of things on their own. As we all stood there in the garage weeping, nobody said a word. We didn't need to.

I'm not sure why, but by the time we got to the hospitality boxes where the rest of the team were supposed to be, Luciano, Flavio and Alessandro had gone. According to those who'd been there, their mood had not been a happy one. I could under-stand Sandro not being happy – after all, he'd just been beaten fair and square by a disabled rookie driver – but the reasons for Luciano's and Flavio's unhappiness would always remain a mystery. Neither was flying off anywhere that evening so why not stay and congratulate me? Or at the very least leave me a message saying 'well done'. It didn't really bother me at the time because neither Peter nor Becky allowed it to, but their behaviour seems pretty pathetic with hindsight. Was it because I was disabled? Did that go against the macho Italian image they wanted to portray? I'm not sure.

On a slightly lighter note, I'll never forget watching the mercurial Mr Mansell descend from the podium, carrying the winner's trophy. He'd somehow managed to cut himself on it, and as he passed the waiting band of reporters he made a point of showing them his flesh wound, not to mention the two or three drops of blood he'd managed to squeeze out of his finger. 'Look, I cut myself,' he said, quickly turning white. I thought, *Catch him, somebody, before he faints.* What a big jessie. No way for a special constable from the Isle of Man to behave.

One interesting side-note to the race is that the two drivers with whom I would eventually go on to win Le Mans, Volker Weidler and my old mate Bertrand Gachot, were also due to make their Formula 1 debuts at Rio that year but unfortunately they failed to qualify. This was one of the few times in Formula 1 history where there were more cars entering the race than places on the grid, which meant pre-qualifying had to be used to help reduce the field. Bertrand, who was driving for the Moneytron Onyx team, and Volker, who was driving for Rial, both failed to make the grade, although that had little to do with their driving skills. Come 1991 things would be very different and a little bit of history would be made once again.

Nine

IF YOU SEARCH the meaning of the phrase 'false dawn' on the internet, one of the first results you're bound to see is 'The start of Johnny Herbert's F1 career'. Back in the spring of 1989 I had no idea the walls were about to fall in, but I should have had at least an inkling. Maybe I was in denial. I think you probably know by now that I used to take life one day at a time, but although that had worked well for me up to that point, and especially with regard to recovering from the accident, it was not the right attitude to have going into a full Formula 1 season. What's that old saying? 'Fail to prepare and you prepare to fail.' Well, that was my situation to a T, although there was certainly no blame to be apportioned.

Despite the steps to recovery I had made in Austria, I felt that I could have done with some more physio work while I was there. The trouble was that because of the time constraints involved, I couldn't do both fitness and physio, which meant one of them had to give. I was fit all right, but my injuries hadn't been given time to heal, which meant that by putting them through a Grand Prix every other weekend, not to mention testing, I'd actually be preventing that healing process from taking place. In an ideal world I'd probably have gone away to Japan for a year or two, had a load of physio and recuperation, and raced in Formula

Nippon just to keep my hand in. But what would have happened when I returned? Formula 1 wouldn't have sat waiting for me, would it? I'd be a forgotten man with a limp and a sticky-out bum. Like it or not, this was the only way it could happen. It wasn't ideal but I'd just have to make the best of it.

My Achilles heel now (so to speak) was braking, although I didn't accept this at first. In Rio, because of the way the track was laid out, I didn't have to brake a great deal and in many cases I was able to use the gears. This meant that although I found it difficult I didn't hear any alarm bells ringing. Or if I did, I was just ignoring them. The next race, at Imola, was a bit of a disaster, and that was partly down to my attitude. I went over there thinking, *This is a doddle. I'll just turn up and get myself in the points again.* But, after qualifying on the second-to-last row, I managed to get up to sixth before spinning off and then finishing the race two laps down. I raced well enough, once I'd got my head together, and finished eleventh, but something was definitely amiss.

If I had to blame one person in particular for what happened at Imola, it would have to be Jean-Marie Balestre, the president of the FIA. I'm joking, by the way, but at the drivers' briefing on the morning of the race he did something that would have boosted the ego of even the meekest individual. Jean-Marie was quite a dour character, and as we all took our seats he started tapping his desk with a pen.

'OK, gentlemen,' he began, 'before we start I just want to say something. Johnny Herbert, stand up, please.'

I thought, *What the bloody hell have I done?* Up I stood.

'Johnny, I just want to say that your result in Brazil was absolutely unbelievable. Well done.'

And then he and all the drivers started clapping.

So the race at Imola might not have gone the way I'd wanted it to, and to be honest things were about to get a whole lot worse, but to have had the likes of Senna, Mansell, Prost, Piquet and Patrese acknowledging the result of my F1 debut, and being led by the president of the FIA . . . well, it was the ultimate tribute really. In fact I don't know why I didn't retire from the sport there and then.

The next race on the calendar was Monaco, and once again I qualified on the second-to-last row. The problem here was that I just didn't have the strength to depress the brake pedal adequately. Somebody had worked out that in order to depress it fully you'd need to deploy between 700 and 800lb of pressure and the most I could muster was about 250 to 300lb. The muscle wastage had become so bad since the accident that I didn't have any calf muscles to speak of. It was just skin.

In the end, after one or two trials and a lot of errors, I discovered that the only place I could find that kind of pressure was from my hips and thighs, so instead of failing with my foot I tried using my heel and straightening my leg. Monocoques were actually quite spacious in those days which meant I had plenty of room to manoeuvre. This was a solution, of sorts, but instead of going throttle-and-brake, I was going throttle-feel-and-brake, so the movement wasn't smooth at all. But even when I did think I'd found the right position I was always taking a chance because without being able to feel very much I just had to take a punt. This meant that for every corner I got right, I'd end up getting the next three wrong. So much is left to chance in Formula 1 that anything you *can* control needs to work like clockwork and be absolutely on the button. This was not the case for me, I'm afraid, and despite my resourcefulness and never-say-die attitude I was simply papering over an ever-expanding crack.

I was now having physio, but because of my driving schedule it was intermittent and therefore not very effective. One day I'd have two hours on a trampoline, the next I'd be flying off somewhere to test, whereas what I really needed was intense physio, five hours a day, six days a week. As long as I was driving, that was never going to happen. Even if, like these days, I'd had a strength and conditioning coach with me twenty-four hours a day I honestly don't think I'd have had the time to get myself back. I also needed to recuperate so I could never have done both. In all it would take me two years to get up to full fitness again, so you can appreciate how far off I was in the early summer of 1989.

We're getting to that point where something's going to have to give again, aren't we?

The next race after Monaco was Mexico, where I qualified eighteenth and finished fifteenth – one place worse than in Monaco. By now I was beginning to get a bit depressed, and, unsurprisingly, some questions were being asked. Peter's mood was starting to change too and he seemed to be spending more and more time over in Italy, probably making excuses for me. There was no hiding place now, with Rio just a distant memory.

At Phoenix, qualifying was a disaster, and I started the US Grand Prix on the back row. I ended up finishing fifth in the race, but more by luck than any heroics behind the wheel. My right foot was also giving me a lot of gyp by this point – the Phoenix track was even more uneven than Jacarepaguá, and you had to walk miles to get to the track – and I cried again during the race. This time, however, I wasn't just crying because I was in pain; I was crying because I knew that I was fighting a losing battle and that it couldn't continue much longer. The frustration I felt was overwhelming, although I promise you I never once felt sorry for myself. There was nobody at all to blame, and in a way I hated that. Everyone had played this completely by the book, even Luciano and Flavio. The fact that their suspicions were about to be vindicated was immaterial. They had to look after the best interests of the Benetton Formula 1 team, and as much as it pains me to say this, I was not helping them do that.

People often ask me if I ever received preferential treatment in the paddock and I always say, 'Yes, I did, although not the kind you're expecting.' With hindsight – and there's an awful lot of that in this book – I probably shouldn't have been racing at all, so the preferential treatment I received was from Professor Sid Watkins, Bernie Ecclestone and Jean-Marie Balestre, who granted me my Super Licence and allowed me to race. Sure, it didn't work out this time round, but I'll tell you what, I wouldn't have changed it for the world and I consider myself to be a very lucky man. I was the world's first disabled Formula 1 driver, and nobody can ever take that away from me. Nor can they take away the fact that I came fourth on my debut and even sneaked a fifth at Phoenix. I wish to hell they'd take away one or two of the other results, especially the couple you're about to read about, but then you can't have everything, can you? Do I have any regrets? Only one, at least in this chapter: I wish I'd per-formed better for the team, that's all. I never let myself down, because regardless of the situation I always tried my best, but the team, and especially Peter, needed a lot more than I could give them.

My final race before being 'rested' was the Canadian Grand Prix on 18 June. Not to put too fine a point on it, it was an unmitigated disaster. In the untimed session on Friday morning I came twenty-sixth, and then twenty-eighth in first qualifying. Then, on the Saturday morning I came twenty-fifth in the untimed session and twenty-second in second qualifying, which put me on the grid with four places to spare. Unfortunately, every single one of the four drivers behind me improved in third qualifying, as did a further two drivers behind them, which left me twenty-ninth overall, three places off the race. It was the lowest point of my career so far and at the time I was inconsolable. Heartbroken, in fact. It was a completely new experience, a new kind of pain, and if I'd had to choose between that and the physical kind I honestly think I'd have gone for the latter.

On 5 July, a few days before the French Grand Prix, Benetton issued a statement regarding my future. I'm not so naive as to believe these things are always a joint effort written by everyone concerned, but I can honestly say that I had nothing to do with this, and although parts of the statement are true, much of it is cobblers.

Following discussions between Benetton Formula, Johnny Herbert and the medical advisors, it has been agreed that Johnny Herbert will cease driving in World Championship Grand Prix for the next three months. His replacement in the Benetton Ford Team for the French Grand Prix on Sunday 9th July is to be the Italian driver Emanuele Pirro. However, Herbert is to remain under contract to Benetton Formula and will play a major role as a driver in the development of the Benetton Ford B189 and a computerized active suspension system which has been designed by Benetton Formula.

'During the past two months, the brief intervals between each Grand Prix have not allowed me to devote adequate time to the exercise programmes which are so necessary to ensure my full recovery,' said Johnny Herbert. 'Although I have not been in pain during Grands Prix, the muscles in my right leg do not yet have sufficient strength for me to drive to the full extent of my ability. In the interest of my long-term future and ultimate recovery I believe that this temporary withdrawal will give me adequate opportunity to work on my legs, free from the pressures created by competition in Formula 1. Everyone in the Benetton Ford Team has been very supportive and I will continue with the testing and development of our new car.'

'We have no intention of releasing Johnny Herbert from his contract,' said Peter Collins, Team Manager of Benetton

Formula. 'On the one occasion when Johnny was not limited by the lack of strength in his right leg, he more than demonstrated his potential by finishing fourth at the Brazilian Grand Prix which was his first ever Formula 1 race. We are all convinced of his long-term potential. In the meantime, he will play a major role as a driver in our test and development programmes.'

There were a lot of tears when Peter told me I was being rested, and I didn't believe for one minute that it was just a temporary measure. Come to think of it, neither did he. Resting me at the time was still the right thing to do, however, and at the end of the day I had a short but pretty promising F1 career on the CV. So at the time I knew I had a chance of coming back – just not with Benetton.

Which again just goes to show how wrong you can be.

Ironically, Peter was about to suffer a similar fate to me, except that his departure would be a lot more clear-cut: after several weeks of to-ing and fro-ing he left Benetton overnight. How much of that was to do with my appointment I'm not sure, but I suspect his leaving the team was more to do with Flavio wanting his job, and because Flavio had the ear of the boss he was always going to come out on top. These kind of power struggles are commonplace within sport but it was the first time I'd witnessed one first-hand, and I have to admit that it made me yearn for the days when I could just get up on a Saturday morning, jump into the car with my family, and go and race. It's so easy to lose sight of what motorsport is ultimately all about, so if one good thing was going to come out of all this, apart from me being able to recuperate and my injuries being allowed to heal properly, it was going to be a renewed appreciation of exactly why I was doing this.

After a few weeks of intensive physiotherapy I began to feel a hell of a lot better, and when in mid-August I was asked to test for Benetton at Pembrey in Carmarthenshire, my calf muscles had recovered sufficiently for me to be able to brake using the ball of my foot occasionally, something I hadn't been able to do since the accident. I put in a few good times that day and came away feeling pretty pumped.

While this was going on, a deal was being done in the background to get me back into an F1 car straight away – which was just ridiculous. The Tyrrell F1 team had fallen out with one of their drivers over a sponsorship issue and had brought in Jean Alesi as a replacement, but because Alesi was in the middle of a promising F3000 season, which he would ultimately go on to win, he couldn't commit to every race. When looking for a stand-in for Jean, Ken Tyrrell had approached Benetton about me.

When I was asked if I might be interested in driving for Tyrrell I jumped at the chance. I was feeling a heck of a lot better, and I had a massive amount of admiration for Ken. Even so, what I should have done was politely refuse the offer, keep my head down and carry on working. Yeah, whatever. I don't think you'll find a racing driver anywhere on earth who would have done that. Can you imagine it? 'Sorry, Ken, I'd love to come to Spa with you and race in the Belgian Grand Prix but I'm afraid I have a two-hour trampolining session followed by some yoga and a good rubbing down. Oh, yes, and then I'm having tea with my mum.' Absolutely no chance.

First I went for a test with Tyrrell at Monza. I managed fifty-five laps, and the car itself felt a lot softer than the Benetton, which at the time suited me down to the ground. When it came to braking, the only problem I had now was mental: although my calf was almost normal again and functioning well, something was preventing me from attempting to depress the brake pedal fully, which meant my braking was just as unpredictable as it had been earlier in the season. I managed to overcome this problem before we got to Spa but only because the braking there was minimal.

The weekend started off far from promisingly because when I went out on the Friday morning I spun off almost immediately. I remember being pretty pissed off at the time because my confidence had been returning by the day and I couldn't wait to get out there. I think if anything I was a little bit too enthusiastic. Saturday went better and I managed to qualify sixteenth, five places in front of my team-mate, Jonathan Palmer. It was all to no avail, though, because on lap 4, at what was a very wet Spa, I spun off at Eau Rouge, and it was back to the pits to apologize. My God, I was angry.

Jean Alesi was back in the seat for Monza, but for the race after that, at Estoril on 24 September, I took his place once again as he was driving his final F3000 race of the season at the Bugatti Circuit at Le Mans. The Portuguese Grand Prix was a disaster for me and for a number of different reasons, but at least it made me appreciate once and for all that if I was ever going to get back into Formula 1 on a permanent basis, I was first going to have to spend a bit of time away from it.

Looking back on it, my Estoril adventure was more akin to a kind of *Carry On* film than a Grand Prix, and it started off with my left foot becoming infected a few days before the race. This used to happen occasionally but never before in the run-up to a race. I admit there's nothing especially funny about a foot infection, but this was no ordinary foot infection. It was always the left foot that would suffer, and what used to happen was it would get bigger and bigger until my socks and boots would no longer fit, which meant I couldn't walk. I have a little hole in my left heel which was used after the accident to drain all the gunk, and whenever the foot became infected this hole would come into service again and start churning out all kinds of stuff – pus, blood, pieces of grass, even tiny balls of rubber. Seriously:

I had remnants of the accident emanating from me for about three years after the shunt, and it was never pleasant. (A year on from this point, when I was racing F3000 in Fuji, Adrian Reynard came to see me and unfortunately I had exactly the same problem. Luckily for him he was just in time to see one of the blisters pop – I used to get them too – and I was able to present him with his very own piece of Brands Hatch turf. I know he's always been grateful.)

Toni Mathis was still dropping in on me from time to time, and he came to Estoril. He put my foot in buckets of ice and tried all kinds of different things, but none of it worked. I was finding walking almost impossible. I remember trying to make my way down the paddock one afternoon and realizing that everyone was staring at me. I couldn't bend my ankle at all, and my foot was about twice the size it normally was. I was just a walking freak show, so God only knows what people must have been thinking. One thing's for sure: I wasn't doing my future prospects in F1 any good whatsoever by being there. Old Mr Damaged Goods looked like he was in danger of being beyond repair.

It got worse, though. The night before second qualifying I went out with Mike Thompson for a meal and chose the one thing that, if it happened to be off, would go through me like a Cosworth turbo: lobster. Sure enough, the following day I was vomiting like some kind of crippled tribute to *The Exorcist*, and because I was still puking I had to stop every couple of laps, run to the back of the garage and puke into one of the bins. If this was nature's way of telling me to take a rest from Formula 1, it was making its point loud and clear. When the car arrived to take me to the airport I literally threw myself on to the back seat, complete with stomach cramps, a huge infected foot full of all kinds of everything, a bruised ego and a massive complex.

My ambitions in F1 hadn't changed though, not one little bit, and despite looking like a disabled tramp I was adamant that if my injuries had time to heal properly, or at least as well as they could, and I then got a seat in a competitive car, I still had a world championship in me. No driver enters Formula 1 with a dream of just being there, or at least not in my experience, and if just taking part ever became the most I could do I'd go and do something else. What gave me the strength to keep going now was acceptance, and a feeling that I was more than a match for anything fate could throw at me (apart from death, I suppose). Going forward, that feeling would become more and more pertinent. The sense of invincibility was gone for ever, as were certain elements of my natural ability, but accepting the fact, putting a smile on my face and getting my head down was the only way I could move forward. It was a poor substitute in the sense that it didn't affect how I went into a hairpin or a chicane, but it allowed me to attempt such things with as few distractions as possible. Things like bad luck would no longer exist in my world. They couldn't. From now on it had to be *whatever will be will be*, and, barring another bad shunt, I figured I could handle just about anything.

Since leaving Benetton, my fairy godfather, Peter Collins, had been busy working in Japan, and while I was putting my feet up and wondering what I was going to do next he called me and suggested that I might like to try my luck out there. Rest, recuperation and physiotherapy were going to be important, but whatever happened I had to carry on racing, both for the sake of my career and my sanity, so before hanging up my helmet for the year I went out to Japan to partner Martin Donnelly in the Fuji 1000 sports car race, which is now the Japanese leg of the FIA World Endurance Championship. I'd always wanted to have a go competitively in a Group C car – something you were never usually allowed to do if you were in F1 – and we ended up coming a very respectable sixth driving a Porsche 962. This hailed the beginning of what would become a long and happy association with sports car racing, one that would yield a bit of success as well as a bit of a hoo-hah with Bertrand Gachot.

Lobster-gate and the world's biggest foot notwithstanding, my options for 1990 were actually looking quite rosy by the end of 1989. Despite what had happened in Portugal, Tyrrell had made an enquiry about signing me full-time, but this came to nothing – luckily, because I doubt it would have done me any good to get back into F1 at this stage. As well as still having a testing contract with Benetton to fall back on, I'd also been approached by Nissan about driving for them at the 24 Hours of Le Mans. This also came to nothing, although I did visit their factory in Milton Keynes, which filled an afternoon. Then, just before Christmas, I was approached by the small and rather up-and-down Osella Formula 1 team in Italy, and for once my feet did me a favour by persuading them not to sign me.

We all knew it would be a bad idea, but . . . I always had this nagging feeling that if a drive in Formula 1 ever did materialize I should at least consider it. Yes, I know I've been going on about the importance of allowing my injuries time to heal and it must seem like I changed my mind as often as I changed my pants, but look at it from my point of view: I had no idea what the future was going to hold and my only ambition was to race in F1 and become world champion. I might not be in the same league as Damon Hill when it comes to brains – in fact I do believe he's even got a little goatee 'professor' beard these days, which lends a marvellous effect to his visage – but even I know that if you want to win the Formula 1 World Championship, you have to have a drive in a Formula 1 car. See, not bad eh? Sharp as a spanner.

After having a medical for Osella, some X-rays were taken,

and on seeing the one of my left foot they couldn't believe that I could move it, so they asked me to do the tests again. In the end they gave the drive to Olivier Grouillard, who'd been involved in my shunt at Brands; as well as failing either to pre-qualify or qualify at seven of the sixteen races, he also retired at five others. This has no bearing whatsoever on Olivier's skills as a racing driver but it certainly goes to prove that my ambitions of world domination would have been poorly served had I been chosen above him.

The next F1 outfit to show an interest in me were the Coloni team, which ran cars in F1 from 1987 until 1991. This lot made Osella look like Ferrari, and because I'd have to pre-qualify for every race I probably wouldn't have spent much time on the track, so that particular discussion didn't get out of first gear. Bertrand Gachot, on the other hand, of whom you'll hear yet more in a moment, did decide to work with Coloni, and after joining the team midway through the season, by which point they'd achieved not one qualification in eight races, he went on to do exactly the same again: eight races and not one qualification.

Come the new year I had been released from my contract with Benetton but had in its place a testing contract with Lotus – a role that was ideal for me, as in addition to remaining on the periphery of Formula 1, and therefore on the radar should anything interesting come up, I wouldn't have to speak to Flavio again via any of his secretaries. I was going to miss them, but it was definitely for the best.

To fill in the gaps, I also had nine races in the 1990 Japanese Formula 3000 Championship to look forward to, as well as six in the All Japan Sports Prototype Championship, and the 24 Hours of Le Mans with Mazdaspeed. Not bad, when you think about it, and by not putting all of my eggs into one basket I didn't feel anywhere near the amount of pressure I'd felt before, so hopefully I'd be able to start enjoying myself behind the wheel again. Remember what I said about wanting to just race? It almost felt like my career had been split into parts, with the end of part one finishing when I managed to vomit my way around Estoril. Part two, which I'd already had a sneak preview of thanks to the race at Fuji, had the makings of being as good, if not better, than part one. Would it be as eventful?

What do you think? This is me, remember.

Ten

BECAUSE OF RELIABILITY ISSUES, 1990 yielded few successes, but what it did provide me with was an awful lot of driving experience so from a rehabilitation point of view it was the perfect year. My braking, although painful and slightly unorthodox, was good, or as good as it was ever going to be, and even heel-and-toe was becoming far less of an issue. Best of all was the lack of politics and the lack of non-performance-related pressure, and when I wasn't racing, I was either at the gym, putting my two gammy feet up, or receiving physio. I even learned a few words of Japanese while I was over there and became a bit of a sushi connoisseur. あなたはそれでいくつかのわさび醤油をご希望ですか?

Despite the lack of podium action there were still one or two highlights to be had in 1990, the most significant of which took place roughly ten thousand kilometres west of Japan at the Circuit de la Sarthe in Le Mans, France. If winning the Formula 1 World Championship, or at least a Grand Prix, was at the top of my professional bucket list, winning Le Mans wasn't too far behind, so when I was approached by the man at Mazdaspeed responsible for booking the driver teams, a former racing driver named David Kennedy, I gave him a big fat yes. He and the team had decided to put together a line-up consisting of young

164

Formula 1 drivers. This race also fell foul of reliability issues, but as an experience it was amazing, and one that I was desperate to repeat.

Endurance racing is all about teamwork, which suited me down to the ground. I've always loved working as part of a team. Some of the best times I've ever had in motorsport have been sharing a success with those who've helped make it possible. That's why prima donnas aren't tolerated in endurance racing. If you're ever going to succeed in the sport you have to surrender your ego, leave your halo at the garage door and just get stuck in. There's no hierarchy as such; everybody, regardless of what job they do, is working towards one common goal. Formula 1, on the other hand – although it does try to position itself as a team sport – is all about individuals, but that's one of the things that makes it so entertaining. It can be divisive, political and downright nasty sometimes, and I've had first-hand experience, so obviously it generates a lot more headlines. People want competition, in all its forms, and if that takes place off the grid as well as on it, all the better.

Personally I've always preferred to do without the politics, the power struggles and the infighting. They didn't bother me as such, just annoyed me; but then perhaps I'm a bit of a purist. As I keep on telling you, I just wanted to race, preferably in a competitive car, and if anything ever jeopardized that I'd get pissed off. When it comes to what we do on the track I'd still say Formula 1 is the ultimate test on four wheels, but mark my words, driving hundreds of miles in the middle of the night at an average speed of about 140mph is pretty exhilarating, and all things considered I'll miss it just as much as I do F1.

Now you're probably not going to believe this, but the boss of Mazdaspeed, Mr Takayoshi Ohashi, started expressing doubts as to whether I could do a job for the team as early as the first week. 'Are you sure he's OK?' he kept saying to David. 'He looks like he can hardly walk.' Of course, he wasn't that far from the truth. You see, Ohashi-san always seemed to arrive first thing in the morning on the day of a test, and from a mobility point of view that wasn't my best time. Back then it was taking me about an hour to get out of bed in the morning, and even though I was usually quite chipper I both looked and felt like the Tin Man prior to being oiled. Ohashi-san's fears were finally put to rest the day we travelled to Paul Ricard to begin a twenty-four-hour test, as after I'd managed to hobble my way up to the garage at about 8.30 a.m., I then manoeuvred myself into the cockpit of the rotary-powered Mazda 787B and proceeded to do what I did best. By the time I came back in Ohashi-san was a happy man, although after that he did always look a little bit suspicious whenever he saw me.

The test at Paul Ricard was supposed to be our dress rehearsal for Le Mans but because of some ongoing electrical issues we failed to complete it so naturally everyone was a little bit nervous. As it turned out we had good reason to be, although in both practice and in qualifying things went without a hitch. That was the frustrating thing about this car: from a speed point of view it was nowhere near as competitive as the Jaguars, the Porsches or the Mercedes-Benzes, and it was even a bit slower than some of the mid-table Japanese cars. This, I think, is why Mazdaspeed went for three young Formula 1 drivers – me, Bertrand Gachot and Volker Weidler – as opposed to more experienced endurance racers, the idea being that we'd drive flat out and just see how it went. It was a big, big gamble, and diametrically opposed to the classic Le Mans strategy: drive fast, but whatever you do, look after the car. Le Mans was, and still is, the archetypal motorsport marathon, yet Mazda, who lacked speed, had just hired three sprinters to compensate. The thing is, this approach was only ever going to work if the car was at least as reliable as the rest, and at the time it just wasn't. The engine itself was absolutely fine, probably one of the most reliable on the grid; it was the heat it generated that seemed to cause the majority of the problems, and, as I said, it played havoc with our electrics.

I forget exactly when we had to retire the car in the end – it was about one a.m. on the Sunday morning – but when we did I was driving, and after getting out and taking off my helmet I shook everyone's hand, said 'bad luck', and then decided to have a little bit of fun at somebody else's expense. Us drivers had a lovely caravan parked at the back of the garage and in there, fast asleep, was my old friend and adversary Bertrand Gachot. He'd been due to drive next, so after I'd finished talking to the team I shuffled off as fast as I could, barged through the caravan door, shook Bertrand to within an inch of his life and screamed, 'BERTRAND, YOU'RE LATE! GET UP! YOU'RE SUPPOSED TO BE IN THE CAR! GET UP QUICK! THE TEAM ARE GOING CRACKERS!'

I have no idea what Bertrand was dreaming about – money, probably – but whatever it was he was reluctant to let go; yet when my words did start to register with him he was up and at 'em like you wouldn't believe. (He's French, by the way, so you'll have to imagine what follows in a French accent. I've tried, but I always end up sounding like a French Indian.) 'Oh my God, Johnny,' he screamed. 'Why didn't somebody wake me sooner? Quick, throw me my boots!'

I never did throw Bertrand his boots, for the simple reason that I was in the process of weeing myself on the caravan floor.

'Why are you laughing, Johnny?' he cried, suspicion now taking hold. 'What is uuuurp?'

Just then Bertrand realized what was uuuurp and went ab-so-lutely mental.

'You English sink you av zis amazing sense of 'umour, but really, Johnny, you are a dick!'

. And then he went for me.

'You can't hit me,' I protested, 'I'm disabled!'

Bertrand did eventually see the funny side, although not until the following year's race, by which time Mazdaspeed had worked out how to cool the electrics.

On the Formula 1 side of things 1990 was again lacking in any visible success, although as a test driver my options were always going to be somewhat limited. It had certainly gone well though, my job at Lotus, and when my old Jordan team-mate and one of the regular Lotus drivers Martin Donnelly was involved in a horrific accident during first practice at Jerez, I was asked to fill in for him at the final two Grands Prix of the season. It was desperately unlucky for Martin, as the injuries he sustained curtailed what was a very promising career in Formula 1. With all the humour you'd expect from an Irishman, he was a very, very talented driver who, unfortunately, we never saw the best of.

True to form, those final two races ended in retirement, Suzuka with an engine problem and Adelaide, the clutch. It was ironic, really, as at first glance the Lotus 102, which was powered by the Lamborghini 3512, resembled the Reynard I'd driven during that fateful F3000 season – both cars were yellow with Camel branding – but I'd hazard a guess that the Jordan may well have outperformed the Lotus. It would certainly have spent longer on the track. Retirements aside, that call-up to Lotus still provided me with some very welcome experience and made me realize just how much I was missing Formula 1. I was in the right place, though – mentally, physically *and* professionally – so the trick was simply to bide my time, carry on driving to the best of my ability, and see what happened. Actually, one of the most enjoyable aspects of that short stint at Lotus was having Derek Warwick as a team-mate. A great driver, of course, he's also a good lad and one of the true characters of motorsport.

New opportunities were bound to arise in 1991, and in the closing months of 1990 I'd already been offered yet more drives in the All Japan Sports Prototype and F3000 Championships, as well as a return fixture at Le Mans with Volker and Sleeping Beauty. The only thing that was missing was a drive or two in F1, but because the current Lotus team had now gone to the wall I was left wanting in that particular area. It didn't bother me, though: I was just grateful for what I had. I was driving as well as I ever had since the accident and figured that if I was good enough, somebody would pick me up. Yes, I know it doesn't always work out like that, but I was buggered if I was going to waste my time worrying about it.

As it turned out, I wouldn't have to wait that long for a new F1 opportunity to materialize, and there are no prizes for guessing where it came from.

My first four races of 1991, which were all Japanese F3000 events, yielded a fifth, a seventh, a retirement and a second. The team I was driving for, Team Le Mans, weren't that competitive I'm afraid, with a below-par Ralt, and in a grid consisting primarily of Lolas and Reynards, with Mugen-Honda engines, the only two cars that were competitive, and which were ultimately driven into first and second place, were a Reynard using a Mugen and a Lola sporting a Cosworth. Even so, I still managed to finish a very respectable tenth in the championship among a pretty impressive field of drivers, two of whom, Michael Schumacher and Eddie Irvine, would become team-mates of mine.

Unbeknown to me, right at the very end of 1990 my old mentor Peter Collins and a wonderful chap called Peter Wright had purchased the rights to the Lotus name with a view to relaunching the brand and starting a new chapter in its proud racing history. It wasn't going to be easy, though, and after two DNQs and a retirement in the first two races of the 1991 F1 season things were looking pretty bleak.

Money was tighter than ever, and during a test session at Imola at the end of April, just prior to the San Marino Grand Prix, Julian Bailey, who was one of the Lotus drivers, was seen driving yet another car that resembled my F3000 Jordan. Unfortunately it resembled the car prior to Eddie doing the sponsorship deals with Camel and so was virgin white. Without a known driver on the team they were always going to find it difficult, and the Lotus name alone was not enough. Had Bailey's team-mate been a few years older they'd have been absolutely dripping in cash, but at the time Mika Häkkinen was just twenty-two and despite winning the 1989 British Formula 3 title was still a long way off being able to attract big money to F1.

After Monaco, which was the fourth race of the 1991 season, Bailey had failed to qualify for three of those races, so in a drastic bid to change things around Peter called me and asked me if I'd be interested in a full-time drive. I wasn't in a position to drive every race for the team as I wanted to fulfil my Japanese commitments, and I certainly didn't have any money to bring to the table. Peter knew that, though; he also knew that because I'd made a few headlines here and there and could drive a bit, he might be able to raise some money on the back of signing me. But on top of that I think he was keen to pick up where we'd left off at Benetton – as was I, it has to be said – and with me now approaching a full-ish recovery and without any Flavios around messing up the game, the feeling was that as long as he could raise the money we might just stand a chance of making it work.

My first race in my second stint with both Peter and Lotus was the Canadian Grand Prix in early June. As well as the car feeling OK I felt very much at home with the team and immediately hit it off with my new team-mate. Mika, in addition to being a consummate racing driver, is a really nice guy. Of course, as well as having more than our fair share of laughs together over the years he has also fallen foul of one or two rather naughty tricks. I'll divulge the details of my favourite later on.

During first practice at Canada, Mika and I were about level-pegging in terms of lap times, but because we were still driving the old Lotus 102 (now with a Judd V8), we were languishing around the mid-teens. We knew that was going to be the case though, so until the two Peters got things sorted out we'd just have to race each other and hope for the best. When it came to qualifying, Mika went out first and ended up on the second-to-last row. Once again, it wasn't ideal, but because our expectations had been managed correctly he was happy just to be there, and if I could do the same I'd be happy too.

Unfortunately (there's that bloody word again), when I went out the car died on me before I could post a time. In those days qualifying lasted an hour so I just had enough time to run back to the pits, jump in the spare car and get out for a couple of runs. I know it's wrong for a workman to blame his tools, but if that spare car had been a pop band it would have been Milli Vanilli. It was an absolute pig of a thing, and in the end I failed to qualify by over two seconds and was probably about a minute down on Riccardo Patrese on pole. I know I'm making light of all this, but I promise you I was devastated at the time. This was supposed to be the first real race of the second half of my Formula 1 career, so failing to qualify was the worst possible outcome. Racing in Japan had been great, and I couldn't wait to get back to Le Mans, but at the end of the day it had all been done with a view to getting back into F1. Before I caught the plane home I had a very tearful conversation with Peter Collins. Once again I thought I'd let him down. It took all of his legendary motivational skills to bring me round and reassure me that all the hard work hadn't been in vain.

These days you can pretty much guarantee that if a spare car comes into use it'll provide a similar performance to the ones it's there to replace, and would be unlikely to be more than two-tenths off the pace. Our two seconds would actually go on to help the team because from then on they would work on ensuring the spare car enjoyed parity with the other two, but this had happened at the expense of what was supposed to be an important milestone in my career, and at the time I felt some-what crestfallen.

Come the next race, in Mexico, everything was tickety-boo again, or at least on the up. As well as Mika and I qualifying a mightily unrespectable twenty-fourth and twenty-fifth on the grid, just behind a Minardi, we finished the race ninth and tenth which, bearing in mind where we'd qualified and what we were driving, was a massive result for the team. It gave everybody a huge boost.

Just three or four days after completing the Mexican Grand Prix I was in France preparing to drive at Le Mans again for Mazdaspeed. We'd already done quite a bit of testing by this point and we were satisfied that all the problems that had hampered us the previous year had now been ironed out. We certainly wouldn't be favourites for the race, in fact we were way down the field in that respect, but we were all very confident of doing well, and with things potentially improving again at Lotus I walked into the Mazdaspeed garage at the Circuit de la Sarthe with a pretty big grin on my face.

For all my talk of teamwork earlier, and despite there being plenty of competition on the grid, I have to admit that Bertrand, Volker and I, although team-mates, were watching each other's performances like hawks, so a little bit of rivalry within the team was going to be unavoidable. We were all young at the time and pretty full of ourselves, and on top of that we'd also been rivals for nigh on five years, so by the time we all arrived in France a rather large competitive elephant had entered the room – or, in our case, the garage. The trick was to take all that internal competitiveness and make it work for the team; after all, if we were all watching each other's lap times, the chances are it would lead to trouble. In the end we had a competition to see who could achieve the best fuel economy. That was arguably our most important task when it came to the overall strategy so turning it into a competition was a masterstroke. Fuel economy notwithstanding, we were all acutely aware of why Ohashi-san had hired us, so when it came to the race proper we drove almost as we would a single-seater.

The Sauber Mercedes featuring Michael Schumacher, Karl Wendlinger and Fritz Kreutzpointner took pole position and was miles faster than anyone else. Karl was being touted as the next big thing in Formula 1. He did well, of course, and as well as seventy-two starts in F1 he won a couple of GT Championships, but who on earth could have imagined what his team-mate would go on to do? Well done, Fritz!

Tom Walkinshaw's Jaguars were placed two, three and four on the grid so everyone sitting in the famous Auberge des Hunaudières was expecting either one of them to prevail, or one of the Mercedes-Benzes. One of the many cars they weren't expecting to do well was the flame-throwing rotary-powered lump being piloted by the three sprint drivers. You underestimated us at your peril.

Believe it or not it was actually the Fédération Internationale du Sport Automobile that gave us the advantage we needed to have a chance of winning. The governing body! Back in April they'd

173

slipped through an amendment to the rules which, without going into too much boring detail, gave us a better power-to-weight ratio than the Mercs, the Jags and the Porsches. The upshot was that we were now achieving 760bhp per tonne whereas the other three were achieving around 720 to 730bhp per tonne. Because of this we were able to be a little bit lighter on the brakes (we were using carbon-fibre brakes, whereas Jaguars and Porsches weren't), the suspension and the tyres, which in turn gave us a more reliable car, a far better fuel economy, and overall about three seconds per lap. According to one of the reports I've read, the other three teams had been so busy eyeing each other up that they hadn't even noticed the amendment. Come the race they must have been kicking themselves.

Another factor on our side was having the six-times Le Mans winner Jacky Ickx as part of the team. He didn't have that much to do with me personally but just having him around was a great motivational tool. He always carried with him an aura of success, probably pretty similar to the one I'd had leading up to Brands.

My memory of the race itself is pretty sketchy, and in a moment you'll find out why, but we were all doing double stints which would have been about an hour and a half each. Back then none of the cars had power-steering, and with it being one of the hottest Le Mans in years this helped to demonstrate the scant regard designers had for installing effective cooling systems. It's a lot better now but in 1991 that cockpit was like a bloody greenhouse, and two of the drivers, whose names begin with a V and a B, were suffering from pretty serious personal hygiene problems. No matter, though. Douglas Bader didn't let a little thing like no legs stop him from flying during the war, and although I wasn't quite in his position I was damned if I was going to let a couple of smelly Europeans spoil my drive. To be fair to Nigel Stroud, who designed the 787B, he was kind enough to ensure we always had just enough air to be able to breathe.

After the first twelve hours things were going so well that we waived a chance to change the brake discs. 'PUSH, PUSH, PUSH!' is what I remember hearing over the radio. The fuel economy required to complete the race had been stuck on the dash and because we were managing to stay below the required rate quite easily we were able to push a bit more. That competition we had on fuel economy had gone out of the window by this time as all we could think about now was the fact that we were in with a chance of winning. You could hear the anticipation and the excitement growing every time somebody came through on the radio, so that obviously filtered through to us. Could we, the lowly Mazda, with that ear-splitting rotary engine, actually go on and beat the might of the three big teams? Well, as a matter of fact, yes, we bloody well could!

Come the Sunday morning we were in second position and still, all the time, we were being told to 'PUSH, PUSH, PUSH!' The Mercedes that had been on pole was still winning by about the eighteenth hour, then all of a sudden I remember hearing a lot of shouting coming from the Sauber Mercedes garage. Bertrand was driving for us at the time and when we saw the commotion everyone started running round shouting, 'Are they out? Are they out?' Never before had I wanted to see a car enter a garage in a state of disrepair more than that Mercedes, and when it finally appeared we were elated. It did go out again, but by then it was too late.

With about three hours to go I took over from Volker to begin what was supposed to be my last double stint, with Bertrand then coming in to finish the race. We had a lead of about a lap by this time which should have given me a nice easy drive, but Tom Walkinshaw's Jaguars, who were running second, third and fourth, had other ideas. John Nielson, who was driving the

Jag running fourth, pushed me hard for quite a while but I was feeling quite fresh at the time, having only just set off, and had enough experience to see me through the scare.

Just under ninety minutes later I came in after what was supposed to be my final stint, but because the lap times were so good I was asked if I'd stay in the car and complete the race. 'No problem,' I said. I still felt fresh and I had enough adrenalin running through me to start a mass brawl.

'We'll see you at the four p.m. flag then, Johnny,' said the team manager, Mr Ohashi. 'Good luck!'

And off I went.

As well as refuelling the car when I came in, they should also have refuelled me – or I should have asked – but with all the excitement going on and with Mazdaspeed being on the brink of making history I went off again without any water. I'm pretty sure I'd run out about half an hour before I came in, so I was already becoming dehydrated. As I said earlier, this was one of the hottest Le Mans for donkey's years and if it was thirty-odd degrees outside the car it must have been at least forty-five in it.

Within about twenty minutes of my setting off again I started to feel the effects. My eyes and head were OK; it was my stomach that was starting to misbehave, but because I had no fluid inside me I couldn't actually vomit, thank God. Come the last couple of laps I was an absolute wreck, and for the first time in years I wasn't being distracted by my feet. It was the rest of my body that was falling apart, and in addition to feeling bilious I was also starting to get cramps everywhere. The funny thing is that my energy levels were fine (that would change the moment the race finished) which is the only reason I kept going. I already knew exactly how to retch in the cockpit of a sports car, with or without a helmet, and cramps compared to pulverized feet were child's play.

Twenty-five years ago at Le Mans, when the flag went down at four p.m. it didn't matter where you were on the track, that was the end of the race, so you never actually took the chequered flag, or if you did you were bloody lucky. I was at Mulsanne's Corner when the race finished which is about halfway round the track. This meant I still had another four miles to drive before I could have a drink, but it didn't matter, I was absolutely buzzing, and when I got to the Ford chicane just before the pits the team had come out and they were going crazy too, as were the crowd. Winning a Grand Prix is very special, but at the end of the day it's part of something much bigger, the Formula 1 World Championship. Le Mans is also part of something wider, but it has a stand-alone quality to it and a history like no other race on earth.

People have often said that by winning Le Mans I proved to the world that I was well enough to compete in F1 again, and I suppose that was always part of the plan, but I would never let that detract from the fact that winning such a prestigious race (in very Herbertesque circumstances) in an unfancied car has to be up there with anything else I achieved. Had I gone on to win the Formula 1 World Championship, it would still have been right up there. Incidentally, until 2015, when Nico Hülkenberg won Le Mans, Bertrand and I were the only active Formula 1 drivers ever to win the race. Thanks for spoiling that, Nico.

As I went through the Ford chicane on the way back, some of the Mazdaspeed mechanics jumped on the side of the car, and because a lot of the crowd had now made their way on to the track, the last few hundred yards resembled a kind of victory procession. I was shattered but I managed to find, somewhere in my body, enough liquid to shed a few tears as I made my way through the cheering throng. All Le Mans winners receive similar treatment, but this car in particular had been very popular with the spectators, partly because of the wonderful scream the R26B rotary engine made, but also because the 787B used to spit out a flame occasionally that must have been about three feet long. In 1990 it had been about six feet long but FISA had ordered Mazdaspeed to minimize it so as not to roast too many competitors. The colour scheme too, a fairly garish bright orange and British racing green which just happened to match the colours of one of the sponsors, seemed to capture the imagination (or turn the stomachs) of the Le Mans faithful. To this day it remains one of the race's most popular entrants.

From Mazda's point of view, the win was historic. Despite both Nissan and Toyota investing fortunes in the attempt to develop a competitive car, neither manufacturer had ever won the race, so for a relatively small player like Mazda to come along and show them how it should be done was a genuine David and Goliath-style achievement. As the first Japanese manufacturer ever to win Le Mans, Mazda captured the hearts of the entire nation.

I forgot to mention that in addition to not drinking anything, my sleep patterns had never really shifted out of F1 mode, which meant I hadn't slept much either before or during the race. Neither had I eaten anything for at least ten hours. This was because of nerves – sometimes before a race they'd get the better of me. Even what I'd eaten prior to that had only been some kind of Pot Noodle, which would have had all the nutritional value of a bag of sand. This was never usually a problem during an F1 race but Le Mans was on a slightly different scale, so when I eventually arrived at Parc Fermé I opened the door of the car, jumped out, gave a few waves and a victory punch, and then all of a sudden my head started to go.

The only way I can describe the feeling that followed is it was as if my head was being separated from the rest of my body. My

God, it was weird. You know the stars you see in a cartoon when somebody gets hit by something? Well, I swear to you I started seeing them, and I remember thinking, *Wooooh, this shouldn't be happening*. Then I saw my dad standing on the other side of the car and I thought, *If I'm going to collapse* – and if I'd been a betting man I'd have put my house on it – *I'd better do it as close to him as possible*. So after making my way slowly yet victoriously around the now famous car – how I did it I have no idea – I found my dad, raised my hands in the air one more time, and then collapsed into his arms.

I'd done the job I'd been paid to do but I'm afraid that really was the end of the line as far as walking and talking were concerned, let alone racing a strangely coloured Japanese car. I had nothing left in the tank. After being piled on to a stretcher I was taken to the medical centre where they rehydrated me and force-fed me some pasta. Because of the time I had to spend there I missed the flaming presentation ceremony, and as far as I know I am the only Le Mans winner in history not to make it on to the podium. How absolutely bloody typical is that?

Did it really matter? No, of course it didn't. Podium or no podium, Bertrand, Volker and I had just won the 24 Hours of Le Mans, and that can never be taken away from us.

A good few hours later I rejoined the team at the after-race party where, as I'm sure you can imagine, there was quite a bit of merrymaking. It had been a tough race, and without wanting to sound like an old curmudgeon, things were a lot tougher back then than they are these days. Sports cars now are much more ergonomically designed, and that's exactly as it should be. A car's no good to anyone without a driver and they can only preserve the car if you preserve them. It was a special win: this flame-throwing, aesthetically unusual scream-machine being driven by a Frenchman with a temper, a German with whom he didn't get on, and an Essex boy with, shall we say, a slightly eventful and altogether erratic career. It was all highly unorthodox.

After that it was back to Formula 1 and the ever-changing fortunes of the Lotus team. I'd also pretty soon be forced to make a major decision – my first ever in the sport, and one that I would very much live to regret.

Eleven

My remaining six races of the 1991 Formula 1 season yielded a tenth, a fourteenth, a seventh, two retirements and an eleventh, which was disappointing to say the least. Even Mika, who raced the entire season, managed to scrape together just two points, although how he even achieved that in the car we had is a bloody miracle. He was actually a pay driver then, but unlike the vast majority of them was rather good – slight understatement there.

He and I got on like a house on fire. It's strange really, because once we were on the track we were as competitive as any drivers I've ever known, but off it we just clicked. Lotus didn't have a pot to pee in so wherever we were travelling to in the world it was economy all the way. Some people might think, *Well, so it bloody well should be,* but you try asking any of today's drivers to travel steerage and see what reply you get. Fortunately for Mika and me there weren't that many people flying at the time, which meant we would usually be able to bag three seats apiece on either side of the aisle, and once we were settled we'd lift up the arms, make a bed for ourselves and read each other bedtime stories. OK, that last bit isn't strictly true, but travelling on a budget held no fear whatsoever for us. In fact we thrived on it. At the end of the day we were two young blokes doing exactly what we'd always dreamed of doing. We'd have travelled by horse and cart and slept on a bed of nails if necessary.

Once we landed, we used to have to go and find our hire car for the weekend and then we'd get the map out and try to find our hotel. As well as things like cars, Mika and I also used to share hotel rooms; on one or two occasions we even shared the same bed. That particular arrangement came to a rather abrupt end one day, and all because of a joke I decided to play on him in Nièvre, which is about five miles from the Circuit de Nevers Magny-Cours.

We were there for the 1991 French Grand Prix, and because it was my first race back after winning Le Mans I was in quite a mischievous mood. I'd also missed Mika. The hotel room we had couldn't have been more than about three metres square, and as well as one tiny little window it had a double bed with a small bathroom next to it. On the Friday night, after returning from the circuit, I asked Mika if he'd like me to run him a bath. 'That would be very nice of you, Johnny,' said my favourite Finn. 'Thank you.' And so I ran him a lovely big bubbly bath.

When it was ready, I grabbed one of the flannels, put it in my pocket, came out of the bathroom and announced, 'Your bath's ready, Mika.'

'Thanks, Johnny,' he replied, and in he went.

While he was disrobing in the bathroom I was doing the same in the bedroom. Once I was sure he was in the bath, I put the flannel over my parts (well, it was more of a bath towel, really) and knocked at the door.

'Can I come in?' I whispered naughtily.

'Erm, yes, I suppose so,' said a rather hesitant Mika.

I opened the door, walked in very slowly – towel, in position – fluttered my eyelashes and said, 'Would you like me to get in with you, Mika?'

Have you ever seen a terrified Finnish gentleman start

splashing about in a bath? Well, if you ever get the opportunity, seize it, because it was one of those sights I shall remember for the rest of my born days. He was absolutely shitting himself, bless him, and with the sight of me standing there starkers with a flannel over my whatsits I'm not surprised.

The following morning the Flying Finn went flying up to Suzanne, the Lotus team secretary, and blurted out his fears. 'Suzanne, I think Johnny is gay. What am I going to do?'

Now I shall tell you the *real* punchline to this story, and I'll leave you guessing as to whether it was intentional or not. The next day I qualified twentieth on the grid and finished tenth in the race, whereas Mika, fresh from his close encounter with yours truly, failed to qualify, and for the only time that season. It was the ultimate mind game really. *If* I meant to do it . . .

Despite the bathroom shenanigans, my relationship with Mika carried on swimmingly well into 1992. As well as having a laugh off the track we'd also help each other on it by sharing little bits of information. For example, I remember trying a different line going into Copse Corner at Silverstone, as by turning in a little bit earlier and clipping the kerb I gained a slight advantage. I passed that on to Mika and the next day he gave it a try. That's how it worked with us; we were back and forth, helping each other out.

This all changed when we got the new car, the Lotus 107, about a third of the way through the 1992 season, and I'm pretty sure Mika's manager, Keke Rosberg, must have had something to do with it. By that time McLaren had started showing an interest in Mika so I completely understand why the change came. He clearly had an ambition to move forward in the sport, as of course did I, and with a team like McLaren showing an interest he had to pull the ladder up and start building 'Brand Mika'. In his position I'd have done exactly the same thing, except when I started receiving overtures from the likes of Ron

Dennis, which would happen the following season, I would be in no position to take them up.

With Mika changing tack, things were never quite the same, but I knew it was nothing personal. It was simply a career move – and a good one at that. By the end of the 1992 season his contract with Lotus would expire and he'd be free to move to McLaren. What happened to him on the track after that I have no idea, although I heard a whisper that he did rather well. Our relationship these days is pretty much back to how it used to be, although we're now *retired* racing drivers as opposed to young upstarts so I doubt we'll be sharing a hotel room any time soon. A bath might be nice, though.

By 1992 I was back to being a full-time Formula 1 driver again, although it has to be said that the season itself was a bit of a shocker. Out of the sixteen Grands Prix we entered I completed only five. Again I out-qualified Mika, as I had done in 1991, but yet again reliability issues prevented me from translating that promise into points. Every one of those eleven remaining Grands Prix ended in retirement. Only Olivier Grouillard, driving the extremely disappointing Tyrrell, retired more often.

There was one rather welcome distraction that year and that was a return to the Circuit de la Sarthe for the 1992 24 Hours of Le Mans. The FIA had banned rotary engines from the race so without the funds necessary to be able to develop a completely new car using the now compulsory V10 power plants, Mazda had decided to approach Judd for the engine – they eventually used their GV10 3.5L V10 which had originally been developed for Formula 1 – and, in a bizarre twist of fate, Tom Walkinshaw Racing for the chassis. This meant that basically we were driving a Judd-powered Jaguar XJR-14 with a Mazda Sport badge, and in the same colours as 1991. We put up a good fight and finished a very respectable fourth (the team also came third in the 1992 World Sportscar Championship) but we were no match for the dominant Peugeot Sport team featuring my mates Derek Warwick and Mark Blundell. They were in the winning car, which was fantastic, and the team also bagged third on the podium, alongside Toyota. I'd eventually go back to Le Mans, but it wouldn't be for another nine years.

There was one moment in 1992, at the Japanese Grand Prix in October, when I actually thought things might be changing. We'd been qualifying well since getting the new car and despite my never being able to finish a bloody race we'd been starting in the top twelve quite consistently; Mika even went on to bag a string of top-five finishes, leaving him eighth in the championship. At qualifying in Japan things seemed to have moved on a step further for the team, with me sixth behind Schumacher in the Benetton and Mika seventh. Reliability issues aside, I honestly thought we were in with a chance of doing well. There was even a little bit of a buzz about the team.

The race started brilliantly, and after three or four laps I went past Schumacher and eventually got up into third. Had I finished the race, this would have given the new Lotus team its maiden podium. It wasn't to be, though: on lap 15 my diff exploded and that was that. This still left Mika, who was now running third in my place, and he ran well right up until lap 44 when he over-revved the engine a couple of times and it blew up. I have to admit that watching him get closer and closer to becoming the first Lotus driver in that incarnation to bag a podium was torture, and when he retired, rightly or wrongly I drew a massive sigh of relief. I love the man to bits but when all's said and done he was as much a competitor of mine as anyone else in the paddock, the only difference being that I actually wanted him to do well – providing it wasn't as well as me or at my expense.

It had been the same in Adelaide the previous season. The race had seen some of the worst rain in years and was stopped after sixteen laps but I remember aquaplaning quite happily and feeling perfectly at home. It was completely on the edge, as close to being out of control as I was ever likely to get without being in a crash situation, and I was almost in touching distance of the unknown. But as good as all that was, do you know what my favourite moment of the race was? Lapping Mika. You see *that's* how racing drivers think. You can be having the time of your life out there on the track, you could even lap the world champion, but if you lap or beat your team-mate there's a kind of vindication that you don't get from beating anyone else. It's a different kind of victory, one that plays a very important part in motivating you, and the more equal things are within the team the sweeter the victory. To be fair to Mika, who was always fantastic in the wet (and especially in a bath), I think he'd been half asleep that day and when he realized I'd lapped him he got his arse in gear and started racing. Just to put all this in per-spective, though, I finished twenty-first in the race and Mika twenty-fifth so, to use some cricketing parlance, it was still very much a view from the boundary.

That Grand Prix at Adelaide was where I signed my new con-tract with Lotus – my new *five-year* contract with Lotus. Peter's reasons for wanting me to commit to such a lengthy deal were both clear and understandable: he needed sponsorship, and he was more likely to get it if I was on board long-term. This was all well and good, but a hell of a lot can happen in five years and what I should have done was meet him somewhere in the middle and at least have one or two release clauses in there should one of the big boys come calling. And it's not as if I wasn't advised to do exactly that.

I remember calling Becky from the hotel where Peter and I were meeting, and she said, 'I've spoken to the lawyer and he says whatever you do *don't* sign the contract until you get back.' Now, what would any sane person do at this point? They'd probably put the phone down, go back to where the meeting was taking place and do exactly that. I, on the other hand, went back and *signed the contract*. With hindsight it was a really stupid thing to do and, as I said earlier, I would live to regret the decision for quite some time afterwards. In fact the saying 'act in haste, repent at leisure' could have been written for that particular situation. When I arrived home, words were had. Why did I do it there and then? I mean, I only had to say, 'Would you mind if we waited a few days until we got back to England?' It wouldn't have been that much of a problem, surely? I suppose I did it out of a sense of loyalty to Peter. After all, without him I wouldn't have been in F1, and as he was the one who'd persuaded me to go out to Japan I probably wouldn't have won Le Mans either. I owed him so much, so signing a piece of paper that would help him to keep Lotus going seemed, at the time, like the very least I could do. What I regret most, in addition to the effect it had on my career, was that it drove a wedge between Peter and me, and that was very hard to bear. We both wanted what was best for each other yet self-preservation was always going to have to pre-vail, and unfortunately our relationship became a victim of that.

It all started in 1993, after Mika went to McLaren. Before that, in 1992, Williams had made a tentative approach for both of us but that had been swiftly rebuffed and then forgotten about. Thoughts of that day at Brands Hatch when Frank had wanted to see me came to mind, but by the time I heard about the approach, the Lotus 107 was about to be introduced, and with Mika already being courted by McLaren and nearing the end of his contract, we were actually quite contented. A year on, Mika had made his dream move to McLaren but I was still at Lotus, and just a year or so into that five-year contract.

Alex Zanardi, whom I also got on with very well, and who was always a very technically minded driver, had joined the team from Minardi, but as time wore on I became more and more unsettled. Frustration was the crux of the problem, and I felt it in all directions. Before I go on I'd just like to say that Alex Zanardi is without doubt one of the most astonishing human beings I've ever had the pleasure of knowing, and as somebody who has also had to ply their trade carrying a knock or two I think what he's achieved since his accident is inspirational. Strangely modest for an Italian, Alex is also a true gentleman and I'm proud to know him.

Testing for 1993 had gone really well and I went on record saying that the 107B was a massive improvement and that its turn-in, in particular, had been impressive. I said this after the final test at Paul Ricard. By the time we got to South Africa for the first Grand Prix of the season we were in all kinds of trouble and both Alex and I ended up retiring, him on lap 17 and me on lap 38.

It was a bad omen, and despite coming fourth in Brazil and then again in April at Donington in the European Grand Prix, a string of retirements would follow that would bring us all crashing back down to earth with a thud. Donington was fun, though. I remember Michael Schumacher overtaking me and then me re-taking him instantly, which he didn't like, and because of the weather – it went from wet, to very wet, to dry, and then to wet again – the lap charts were hilarious. I think Alain Prost in the Williams pitted seven times in all. I pitted just the once and finished in the middle of a Prost – Patrese sandwich, which was rather nice.

What these two performances helped to demonstrate – although a fat lot of good it did me at the time – was that given the right car I could more than hold my own against the big boys. In turn, this helped generate a renewed interest in my services. While Rome was effectively burning – by this time Lotus were getting into some serious financial difficulty – I was starting to hear rumours about teams wanting to offer me an escape route, and the more it went on the harder it was to ignore. Believe it or not, and I only know this because I decided to look it up on a whim, in Greek mythology 'lotus' is the name of a plant whose fruit was supposed to induce an unwillingness to leave somewhere. What horrible irony.

As far as I know, McLaren were the first team to show their colours and make an approach for me, although I wasn't made aware of it at the time. This would have been towards the end of 1993 – after I'd added a fourth at Silverstone and a fifth at Spa to my tally of finishes – when Mika moved up from being their test driver to getting a race seat, so I suppose they wanted me as his replacement. It was reported that Peter wanted something like £21 million for me, which was probably Lotus's debt at the time, but that was never going to happen. As strange as it might sound, I wouldn't have gone to McLaren anyway, even if I'd been given the opportunity, and in a moment or two I'll explain why.

I ended the season ninth in the Drivers' Championship, just one point behind Ferrari's Gerhard Berger who had also been plagued by reliability problems. By this time my relationship with Peter was becoming strained, and although nothing had been said out loud and we never actually fell out, thank God, the elephant in the room was now far too big to ignore. So once the season was over I sat down, picked up a pen and wrote him a letter in which I thanked him for all his support over the years, but might he consider letting me go so that I could try to fulfil my true potential?

Peter was magnanimous in his refusal, and I would have expected nothing less, but he was resolute none-the-less. 'If you go, so will half our sponsorship, so how can I possibly say yes?' he said. I now appreciate just how much pressure Peter must have been under, and when the team eventually did fold it was with debts of about £11 million. He was right, though:

if I'd gone at the end of 1993 they'd have lost a fortune, and at the time there were probably forty or fifty people employed by the team, many of whom would have had families. What right did I have to leave so many people on the brink of unemployment just to further my own career? If only I'd listened to Becky and our lawyer.

Once again the start of the 1994 season came with all kinds of promises, and after four races using the updated 107C – which, shock horror, yielded only one retirement – the potentially team-saving Lotus 109 was introduced, which apparently had enjoyed a development budget running into many tens of pounds. It had potential, that's for sure, but it had the wrong engine, and the last time I looked that sort of thing is pretty fundamental to a car's success. Initially it was powered by the very bulky old Mugen-Honda engine which had almost caused the late Harvey Postlethwaite, who designed James Hunt's Hesketh 308, to scream in horror when he was given it for the Tyrrell 020. With this thing on board, the 109 was never going to be capable of doing anything, so in the end they had to introduce an active suspension system which in itself caused more problems.

On the track there were few pluses to be found, and of course that entire 1994 season was overshadowed by the deaths, at Imola, of Roland Ratzenberger and Ayrton Senna. I didn't know either of them intimately but we were certainly friends and what memories I do have of Roland and Ayrton are pleasant ones. I'd raced against Roland, not only in Formula 1 but in Formula 3, at Le Mans and in Japan, and he was definitely one of the good guys; he was always smiling and he quite obviously loved what he did. Ayrton, it won't surprise you to know, was another of those people who had an aura about him; even before he died he'd attained a kind of godlike status. That's quite rare, I think, as it's usually something that happens posthumously, but he'd been walking on a different plane to the rest of us for quite some time.

Back in the early eighties I'd raced against Ayrton in karting, and in 1983 we went to watch him at the Formula Ford Festival. I remember him walking through the stand where we were sitting and he recognized my dad for some reason and came over to say hello. His English was probably better than mine at the time and he was incredibly personable, like an old friend. By the time I made it into Formula 1 Ayrton was established but he was always very interested in what I was doing and how I was getting on. I think it's fair to say that we developed a kind of cheeky rapport. For instance, he always used to pinch my bum after drivers' briefings. I'd always react with a lot of pretend horror and surprise and then I'd try to get him back. It's a funny thing, but I suppose that's my abiding memory of Ayrton – that and his astonishing ability on the track.

He also used to send me Christmas cards, which was nice. I received the first one after my accident in 1988. I can't find it now, unfortunately, even though it's in the house somewhere, but inside the card there's a lovely message – again, written in perfect English – where he wishes me a speedy recovery and hopes I'll be back racing soon. Ayrton was never afraid of showing his true feelings. If he was ever worried about somebody, he'd let them know. I just wish he'd taken Professor Sid up on his offer and retired and gone fishing.

Thanks to Gerhard Berger I was fortunate enough to be able to attend both Ayrton's and Roland's funerals, which took place on consecutive days but on different continents. Ayrton's was in São Paulo on 6 May and Roland's in Salzburg on the 7th. Gerhard had been close to both men and because he had access to a private jet he was going to have no problem making it from Brazil back to Austria in time. I was also planning to make the journey but was going to be at the mercy of the airline schedules. When Gerhard found out about this, he very kindly offered to take me with him.

Ayrton's state funeral was a tremendously emotional occasion. Even though you could only see the people around you, there were over three million on the streets, and you knew full well that the entire country was in mourning. The vast majority didn't know him, but they didn't have to. He *was* Brazil, and by epitomizing that country's legendary passion and spirit he'd managed to help it through some pretty dark days. Being asked to be one of the pallbearers at Ayrton's funeral was a great honour, and I've since been back to his grave several times, just to say hello. I always shed a tear or two when I'm there.

Directly after Ayrton's funeral had finished, Gerhard and I made our way to the airport where we boarded his jet and began the very long and very sad journey to Salzburg. I knew Roland a bit better than I did Ayrton and I have to admit that I found the journey quite difficult. Gerhard came and sat with me for the first hour or so, but with the conversation being a bit strained he went forward to fly the plane for a bit and I was able to think about Roland. What made his death so tragic, to me at least, was that he was such a happy-go-lucky guy, like an Austrian version of me in a way – or me an English version of him. What makes his death sadder still is that, after years of trying, I don't think Roland could quite believe he'd finally made it into the sport. He was only a few months into a five-year contract. He was in F1 on merit, though, and was a good solid driver who loved life. His funeral was a much smaller affair than Ayrton's but it was no less heartbreaking, and that's important to remember: when motorsport loses somebody, regardless of his success or status, we all of us mourn. I miss them both.

Just a week or so after the funerals, at the Monaco Grand Prix, Karl Wendlinger crashed during the Thursday morning practice session and was taken to hospital in a coma, so we were all starting to wonder if things could get any worse. Unfortunately for my team-mate Pedro Lamy, they could. We were testing at

Silverstone prior to the British Grand Prix and were trying to implement all the new changes that had been rushed through since Imola. I won't bore you with the details, but what they'd tried to do was slow the cars down by shortening the diffuser. Originally it had stretched to the end of the wing but now it only went as far as the axle, and this was supposed to give you slightly less grip and subsequently less speed. We were going through Abbey, which in those days was a flat-out left-hander, so we must have been doing at least 170mph. Pedro was about a couple of hundred metres in front of me. As we went into the corner he disappeared out of sight for a few seconds, and when I emerged on to the straight, under the bridge in front of me, right in the middle of the track, was a smoking engine with the gearbox on the back of it – nothing else.

Straight away I started thinking about Ayrton and Roland. *Please God*, I thought, *don't let there be another fatality*.

I stopped my car and got out. There was no car, no wheels, no pieces of carbon fibre, nothing, just the smoking engine and the gearbox. I thought, *Where the bloody hell has he gone?* I looked to the right but there was nothing except a bank and a fence at the top of it. I looked to the left and it was the same. When I looked again to the left I noticed that part of the fence was missing, and I then realized that's where he'd gone.

When I got to the top of the bank and over the fence the carnage started to become apparent, but although I was spotting things like wheels and bits of suspension there was still no monocoque. 'Where the bloody hell are you, Pedro?' I said to myself, and then, just as I was walking past the small pedestrian tunnel that runs parallel to the track, I noticed out of the corner of my eye a tiny flame. This tunnel could only be about six feet high by eight feet wide so I very nearly missed it, but when I went to investigate, there, about fifteen metres inside the tunnel, was Pedro Lamy and part of his Lotus Formula 1 car, with a little flame spilling out of it. There'd obviously been a handrail running along one side of the tunnel but that had been removed, unceremoniously, by the car.

As I started to run towards where he'd landed the sheer horror of what had happened started to hit me. It's quite hard to describe the scene, but because he'd gone into the tunnel at an angle it was actually the monocoque that had taken away the handrail, and when I found him it looked like he was fast asleep in a deckchair, just at a very strange angle. Part of the front of the monocoque had come away on impact, and as Pedro lay there with his head slumped forward, his feet were crossed on top of it. It all looked very disturbing but at the same time slightly comical.

That changed when I saw him close up. The flame I told you about was coming from the refuelling valve just behind the back of his helmet, and when I looked closer I could see that the paint and part of the helmet itself were already starting to melt. It was then that I began to panic because I wasn't able to get in close enough and for all I knew Pedro himself might well be on fire.

Seconds later a marshal came running in, but before I could suggest to him that it might be a good idea to fire the extremely large extinguisher away from the crash and out of the tunnel, thus preventing anyone from choking, he just set the bloody thing off, which meant the fire went out but we were all struggling to breathe. I used this opportunity to leave the tunnel and take off my helmet. I went back in again once things had died down.

Pedro was still slumped forward, but at least he wasn't on fire now, so after silently rescinding my request for him to die before being burned alive I went to take a closer look. Before I could get to him he sat up suddenly, and the look on his face scared the living shit out of me. His eyes were like Jim Carrey's in *The Mask* – you know, when they're popping out on stalks. His expression was one of pure astonishment and horror. I can still see his face to this day, and I'm sorry, Pedro, but you looked absolutely terrifying. He then tried to get out of the monocoque, but as well as still being strapped in, his kneecaps were broken and he had a badly damaged thigh, so, quite simply, he couldn't. This didn't stop him from trying, though, and in the end I had to restrain him by putting my hands on his chest and then trying to comfort him. 'Sit still, you Portuguese prat,' I whispered softly. 'The ambulance will be here soon.'

The accident pretty much finished off Pedro's Formula 1 career, a real pity, but since then he's become a Le Mans regular and is a very popular driver. He's a bit of a silver-tongued cavalier, is our Pedro, and within a few days of being taken to hospital after the accident he'd already arranged a date with one of the nurses. An accident with a happy ending. How refreshing!

Twelve

AFTER AYRTON PASSED AWAY, McLaren had to start looking for a replacement driver, and one of the names on their list was mine, although once again I was not informed about this until later on. In fact it was a journalist who called me about it. This time the approach went public which forced Peter into making a statement, and you could tell by the words he used that he wasn't happy about how it had been done.

'There is a correct manner in which to deal with these issues,' he said, 'and McLaren have not acted in this manner. They have not acted correctly. It is flattering for Johnny that McLaren consider him a suitable replacement for Senna, but I'm here to look after Team Lotus, not McLaren, and we will be racing this year with Johnny.'

He went on: 'It is irritating to have another team making clear their interest in a driver under contract to you. That can be damaging to your position. They were informed by Johnny and the team of his contractual position, but their subsequent contact with the team has been minimal. Their interest has created speculation which would be damaging if it were to continue, but I do not anticipate it will. Team Lotus have no intention of assisting McLaren in resolving their difficulties.'

By then there were rumours flying everywhere that Lotus

196

were having severe financial problems so in the end I threw caution to the wind, took the advice of my agents, IMG, and went to see Ron Dennis at the McLaren factory. Unfortunately the meeting was anything but a success. First I had a quick look around the factory, which was hugely impressive, then I sat back down in reception and waited to be called in. It was all *very* corporate, I remember, and in my opinion just a little bit soulless. *This is just not me*, I thought to myself. *It's too much like a machine.*

These initial premonitions of mine were confirmed when I was finally called into Ron's office. The first thing he said to me was, 'Right, Johnny, we're going to have to change you. No more of this laughing and joking, that's not the McLaren way. With us it's all about professionalism and conduct.'

And that's when the shutters came down. We went through the motions, but from the moment he set his stall out, my heart was already out of the door. It was a fair enough comment, I suppose, and I dare say that if I'd seen every other team manager in the paddock one or two more would have said something similar, but I was buggered if I was going to sit there and try to explain to Ron, or anyone else for that matter, that when it came to doing the job I was paid to do I was always totally professional, and that if he cared to speak to Peter Collins (although not at that particular moment in time), David Kennedy, Eddie Jordan or even Ken Tyrrell, they would all be happy to confirm it.

Ron wasn't to know this, and I completely respect his way of doing things, but as I mentioned earlier, that side of my personality first came about as a coping mechanism for the pain I was feeling, and to deflect people's attention away from my bloody feet and legs. It had served me well over the years and was now very much part of who I was. I couldn't pretend to be somebody I wasn't – that, as far as I was concerned, would just be ridiculous. Not being willing to turn myself into some kind of corporate machine has probably cost me quite a bit of work over the years, but hey ho. I'd much rather be true to myself.

Back at Lotus, things were going from bad to horrible, and amid all the rumours of liquidation and so on the atmosphere between Peter and me hit an all-time low. We hadn't spoken properly to each other for months. There'd been no huge arguments, but it had got to the point where every conversation we had usually involved me asking him when we were going to get a decent car so in the end I think he'd just started avoiding me. It was a very lonely place to be, and when in July I qualified twenty-fourth at the British Grand Prix at Silverstone – my home Grand Prix – I reached possibly my lowest ebb. Nobody wants to talk to you when you're at the bottom, not even the press (unless you've got any gossip about bankruptcy), and while giving my one and only interview to the TV station Eurosport, I said as much.

The following day a journalist called Christopher Hilton, who's sadly no longer with us, came to see me at the Lotus motorhome. I remember being so pleased to see him.

'I've come to hold your hand,' he said. 'I can't bear to see you lonely.'

'Oh my God!' I replied. 'What do you really want?'

The truth was he'd seen the interview on Eurosport and had come to keep me company. There was no interview, we just sat there chatting about what was going on, and because I trusted Chris I was able to get quite a few things off my chest, and he understood. These weren't self-indulgent petty grievances such as the fact Peter and I weren't talking, they were concerns about my future and that of the team, genuine concerns I had nobody else to talk to about. This state of affairs had been going on for so long now that I was even considering giving up F1 and then trying to get a drive racing touring cars or something, but that was just the result of months and months of ruminating. Simply having somebody there to listen, without a tape recorder on and without having a vested interest in my career, was exactly what I needed. I'm not sure if they saw the same interview, but around the same time I was also visited by some other journalists I knew; people like Ray Matts, Stan Piecha and David Tremayne. Once again not one of them was after a headline. They were just worried for me, and believe me that made a difference. Thank you, gents.

The next three races, in Germany, Hungary and Belgium, yielded two retirements and a twelfth place, and were all pretty desperate experiences. Then, completely out of nowhere, the team announced they'd got a new engine from Mugen which would be ready in time for the Italian Grand Prix. A few days later I went to test this new engine at Silverstone, and the improvement was dramatic. I'm afraid this messed with my head a bit because although I wanted to believe this was the start of a bright new future for Team Lotus – and Peter and commercial director Guy Edwards had clearly been trying to move heaven and earth to make it so – there was always a voice in the back of my head telling me that it would all come to nothing. I determined to give it my all but I certainly wasn't going to get carried away.

The news lifted the mood of the team, and we arrived at Monza pretty chipper, for a change. Friday practice went OK. As well as a touch of understeer I also experienced some instability at the rear end when breaking for the Ascari chicane but fortunately John Miles, who'd raced for Lotus in the 1970s and was now one of their engineers, managed to rectify the problem by adjusting the damper settings. The thing is, every time he made an adjustment I seemed to go faster and so the mood definitely held going into qualifying. Such was the improvement shown I knew that if I drove as well as I knew I could there was every chance of us getting on the podium. I couldn't remember the last time I'd driven something fast and competitive and it was such a shot in the arm. That voice in the back of my head was being drowned out by enthusiastic chatter about what might be round the corner. It was daft but I couldn't help myself. I'm a realist leaning towards optimism, and despite the potential pitfalls involved I probably wouldn't have it any other way. (Notice I said probably!)

We spent the morning session on the Saturday just doing a little bit of fine-tuning – not that there was much to do – and I could feel that I was getting better with every lap. I'd started doubting myself months earlier – who wouldn't have, for heaven's sake? – to the point where I'd even been thinking the problem might be me and not the car, but every lap I drove in those first sessions at Monza brought me closer to being my old self again. When qualifying eventually arrived I had *never* been as desperate to get on the track.

Qualifying for the 1994 Italian Grand Prix finished like this:

Jean Alesi (Ferrari) 1m 23.844s (pole)
Gerhard Berger (Ferrari) 1m 23.978s
Damon Hill (Williams) 1m 24.158s
Johnny Herbert (Lotus) 1m 24.374s

For a time during the session I'd even been quicker than Damon, although he managed to pip me to the post. This was an astonishing achievement, though; not for me, but for the team as a whole – for Team Lotus. If you happened to see the interview I gave Eurosport after qualifying it demonstrated perfectly the effect this new engine had had on us all. We were alive again, and as well as talking optimistically about the future and extolling the virtues of the new package, I do believe I even made a joke about Damon Hill. Nothing new there then.

The Ferraris and the Williams were all on two-stop strategies whereas I was supposed to be on a one-stop, something that had worked well in the warm-up. Even with them being lighter than me I was still close enough to them time-wise to be able to turn it into an advantage. But then, when I was on the grid, the two Peters came up to me and told me that we'd changed to a two-stop. 'But that just makes us the same as them,' I said. Unfortunately they were resolute. It was the wrong decision, I was sure about that, but in the end it was all academic as thanks to a certain Edmund Irvine Jr, who was driving, of all things, a Jordan, I never even made it past the first corner.

At the start at Monza there's this great rush to the first chicane, and because everything compresses, things become very tight. With Berger and Alesi leading, I passed Damon as I went towards the chicane, but then just as I was turning into it Eddie, who'd had a cracking start, rammed me from behind, twisted the car, and I ended up beached on the kerb. Straight after that David Coulthard, who'd also been hit, went over the front of the car, which obviously caused further damage. After this the race was stopped, but because my car was so badly damaged, I had to take the restart from the pit lane using – yes, you've guessed it – the *old* car with the *old* engine. I think I was running fourteenth when the engine failed, and, although we didn't know it then, that signalled the final death knell for the team.

To be fair to Eddie he was extremely apologetic afterwards – he'd just got caught up in the moment. To coin a popular phrase, it could have happened to anyone – anyone who was incapable of using their bloody brakes. Only joking.

I know it's easy for me to say this but I honestly believe I would have gone on to win that race had I been spared. The car really did feel that good. It might have made a difference to the team too. As it was, the following day, Monday, 12 September 1994, Lotus applied for administration and it was granted by the court. With all the promise the new Mugen engine had given us they must have thought there was an outside chance they'd be able to find the investment necessary to keep the team afloat. That possibility would have been a lot more realistic had I at least got a podium finish in Italy.

By the time we got to Portugal the administrators were making their presence felt; they'd been strutting around like peacocks ever since the courts had appointed them. I know they had a job to do but they seemed to have this habit of treating everybody at the team like naughty schoolchildren, and I remember wishing they'd all just naff off. They didn't though, and because I thought they might block my wages I was too scared to ask them to, so we had to just get on with it.

Perhaps unsurprisingly, although at the time it was a big shock, in Estoril we seemed to have lost almost all of the speed we had at Monza, and I ended up qualifying twentieth and finishing the race eleventh. The following week we went straight into a four-day test to try to rectify things but by day three we were still scratching our heads; in fact I'm pretty sure we were even slower in those three days than we had been at the race. How the hell can you lose three seconds from one race to the next? The entire team was completely nonplussed.

In the end, and this was purely because we'd run out of ideas, I suggested using the wings we'd had on at Monza. The wings we'd used at Portugal had produced medium-to-high downforce and the ones at Monza the lowest of the low, so when I suggested using the Monza wings I was almost laughed out of the garage. 'Let's just see what it does,' I insisted. 'This is a test, so let's test them. It probably won't solve the problem but you never know, we might learn something.' And so on went the wings and out I went again, and on the first lap I knocked a second and a half off the fastest time I'd posted so far. This made us realize that it wasn't just the engine that had made the difference. It also helped demonstrate that the wings producing medium-to-high downforce simply didn't work, and as well as creating drag on the straights they made very little difference going through corners.

Although we hadn't meant to, what we'd actually done was bring an end to Team Lotus. By discovering that we weren't as competitive as we thought we were there was now nowhere else to turn, so the administrators, who had let us perform the test as a last attempt to save the team, finally ran out of patience.

The team would complete the season before finally being wound up, but it did so without me: on the Tuesday before the European Grand Prix at Jerez I signed for the Ligier team. This was all down to the administrators, because one of the few assets the team owned outright at the time was my contract. In other words, in order to raise some funds, and probably to cut the wage bill, I was put out to the highest bidder. It was a sad end to what had been a tumultuous four and a bit years, and one of the few regrets I have in life is that Peter Collins and I didn't manage to get on the podium together. That would have been the perfect way to repay all the faith he'd shown in me ever since spotting me at the Formula Ford Festival back in 1865, or whenever it was. But it never came to pass. Despite us going through some very difficult periods, I'd just like to put on record that I will always be extremely grateful to Peter Collins, and the respect and admiration I have for him is without measure.

Tom Walkinshaw – who together with a very tall and beautifully tanned Italian gentleman by the name of Flavio Briatore ran the Ligier team – was the man responsible for purchasing me from the administrators. Whatever problems I'd had with Flavio in the past, it was now all water under the bridge, and I had an awful lot of respect for Tom. I was relieved, albeit reluctantly, no longer to be tied to Lotus, and because the transaction had had very little to do with me personally – I was merely doing as I was told – I was able to start work straight away at my new

203

team, free from any baggage or bad feeling, and that was a big plus. I've told you what my only regret was from that period (apart from signing that bloody contract), and as far as I was concerned what had happened at Lotus was now history. I still had this belief that I could win, and win big, in Formula 1, and even though Ligier were usually in the top ten, they were affiliated to Benetton who, thanks primarily to the soon-to-be newly crowned world champion Michael Schumacher, were currently running second in the Constructors' Championship. Everything, then, was still very much to play for.

One person I did feel a bit sorry for at the time was Éric Bernard, the Ligier driver I'd replaced. As I said, Lotus were going to finish off the 1994 season come what may, but in order to do so they'd need a replacement for me, so as part of the deal for me moving to Ligier, Éric moved in the opposite direction. As far as I know he only found out about this when he was setting off for the European Grand Prix. 'Éric, you're reporting to the Lotus garage this weekend, not Ligier, OK?' I'd have been bloody furious if that had happened to me.

Come to think of it, that's exactly what *did* happen to me, and just a few days on from that, although I'm happy to report that my own extradition took place in what were far happier circumstances than poor Éric's. It would all go tits up in the end, of course – Flavio would see to that – but at the time it was quite a nice surprise.

The other driver to join Lotus at the end of their final season was Mika Salo, who I've since learned had never driven an F1 car in his life when he was offered the seat. A week before the Japanese Grand Prix he got a call asking if he'd mind doing the race without any testing. I wonder how many other F1 drivers have made their debut having never driven an F1 car before? I don't think Mika minded though.

I got the call about going to Ligier at about eleven p.m. one evening and was told by Tom Walkinshaw to drive immediately to his house in Oxfordshire. I was all tucked up in bed at the time and had it been anyone else I may well have told them to bugger off. Tom, though, was not somebody you could easily say no to, and besides, he was asking me to drive over and sign a piece of paper that would free me from Lotus and secure my immediate future in Formula 1. About an hour or so later, then, I was standing in Tom's home with a pen in my hand, and a few seconds after that I was part of the Ligier Formula 1 team.

The following day I was on a plane bound for Magny-Cours where I'd test the Ligier prior to the European Grand Prix at Jerez. It was balanced, had good aero, and had a great engine. Chalk and cheese compared to the Lotus. The team's then star driver, Olivier Panis, had suffered only one retirement all season and was currently running a relatively impressive eleventh in the Drivers' Championship with 9 points. *I'll have a bit of that*, I thought to myself. Even poor old Éric had only had to come in three times that season, and he'd also bagged himself a podium. Perhaps Ligier *was* a long-term option after all.

In Jerez my feelings of optimism were all but confirmed, and after qualifying seventh on the grid (Olivier was back in eleventh), I finished the race an encouraging eighth, ahead of Olivier. I was still a lap down on Michael Schumacher in his Benetton but that was a damn sight better than being two or three laps down, which is where the poor boys at Lotus were.

One thing I will say about that Ligier is that despite the improved performance and reliability it was one of the most uncomfortable cars I've ever driven. As far as I know, the design had been based partly on the Williams car – I think they'd done some kind of deal – and for some reason the steering wheel had been placed so low that it was almost in between my knees, so in a way it was like driving a Sinclair C5. The day after the race I was in agony because I'd been using a completely different set of muscles. I didn't mind though, and it was nice for something else to ache for a change instead of my feet. I'd also had a great weekend and was as contented as I had been in years.

The following Wednesday both Ligier and Benetton were due to be testing in Barcelona so on the Tuesday evening I got on the plane, and when I arrived at the hotel I readied myself for the following day. I remember feeling pretty damn good about things. They could have put that steering wheel on the bloody floor of the car and I wouldn't have cared. Everyone had been very welcoming at the team, which was encouraging. It was early days, but that family atmosphere I always craved seemed to be part of the Ligier culture.

The next morning I made my way down to the Circuit de Barcelona-Catalunya where I was due to report at about eight a.m., but as I walked into the garage I was immediately stopped by one of the mechanics.

'What are you doing here?' he asked.

'Well, I'm here for the test, obviously,' I said in a jokey manner. 'I'm one of your drivers, remember?'

'Not any more,' said the mechanic. 'You're testing the Benetton. You're two garages down.'

Well, you could have knocked me down with a feather.

'Really?' I said. 'Nobody told me.'

'Flavio's orders,' said the mechanic. 'Best of luck.'

It was typical of Flavio not to say anything, and why he didn't get one of his famous secretaries to call me I have no idea, but once again I certainly wasn't going to be putting in any grievances with the HR department.

I spent the rest of the day with the Benetton team making a seat, and the next day I was ready to take the car out. It was almost like going back in time in a way because the feelings I experienced driving the Benetton were very similar to those I'd had at my first ever F1 test, which was also in a Benetton. The jump I'd made on that day was from an F3 car to an F1 car and was pretty damn dramatic, but this was also one of those smile-inducing occasions that you never, ever forget. For the first time in my career I was sitting in a car that was on the brink of winning not just one but both Formula 1 championships, and it was because of one of those, the Constructors' Championship, that I had been seconded to the team.

At the time Benetton led Williams 97 points to 95 in the constructors' table and neither J. J. Lehto nor Jos Verstappen had been able to lend Schumacher much in the way of support, Lehto picking up just the one point in six races and Verstappen ten in nine. At Lotus we'd have killed for figures like that, but with Schumacher currently on 86 points the variance was not as acceptable, even if Michael did enjoy more by way of support. Flavio had brought me in to try and help secure the points necessary to pip Williams to the post, although once again that was never relayed to me personally.

By the end of the test I'd got within four-tenths of Michael, which apparently was quite impressive, so I was duly confirmed as Jos's replacement for the final two races of the season, both of which – and I can't believe I'm having to write this – ended in retirements. Having said that, only one of them was mechanical; the other was down to weather (that's my excuse), so I didn't really experience the same doom-laden feelings of *déjà vu* as I had at Lotus.

In Japan I qualified fifth, just 0.61s off Michael, who was on pole, and with neither Jos nor JJ having been able to get anywhere near that, things were looking good. Come Sunday the rain was atrocious, but after Heinz-Harald Frentzen spun off in the Sauber on lap 2 I was running third, so providing I was careful I was on for my first ever podium finish and a dream debut. A lap or so later the rain became biblical and the safety car was sent out as a precaution. The trouble was, literally a few seconds before that happened I had been coming through the chicane and was experiencing what was known as the 'Benetton Wiggle'. I'd never driven the car in the wet before and was having to indulge in a little bit of 'trial and error', but it seemed that even the slightest acceleration resulted in the car spinning like a top. Just as the team came over the radio telling me that the safety car was coming out I began aquaplaning, and before I could back off and save myself, I was saying hello to a very big wall situated down the pit straight. What an absolute bugger! I was furious, not only with myself but also with God for ruining my day.

I struggled against Michael in Australia, qualifying in seventh about a second and a half off the pace, but unlike me, pushing hard and trying to win some points, Michael was on the brink of winning the 1994 Formula 1 World Championship – his first of about thirty – and was right at the top of his game. And let's not forget that for all the controversies and confrontations Michael had during his career he's one of the greatest racing drivers who ever drew breath. Despite what you may think of either him or his methods – my own issues were with his methods – he could go toe-to-toe with anyone who's ever put on a helmet. Winning the 1994 championship against what was a highly talented field was a tremendous achievement.

Just for the record, I ended up coming in on lap 13 in Adelaide with a gearbox problem and left Australia with no idea what I'd be doing in 1995. I hoped I'd get a drive at Benetton, but had I done enough? It appeared that I hadn't, as on 28 October it was announced that I'd be partnering Olivier Panis back at Ligier, which meant somebody else would be alongside the new world champion.

Come January things were still the same, and I'd forgotten about Benetton completely. Then, out of the blue, my agents, IMG, received a telephone call from one of Flavio's secretaries (naturally) informing them that he wanted me to drive for

Above: Of all the teams I raced for, it has to be said Sauber had by far the most imaginative launch parties. Half the time I had no idea what was going on but I always got involved. Here I am in 1997 with the Argentinian driver Norberto Fontana and some friends of ours.

Right: Back on stage for a sing-song after the British Grand Prix in 1996, with Eddie Jordan and Martin Brundle. Those Sauber years were fun, and the fans seemed to enjoy my efforts too (**below**). F1 needs teams of all shapes and sizes, not just the big guns.

Some more memorable moments from the 1997 season, when I was given a rather nice present in honour of my 100th Grand Prix at San Marino in April (**above**) and got an unexpected third place at the Hungarian Grand Prix in August (**left**). The sport never forgets its fallen though, as Murray Walker, Damon and I observed a minute's silence at Monza in September (**below**).

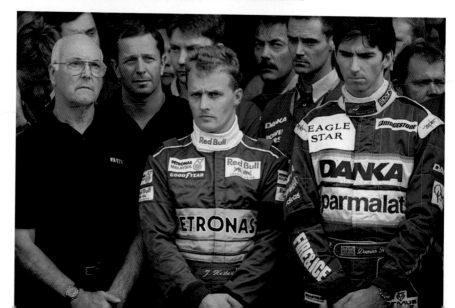

Left: The long walk home. This was with Jacques Villeneuve after we collided on the first lap of the 1997 Australian Grand Prix. Crashes seem to be a constant theme in this book, for some reason, so here are another couple of mishaps – not my fault, of course – from Italy in 1997 (**below**) and Canada in 1998 (**bottom**).

The family-friendly world of Formula 1. The wife and kids join me at Silverstone in 1997 (**top**), followed by my mum and dad the following year (**above**).

Left: The Herberts have nothing on the Stewarts though! This was the launch of Ford Stewart in January 1999, with Paul and Jackie keeping a watchful eye on me and Rubens Barrichello.

Above and left: The fourteenth round of the 1999 Formula 1 season, the European Grand Prix, brought one of the most shocking results in the sport's history. I read the conditions correctly, drove the perfect race and beat Jarno Trulli to win at the Nürburgring and send the Stewart team suitably wild.

Right and below: Celebrating with my team-mate Rubens, who finished third, and of course with Jackie Stewart, who achieved the seemingly impossible dream of winning a GP, and just three races before the end of his career as a team owner. Amazing days.

Left: 'You've got to be smoooooooooooooth with the car, Johnny. Smoooooooooooooooth.' The 2000 season with Jaguar would be my final one as an F1 driver.

Below: My dad Bob, mum Jane and wife Rebecca joined me for my farewell party in Malaysia, where Jackie presented me with, of course, a tartan hat, which went nicely with the tartan suit he had made for me earlier. I wear both regularly.

Above: Life as an ex-Formula 1 driver has been, it has to be said, a lot of fun too, even when J. J. Lehto tried to set me on fire during an American Le Mans series race in Miami. We won the race though, and the next morning I swore never to drink vodka with him ever again.

Right: The 24 Hours of Le Mans remains one of my favourite races, as well as opportunities to refuel, as I demonstrate after finishing second (again!) with Bentley in 2003.

Below: A celebration with the Mazda management to mark twenty years since my Le Mans victory of 1991, one of my proudest memories from my life in motor racing.

Top left and right: Working with Sky Sports F1 has given me the opportunity to see the likes of Sebastian Vettel and Lewis Hamilton at close quarters, as well as indulge in a little bit of crowd-surfing with the fans (**above**).

Left: My daughters Chloe and Aimelia. I'm so proud of them.

Benetton in 1995 and would I like to go out and see him at the team's headquarters in Italy? Happy days! Despite the fact that Flavio Briatore didn't actually own the team (although he did own Ligier), Benetton was, to all intents and purposes, his baby, and he was persuasive in his argument that the number-one priority for the team was not simply the betterment of Michael Schumacher but the Constructors' Championship, and that in addition to Michael being happy having me as a team-mate, I would enjoy exactly the same support and resources as him.

What is it they say? 'Beware the man bearing gifts.'

Flavio's claims that the Constructors' Championship was key were backed up in my contract as there was a performance-related clause in there that said I had to achieve a certain number of points by Silverstone, otherwise they'd have the right to replace me. I forget how many points exactly but he'd clearly thought it through carefully. I have no problem with things like this – a little bit of pressure and uncertainty can often result in a positive reaction – but they have to be managed correctly, other-wise they can be destructive and because I was pretty sure Flavio had included the clause because either he didn't like me or he didn't rate me, I was always too embarrassed to tell anyone it was there, in fact this is the first time I've ever confirmed it. With hindsight – and this is just a theory, by the way – I'm pretty sure that Flavio's ambitions for me personally were capped at winning the required number of points, in that it was a total and not simply an ideal, which would obviously leave Michael to fight for the championship unchallenged (internally, at least), and with the points from me in the bag they could potentially go one better than the previous year and lift both trophies. Given the relationship that already existed between Flavio and Michael, who on earth could blame them? They wouldn't have been the first to cook up a plan like that and they certainly wouldn't be the last.

As I said, though, this is just a theory, and at the time of signing my contract I was blissfully unaware of anything other than what Flavio had told me. In fact, I trusted him. What I think they thought they were getting by signing me was a talented yet ultimately grateful and, with any luck, subservient number-two driver who would do as he was told, and that may well have been down, partly at least, to my injuries and that cheeky-chappy persona. 'Look at him smiling. He's just happy to be here, bless him.' I couldn't possibly say if there were drivers out there who'd have been willing to fulfil such a role, but if there were, I was most certainly not one of them. Once Flavio and Michael realized this, things would start to change very quickly indeed. I may have been short, blond, beautiful and innocent-looking, but I'd also been through quite a lot in my years as a professional racing driver and I had never joined any team nor competed in any race just to make up the numbers. I wanted to win the 1995 Formula 1 World Championship, which is why I joined the Benetton team, and I firmly believed that if I kept my part of the bargain and helped them to win the Constructors' Championship they, in turn, would allow me a clear and equal run at the Drivers' Championship alongside Michael Schumacher. That's what Flavio had made me believe and at the time I had no reason for thinking otherwise.

Was that a little naive of me? Yes, I suppose it was, and when you consider what happened with Michael at Ferrari it was bloody ridiculous, but I was an optimist, remember – I still am – yet one who was without the benefit of hindsight. Did Flavio really see me as an also-ran who'd dance to whatever tune he played? You'd have to ask him that. If he did, he was wrong.

But as resilient, determined and battle-worn as I had become on the track, nothing on earth could have prepared me for the battle I was about to go into off it.

Thirteen

IT TOOK ME a good two or three days to get Michael's back up at Benetton, which was quite good for me. In one of the first interviews I gave after signing my two-year contract, I said to the journalist, 'It doesn't matter if the car has been set up around Michael; as far as I'm concerned, I want to win races, I'm in a competitive car, and I will be challenging for the 1995 world championship.' Or words to that effect.

It was all quite innocuous, and pretty much every driver in the top four or five teams would have been coming out with something similar. But Michael, who had clearly been told I'd be a good little boy, wasn't happy, and the following day he remarked to another journalist that he hoped I wasn't going to get all political, and that if I thought I was going to be challenging for the championship I had another think coming.

He wasn't wrong. Political, though? All I'd done was outline my ambitions for the season, just like every other driver on the grid. I wasn't expecting much from him, and because I knew he too would be hoping to win the Drivers' Championship I wasn't even expecting him to be nice to me, but to come out and counter a fairly predictable soundbite was just ridiculous. After that the alarm bells started ringing . . . and if you examine the results of the three previous seasons at the team in terms of

Michael versus his team-mates, they'll demonstrate not only his talent as a driver – let's not forget that – but also how his grip on the team had tightened year on year:

1992 Schumacher 53 points Brundle 38 points
1993 Schumacher 52 points Patrese 20 points
1994 Schumacher 92 points Lehto and Verstappen 11 points

Michael Schumacher considered himself to be the number-one driver at Benetton, in the sense that he should be the team's number-one priority, and as far as I could tell nobody at the team had ever said anything to the contrary. Given that, from that interview on he saw me not as his obedient team-mate but as a threat. So thank God for Damon Hill, because if Michael hadn't been battling Damon for the championship I'm pretty sure he'd have set his sights purely on me, and, all things considered, I think I might have lost.

At Brazil I managed to equal my best ever qualifying position of fourth, and this was without getting a run-out on the Friday, as Michael had crashed heavily and the team decided to keep me in until they'd discovered the cause. Even so, I managed to line up on the second row of the grid alongside David Coulthard (Damon got pole, by the way), and because I'd been faster than Michael in the latter stages of the session he'd had the trace sheets out looking to see where, and that was completely understandable. Had there been any kind of rapport between us, or had a team mentality been allowed to exist, I'd have been only too happy to discuss it with him, though I wouldn't have given him chapter and verse. We were team-mates, but I go back to my earlier comments about Formula 1 not being a team sport.

Having two arch-rivals in a team makes it more interesting for the spectator, but surely a balance can be found where you can keep the competition going on within a team yet share information for the *good* of the team, and, most importantly of all, keep things equal. Let them race and see who wins. Lewis Hamilton and Nico Rosberg seem to have exactly that going on at Mercedes and the battle between them is the most exciting thing to happen in Formula 1 for years. In 2014 and 2015 they had the best car by a mile so if there hadn't been that internal war going on and one driver had been favoured over the other, like at Red Bull, it would have resulted in a foregone conclusion – and they, as we know from Ferrari in the early to mid-2000s, are not fun to watch.

For me personally it was frustrating, as in that respect Michael and I were operating in parallel universes. Achieving parity with him was a complete non-starter. Michael was always pleasant to me but it became clear very quickly that he would be operating alone and that what he wanted, should the need arise, was not an ongoing ally but a butler on wheels. Ultimately, though – and once again, this is just my opinion – surely it's up to the person in charge to create the culture at a team. It shouldn't matter how strong-willed a driver is, he should not be allowed to become so dominant that a level playing field cannot be created – or at least level-ish. That's what was happening at Benetton, more's the pity – it had been for some time – and it would take only another two weeks before I realized exactly where I stood.

The 1995 Brazilian Grand Prix was full of incident, so I'm going to cut what was a very long story short. I'd managed to damage the bottom of my monocoque during qualifying, which had forced me into the spare car for the race, and while running mid-table on lap 31 I collided with Aguri Suzuki (in the Ligier, goddammit!), and that was the end of that. Overall, though, it had been an extremely positive and encouraging weekend for me, and because I was still unaware of how Flavio and Michael operated and where they thought I fitted into the team, I travelled to Argentina for the second race of the season full of confidence. Now where have you read that before?

In first practice at Argentina I was just 0.012s slower than Michael so I'd managed to carry my form over from Brazil. This ruffled Michael. That evening, as we were walking from the car park to the hotel, he said, 'Johnny, there are things to do with my driving that I do not want you to see, and at the same time there will be things about your driving that you will not want me to see.'

'It doesn't worry me what you see,' I replied. 'Whoever's quickest is quickest.'

'Ah, you think so, do you?' he said. 'Well, from now on I don't want you to see my data.'

I honestly thought he was joking, but the following morning Ross Brawn, who was then the Benetton technical director, sat me down and told me that Michael had spoken to Flavio about my not seeing his data and that Flavio had agreed to that. He could still see mine, though. I could tell Ross was embarrassed, but what could he do? Flavio was King Henry, Michael was Cromwell, and the rest of us were just peasants – peasants who wanted to keep their jobs. Prior to that, my wife Rebecca and Michael's wife, Corinna, had been spending quite a bit of time together during race weekends. Sadly, even that changed after the data fiasco and Corinna started keeping her distance.

Michael's strategy was never, ever to let anyone get a crack at him, and to cut every bugger off at the pass, and even though his team-mate would always be the first to go, which for me was a bit of a bummer, it was an extremely effective strategy, one that he created and developed at Benetton and then perfected over at Ferrari. It wasn't something I'd ever have considered – I'm a bit too old-fashioned for that. There will be people saying, 'Well, that's why you never won a world championship.' I'll live with it. Once again, though, it only happened because somebody upstairs allowed it to. Drivers are always going to chance their arm and try their luck here and there; it's up to those in positions of authority to ensure it doesn't get out of hand. In my opinion, what Flavio should have said when Michael requested that I not see his data was 'No, Michael, that's not fair', or 'OK, but as long as you're not allowed to see his'. Only Flavio would be able to tell you why he didn't. Just for the sake of balance, I probably should have done exactly the same when Ross and I had the meeting – said 'No, that's not fair' – but I think I was in a state of shock.

Ross always tried to be as fair as he possibly could with me, as did virtually everyone else at Benetton, but he was working within parameters that had been set out by somebody else, as was everybody at the team. We're back to what I said towards the beginning of the book about gaining an unfair advantage. Michael Schumacher is undoubtedly one of the best drivers in the history of motor racing, and given his record – the sport's most successful by a considerable margin – he should at least be thought of in the same vein as the likes of Ayrton Senna and Jim Clark. Is he though? Is he really? I don't think so, and the reason for that is because the methods he used were deemed by some people as unfair, although technically they were perfectly legal. He was simply indulged by people.

You won't believe this, but after being just 0.012s slower than Michael on the Friday in Argentina, come the Saturday I was a tad over three seconds off, and I'm afraid that started causing me all kinds of problems mentally. Nobody is that much slower than his team-mate in Formula 1, and after what had happened with Ross I started to become slightly paranoid and began feeling detached from the rest of the team. Was it just a coincidence that ever since Michael had spoken to Flavio my times had gone from being within a whisker of his to pretty much mid-grid? At the time I did not think that was the case, although the mistake

I made was going public with my fears. That, I realize now, did me quite a lot of damage within the sport. I should have kept my gob shut. People only knew one side of the story so in their eyes I was just a driver failing to do his job. I wanted people to know that was not the case and that I was not being treated as an equal, but it backfired on me and I just looked like a bit of a sore loser.

What I desperately needed at this particular point, and what I should have sought out, was some kind of intermediary – somebody who could go in there and speak to Flavio, clear the air and try and find a way forward. And it's not as if I didn't have people on my side. In fact I had a lot of people I could confide in – friends and agents – and sometimes did. Or at least I tried. The thing is that every time I started talking about the really serious issues like my injuries or what was happening at Benetton I'd end up laughing it off and changing the subject: 'Let's not cause a fuss, eh? It'll all work out in the end.' It felt so unnatural, and in a strange way I felt protective of what was bothering me and just didn't want to worry people. I was my own worst enemy in that respect.

This is the first time, either verbally or on paper, that I have ever talked in any detail about my injuries or about the problems I experienced at Benetton, friends and family included, and even as I write this I still feel compelled to say everything's OK and turn everything into a joke.

After a chaotic first lap in Argentina I managed to finish fourth in the spare car, and we moved on to Imola, a changed circuit after the deaths of Senna and Ratzenberger a year earlier. In qualifying on the Friday the gap between me and Michael was still over two seconds, and even though I managed to close it the following day it was only by a tenth or so. What made me even more suspicious was that Michael had suddenly gone from being quicker than me only on certain parts of the track, as he had been in Brazil and in testing, to being quicker than me everywhere, and that just wasn't right.

After finishing the race seventh, two laps down from Damon, who lifted the winner's trophy for the second race running, a journalist remarked about me that 'he and his engineer Tim Wright appear to be left to their own devices. Frustration is starting to creep in.' He'd hit the nail on the head. The fact that the car had been designed to suit Michael's style of driving was understandable, and shouldn't really have been much of a problem, so long as I was able to acclimatize and get used to it. The only way I could do this was by testing, but, as with the data, it was a privilege that would be made available to Michael and not to me. I had to undertake the majority of my testing during practice sessions prior to races, and that was neither the time nor the place.

After Imola, rumours started doing the rounds that I was on borrowed time and that Jos Verstappen, who'd been shunted to the lowly Simtek team but whose contract was still owned by Flavio, was due to come back in again as my replacement. So on top of everything else I was now living with the fear that the next race could possibly be my last. And – I'm sure you're fed up with hearing about them by now – my feet were absolutely bloody well killing me. Perhaps that had been made worse by the stress, because even though the pain was always there and could be very uncomfortable at times, it had been just about bearable. The moment Benetton-gate started getting into full swing it was almost like being back in Austria again: every time I got in the car it would turn into a full-on screamathon, and those tears of pain I thought I'd said goodbye to were back with me once again.

In the press, conspiracy theories started being aired – not by me, I might add – that there was some kind of plot against me. While Benetton dismissed them all as rubbish, saying that all things between Mr Schumacher and me were equal, Michael came out and said that the reason for me putting in such woeful performances was probably because I was low on confidence. He wasn't wrong, but that wasn't the reason; although to be fair to Michael he did concede that perhaps I hadn't been given as much time in the car as I should have.

Paradoxically, for the fourth race of the season, at the Circuit de Barcelona-Catalunya, Michael, who had spun off at Imola, tried using my set-up, ended up taking pole position, and then won the race by fifty-one seconds. How typical is that? Benetton actually gave me full credit for this, as did Michael, but by far the most important and historic moment of that 1995 Spanish Grand Prix was when the driver running second drove through the chequered flag – *moi*. I remember being just a tiny bit excited.

I'd qualified again about two seconds behind Michael, yet after the second round of pit stops I was running fifth. When I emerged from the pits after my second stop, I did so with a jack still under the back of the car, as you do. Fortunately the jack removed itself soon after that, and without causing any damage either to me or any of the other drivers, and when David Coulthard retired because of a faulty gearbox and then Damon with something similar, I was able to take advantage and come away from the weekend with my best ever finish.

Monaco, Canada and France followed Spain and yielded a fourth, a retirement due to a collision with Mika Häkkinen, and then another one after being tapped by Jean Alesi. I remember being quite annoyed by both incidents but neither was intentional and that's just the way it goes sometimes. They did end up costing me money, however. In Canada the FIA had introduced an electronic eye that was supposed to spot any drivers who jumped the start (it didn't last because it didn't work), and after being judged to have jumped at Canada I was given a ten-second drive-through penalty. I was unable to serve this penalty because of the collision with Mika so I received a $10,000 fine, which was suspended. At the next race the same thing happened again, and because I was again unable to serve the penalty thanks to Jean tapping me early doors, they clobbered me with another fine. Jean flipping Alesi. What a horrible little man he is. I'm joking again, of course. The fact that he won the race in Canada after standing second or third on the podium God knows how many times was just reward for a brilliant driver.

I arrived at Silverstone, the eighth race on the calendar, both poorer and in the knowledge that because I hadn't yet scored the required number of points outlined in my contract, this could well be my final race in Formula 1; anything less than a podium finish would probably open the door for Jos. Not exactly the preparation you need going into your home Grand Prix, but even so, it was preferable to what had happened the previous year and I was ready for it. Conspiracy theories were still rife, so although the pre-race questioning wasn't always about the forthcoming GP, I was happy not to be consigned to the drivers listed under the 'only if you can't speak to anyone else' banner.

I qualified fifth alongside my independent financial adviser Jean Alesi, now only one and a half seconds behind Michael who was second on the grid next to Damon. Alesi got off to an absolute flyer and by the first corner had placed himself between Michael and Damon. After that lap I was still running fifth behind David Coulthard with Mika Häkkinen about half a second behind me. Given what was happening in the championship, the battle everybody wanted to see was Michael versus Damon, but with Jean in the way that would have to wait – although it would come soon enough. When David pitted on lap 16 I was up to fourth, and when Jean eventually came into the pits soon after that I was third. It was early days but I could already sense that Flavio might be twitching. My own stop came on lap 21, and even though I was stationary for a good ten seconds or more I still came out in front of Jean. I managed to maintain position until lap 40, when I came in again for my second and final stop. Now David Coulthard was running third, but when he pitted a few laps later I was back where I hoped I'd stay for the remainder of the race.

On lap 44 it was Michael running first, Damon second and me third. Just one lap later Damon 'Dangerous' Hill made a vicious and unprovoked attack on my poor team-mate, something I will never forgive him for (I'm being ironic, by the way!). While steering wheels were being thrown into the air, heads shaken and hands being put on hips, I was driving by, almost unnoticed, into the lead at the 1995 British Grand Prix.

The only thing that now separated me from my first win in Formula 1, and a reprieve from feeling the full force of Flavio's foot, was a tall Scottish man-about-town with a chiselled chin and the initials DC. Fortunately he was given a ten-second drive-through penalty which he'd incurred for speeding in the pit lane during his last stop. Ross Brawn informed me about this over the radio, but for some reason David didn't know at that time, so when he made another move I just let him go through. Before long he must have realized what was happening and went in to serve his time. After that the race was beyond DC's grasp, which left me with ten laps to see out before victory, with Jean Alesi now trailing me by about fifteen seconds. Jean was good, but there was no way in the world he was going to make up that amount of time on me in ten laps, so providing I kept my nose clean I knew I'd be OK.

Once the crowd had forgotten about the Hill/Schumacher debacle, for now at least, they began to realize that a home win, and an unlikely one at that, was very much on the cards. The closer I got to the finish the more aware I became of the noise of the crowd and the sea of Union Jack flags. *Do I acknowledge the crowd?* I thought to myself. No: I'd look a right twit if I started punching the air and then spun off or got a puncture. But this was *my* time, *my* moment of glory, so with a lap or so to go I threw caution to the wind and became part of the celebrations, trying to acknowledge every flag, clenched fist and cheer that greeted me as I made my way towards the chequered flag. As you now know, I hadn't really talked to anybody about my problems since the crash, but that afternoon it was almost as if the crowd had been with me every step of the way and this was them saying, 'Well done! You've got through it all and this is your reward. Go on, Johnny!'

Then, as I drove around Woodcote, I saw it, the chequered flag, sticking out from the crowds like a beacon guiding me home. Just a split second later, that was it – I'd won the British Grand Prix. When I'd arrived at Silverstone earlier that day the last scenario on earth going through my head was winning the race. I knew I had to get on the podium, and I was going to try my hardest to do that, but because of all the politics, paranoia and rumours that had been plaguing my season I'd probably lost a bit of my belief. What a way to have it restored.

The first person to congratulate me after the race was Michael. He'd obviously had a difficult day, especially for probably the most competitive man on God's earth, yet he was still there to say well done and I'll always remember that. I think he meant it too. We were poles apart in many ways but that was a very gentlemanly thing to do. I know I haven't touched on his skiing accident yet, but I, like everybody else, am still hoping he makes a full recovery and I look forward to the day when we see him at a Grand Prix. Michael has a very English sense of humour, as does Sebastian Vettel, and that's one thing he and I did have in common. On the few occasions when he forgot about being competitive and let his guard down a bit we had a good laugh. In the right circumstances he was great company.

Flavio, I'm afraid, wasn't quite as magnanimous as Michael.

After giving me a rather cold hug and a quick 'Well done' (he stopped short of patting me on the head), he neither said nor did anything else and disappeared from the podium the moment the anthems had finished. Actually, that's not true, he did do something else, and I'll tell you what in a second.

Up on the podium, all I could see were flags, waving hands and happy, smiling faces. Now that I had my helmet off and was stationary it was all very vivid, a scene that I will remember for the rest of my life, one that I can call upon any time, day or night – it's always there. DC, who'd finished third in the race, was naturally gutted at being given the penalty – without it he could certainly have made life very difficult for me – yet when it came to the champagne moment, he and Jean put their bottles down and lifted me up on their shoulders. There I remained for what must have been a minute or so, just savouring the moment, hoping not to fall and trying to spot Mum and Dad. They, by the way, had been selling merchandise for my fan club, which at the time had a membership close to double figures, and for a time they probably had the busiest stall at the track.

After DC and Jean put me down we made our way to the TV press conference, which I think was with the BBC's Steve Rider. By the end of it I was becoming quite emotional. I'm not sure if Steve realized this but it got to the point where if he'd asked me one more question I'd have just burst into tears and made a fool of myself on national television. Fortunately he stopped just in time so I was able to escape and try to pull myself together.

After that it was down to the Benetton garage to start celebrating with the team, and I enjoyed that bit a lot. Some of the people, such as the truck drivers, had been there since my first stint with the team, and whatever Flavio thought of the win they were all as pleased as I was.

My next port of call was a Portakabin where I'd speak to the written press – people like Bob McKenzie and a very young

Oliver Holt, plus all the guys I mentioned earlier. This was also a big high because I'd known the majority of them for years and they too seemed to be really happy for me. But before I could leave the party and get to the journos, Flavio stopped me. 'I want your winner's cap, Johnny,' he said, and without thinking I handed it to him. I know I keep adding to my regrets in this book – by now it must seem like a motorsport version of Monty Python's 'Spanish Inquisition' sketch – but this particular one is a whopper. Why I gave it to him I have no bloody idea. Perhaps I was feeling all generous and conciliatory after the win? Who knows. Whatever it was, I was a bloody prat, and that was the last I saw of it. Come to think of it, I'm not even sure why he wanted it. Maybe he has a hat fetish?

Once all the immediate traffic had gone, Eddie Jordan took to the stage for the after-race party together with a band featuring Damon on guitar, Nick Mason from Pink Floyd on drums, Eddie on spoons, DC on the harp (only joking – can't remember what he played) and me on tambourine, and about fifteen cans of Foster's. I can't play an instrument to save my life so I just stood there banging that tambourine while Eddie got very excited and said some very nice things about me. He's a born entertainer, Eddie. The fact that he's now making a career as a presenter doesn't surprise me one bit. I have to say I felt like a real rock star when I was on that stage, and at one point there were bras, pairs of knickers and all kinds of things being thrown up there. No wonder Eddie does it whenever he can. All in all it was a pretty special end to what had been a pretty special day.

Instead of the win at Silverstone improving my relationship with Flavio, as you might have thought it would given the fact that I'd salvaged a much-needed ten points for the team, it actually made it a whole lot worse. Over the next three races we hardly said a word to each other. Why, I honestly couldn't tell you, but I'm sure I could have won every Grand Prix for the next ten seasons for whatever team Flavio happened to be in charge of and he still wouldn't have given me the time of day.

At the end of July, in Germany, the gap between Michael and me was back to two seconds plus, and after an awful first session I ended up qualifying ninth alongside an equally despondent Jean Alesi in the Ferrari. Now, instead of conspiracy theories being bandied about suggesting plots against me, I was in the firing line; the question wasn't 'Why is Herbert two seconds behind Schumacher?', it was 'How long will Benetton tolerate an underperforming driver?' Once again I could only work with the tools I'd been given and, short of taking out an advert in the national newspapers outlining exactly what was happening at the team, there was nothing I could do except push as hard as I possibly could.

Only eight cars finished in Germany and fortunately I was in one of them, in fourth place, so after starting the weekend kicking myself I left the Hockenheimring feeling like I was genuinely contributing to Benetton's attempt at winning the Constructors' Championship. But by Hungary a fortnight later the gap had turned into a chasm and in qualifying I was over three seconds slower than Michael. Rumours of Verstappen being brought in were mooted once again, but when I finished the race in fourth place again, leaving me fifth in the Drivers' Championship, these were put to bed.

It's usually around August that the rumour mill begins about who might be going where the following year (Schumacher to Ferrari, Alesi to Benetton and Villeneuve to Williams were three I remember from 1995). The only driver who wasn't mentioned in any of these despatches was me, such was my reputation in the paddock. Not only was I seen as damaged goods physically, and therefore always a little bit different, but now there were also questions being asked about my ability on the track and my attitude off it. Apart from keeping my mouth shut, which I now did most of the time, and driving as well as I could, there was absolutely nothing I could do about it. Even Tom Walkinshaw criticized me in public, saying that I didn't seem to want to apply myself to winning races at the top level. The truth was I was desperate to win races, and that had been my downfall.

I promise you things do get a bit more cheerful again soon. I too am getting fed up with having to use the F word so much (Flavio, not the rude one), but at the end of the day this is part of my story so you'll just have to bear with me for a little bit longer. There's another win to look forward to, and a shunt in the next sentence, so it's not all doom and gloom.

The next Grand Prix weekend, which took place at Spa, started on the Friday with me losing control coming out of the La Source hairpin, smashing into the barrier and then performing three beautifully executed 360-degree spins that even Rudolf Nureyev would have been proud of. I remember getting a bit of wheel spin, putting on opposite lock, and bang, that was it. What happened after that I couldn't really tell you, and I later discovered that the impact on hitting the barrier had been a whopping 12G. Bearing in mind you're supposed to black out at 8G, I shouldn't even have been able to find my way out of the car. My journey to the medical centre is, to this day, shrouded in mystery.

By the afternoon I'd been deemed fit to drive by the doctors (although my head continued to hurt when I shook it until after the race), and on the Saturday morning it was Michael's turn to crash. Because it was going to be touch and go as to whether or not his mechanics would be able to fix his car I wasn't allowed out in case he had to use mine. At the time I was quite diplomatic about this, but only because when I eventually got out I put in some good times. Looking back, it was a pretty outrageous request, and had Michael actually used my car I'm not sure what I'd have done. Spontaneously combusted, most probably. Because of all the hoo-hah, qualifying was a bit of a mess. Even though Michael ended up starting down in sixteenth he still managed to pip Damon to the post and win the race, albeit controversially. I qualified fourth and ended finishing seventh after a fuel problem, so it wasn't my best result.

The pressure was definitely starting to get to me, and a few days later things exploded when Gerhard Berger announced that he'd be driving for Benetton in 1996. With Jean also on his way there, this all but confirmed that I would not be retained. Of course there had been no contact from the team about it: I got wind of Gerhard's appointment from a journalist. This was one of the few occasions in my life when I lost my temper, and because it doesn't happen very often there was rather a lot to come out. I might just have said one or two rather derogatory things about Michael and Flavio. They responded in kind, and a mini war of words ensued.

Do I regret it? Do I buggery. I was past caring by that point. In fact I was beginning to find both them and the situation downright annoying.

As if things couldn't get any more bizarre, the following race at Monza produced a situation that has to be one of the most mind-boggling in the history of motorsport. To this day it leaves me speechless.

I qualified eighth for the race, one and a half seconds behind Michael who was on the front row, and bearing in mind what country we were in all eyes were on Berger and Alesi in the faltering Ferraris. At the start I got away well, immediately manoeuvring into the middle of the track and then making a rush for the first chicane, but before I could get there a shunt occurred involving three or four cars and a restart was ordered. Once again I got off to a good start and was running sixth after the fifth lap behind DC, Berger, Schumacher, Hill and Alesi. On lap 23 Damon and Michael collided yet again, which put me up to fifth, and by lap 32, after the majority of pit stops had taken place, I was running third behind the two Ferraris.

Just two laps later Berger had to retire from the race, and in the strangest of circumstances. He was tailing Jean, and at the time it looked as though they were heading towards a very popular Ferrari one-two, but then, on lap 34, Jean's on-board camera broke away and ended up breaking Gerhard's front left suspension. Goodbye, Gerhard, hello, second place.

I spent the next however many laps chasing Jean, and with six laps to go I'd managed to reduce the gap between us from about ten seconds down to four. I didn't know for sure if I'd catch him, but I thought I was in with a slight chance. Before the end of that lap, just as I was coming out of Lesmo, it all became academic as I started noticing smoke coming from the back of Jean's car, and before you could say *arrivederci* he was off back to the pits. I did feel a bit sorry for Jean; after all, it was one of his last races for Ferrari, and to have won the Italian Grand Prix would have rounded things off nicely. Even so, his victory in Canada had happened in similar circumstances so I managed to pull myself round pretty quickly.

The next thing I remember is Ross coming over the radio saying, 'Keep calm, Johnny, keep calm. And remember to preserve the brakes.' This was duly noted, and with a fairly big gap to second I was able to take it easy. And so, after what had been an interesting weekend – an interesting week, in fact – I won the 1995 Italian Grand Prix at my favourite racetrack, wearing what were about to become my favourite underpants. I'd worn them at Silverstone, and Monza was the first time I'd worn them since then.

Now you'd have thought, given where Flavio and Benetton hail from, that it didn't matter who won the Italian GP for them, be it Johnny Herbert, Michael Schumacher, Luciano Pavarotti or Basil Brush – the fact is YOU HAVE JUST WON YOUR

HOME GRAND PRIX, so what on earth is there not to be happy about? There's a photograph in this book of the podium at the Grand Prix that was taken just after my name had been announced as the winner, and Flavio's standing there with his arms folded looking like he's just been told he'll be holidaying in North Korea for the next ten years. What, again, I find frustrating about all this is that I actually have quite a bit of respect for what Flavio achieved with the likes of Michael and Fernando Alonso. We could, and should, have had a good relationship. But with me, regardless of what I achieved, there never seemed to be any of that pride or joy he always showed with Michael; in fact, if I ever did well he just seemed to have this air of mild disgust about him, as if I'd let one go at the dinner table. Some team bosses can cope with pitching two drivers against each other, but Flavio most certainly couldn't, and if you look back over his career in F1 that fact bears out. One has triumphed, but always at the expense of the other.

The only theory I have to offer for why he could never communicate with me or relate to me as a driver is that maybe Tom Walkinshaw had been most influential in re-hiring me, and after what had happened with Peter Collins, Flavio thought he'd been hoodwinked a second time. So with Peter not being around and Tom being as hard as bloody nails, he decided to take it out on me instead. Who knows? I think some of the team were slightly nervous about getting too excited at Monza though, such was Flavio's mood, and after unfolding his arms and disappearing from the podium with the constructors' trophy, that was it, he was gone. I'd won the Italian Grand Prix but the Italian team manager couldn't even bring himself to speak to me, let alone congratulate me. *Ridicolo!*

By the way, just in case there are any people out there saying, 'Hang on a minute, he was gifted those two wins' – and this has been suggested to me a couple of times – don't forget that in order to benefit from things that happen at the front of a race, you have to get yourself in a position to do so in the first place. The same could be said about drivers who are accused of winning races *only* because they have the best car. Is that down to luck? No, it isn't, and for the same reason: they too had to get themselves into the position of being able to drive the best car – it wasn't just gifted to them. Regardless of the circumstances, a win is a win. It's an interesting subject though, and my theory is that it's all down to how you're perceived. If I'd had a reputation as a tough, silent, steely type of driver, the wins at Silverstone and Monza would probably have been described as 'just reward for a determined, focused and mercurial battler', but because I was seen as being an affable guy and a bit of a joker – and we already know this didn't always serve me well – people tended to take me slightly less seriously, and so I was seen as being a bit lucky. 'Aw, bless him. He tries hard, doesn't he?'

Did it bother me? No, of course not. You ask anyone who knows me and they'll tell you that in most circumstances I couldn't give two hoots what people think. As I hope you know by now, I was as steely and determined behind the wheel as anyone else on the track. But I do find how we perceive racing drivers, against how they actually perform, quite thought-provoking, and it creates a lot of very interesting contradictions.

After my wonderful win at marvellous Monza, Michael still led the Drivers' Championship on 66 points; Damon was on 51 and me on 38. The fact that I was now in third position meant I could have some fun, and because – mathematically at least – I could still catch Michael, I started suggesting to one or two journalists that with five races still to go I thought I might be in with a chance of claiming the championship. I knew I didn't stand a cat in hell's chance, but I also knew that the following day Flavio's phone would be ringing and he'd be getting a right ear-bashing. It worked, as far as I know, so instead of keeping my head down and seeing out my sentence quietly and respect-fully, like I probably should have, I threw out the occasional inflammatory comment just to keep them on their toes. I suppose it was immature of me, and also not very professional, but it was sport and at the end of the day I'm a sportsman.

Of those final five races only Japan resulted in a podium for me (third), but had it not been for a dodgy drive-shaft in Adelaide I might well have gone one place better there, as at the time of retirement I was running confidently in second. I remember at the time having this vision of driving past the pit wall in second, and as I did so Flavio was sitting there, his hand hovering over this giant red button, and laughing in a very evil way. Then, when he was ready, he pressed the button and, BANG! Goodbye drive-shaft. It was like something out of a James Bond film, with me as the goodie and him as the evil genius. It still makes me laugh when I think about it. 'I am Flavio Briatooooore and I will destroooooooy your chances of winning this race. AAAAAH, HA-HA-HA-HA-HA-HA!'

It was a pity not to finish the season on a high, but to be honest I was just glad it was all over. My one season in a truly competitive car – my one big chance – and it had all come to nothing (well, apart from winning two Grands Prix that is). In fact the Schumacher–Herbert affair had left a pretty bad taste in quite a lot of people's mouths. I was to blame for some of that, and I hold my hands up. I was naive, I suppose, but I'd had no idea about the true nature of the relationship between Flavio and Michael. If I had, if I'd known how I was going to be treated, I wouldn't have accepted the drive and would have asked to stay on at Ligier. As it was, Michael won the Drivers' Championship and Benetton the Constructors', and regardless of what Flavio thought of me at the time the fact of the matter is that without my 45 points Benetton wouldn't have won that Constructors' Championship.

I was left feeling that Flavio had tried to stop me at every turn, which meant the team policy could easily have backfired at any time. How the hell does that work? I suppose it's one of life's great mysteries, like Bernie's eternal hair.

Fourteen

AS THE 1995 SEASON drew to an anti-climactic close – for me, at least – I started thinking about the future, which wasn't like me at all. Normally I just let things sort of happen, but I wasn't expecting there to be a lot of interest from inside the paddock so in anticipation of becoming a bit of a Billy-no-mates I started making a few enquiries about going to America. I'd always fancied having a go at IndyCar and had been to quite a few races over the years, so after talking it through with Becky I made some calls and slowly started trying to get my head around the idea.

Luckily for me the news of my battles at Benetton hadn't yet found their way across the Atlantic – or if they had, they couldn't give a damn – and within a few days I'd been offered a test out there. This came about because of Rick Gorne and Adrian Reynard, who had been working with a big team by the name of Chip Ganassi Racing. These days they also compete in the World Endurance Championship, but back then Chip Ganassi Racing was focused purely on NASCAR and IndyCar, and Adrian had given me a glowing report. I wanted to feel part of a family again, and according to him that was going to be the perfect place.

A couple of weeks before the test was due to take place I received a telephone call from my agent to say that Sauber had been in touch and would I be interested in doing a test for them

232

at Paul Ricard. As much as I'd warmed to the idea of going to America and racing in the IndyCar Series (also known as the IRL – the Indy Racing League), the pull of F1 was still very strong. The Ganassi test had made me feel hopeful and excited, but when I got the call about Sauber my heart leapt. Formula 1 remained the ultimate test for a racing driver, and it was always the case that if the opportunity arose, particularly in an up-and-coming team like Sauber who had just had a very strong season (and their cars were powered by Cosworth, who I knew well), I'd find it very hard to say no.

From a testing point of view, Paul Ricard had always been a happy hunting ground for me, so when I arrived at Marseille airport I had a smile on my face and a spring in my limp. Like Chip Ganassi, Peter Sauber had created a real family atmosphere at his team, so with things looking good both on and off the track I was keen to impress. The only thing standing in my way, so I'd been told, was a young upstart named Mark Blundell. He'd been at McLaren in 1995 and, because they'd just taken on DC and had Mika signed up on a long-term contract, he too was looking for a drive.

The journey from Marseille airport to the Paul Ricard circuit is about 65km, and because I knew the route like the back of my hand there was definitely going to be no repeat of my Vallelunga fiasco. No way. This was going to be my time: the rebirth of what could still be an ascension to the summit of Mount Motorsport. 'Come on, Johnny!' I shouted as I drove through the gates and headed towards the paddock. 'Let's show these buggers what you can do.'

The scene was set, then. Paul Ricard was where we'd done the majority of testing for Le Mans in 1991, so it was a circuit I associated with just one thing – victory! I could hear Heinz-Harald Frentzen thundering down the pit lane on his way to put in a few laps.

233

'This is where you belong, Johnny,' I growled, punching the steering wheel. 'This is home!'

They'd all be here, the boys from Sauber and Cosworth, and although I already knew some of the Cosworth contingent, the Sauber boys and girls were all new to me so it was imperative that I made a good first impression. When I finally made it to the paddock I gazed at the succession of wagons and vans that had transported every car, computer and component to the track. *Welcome back to the circus*, I thought to myself. And then, as I turned left at the rear of a huge Sauber-branded artic, dreaming of a bright new tomorrow, I drove straight into the back of a Cosworth van. BANG! What a twenty-two-carat arse. I prayed for one of the airbags to deploy, but alas, nothing, so I had nowhere to hide my crimson mug.

'Oh, bloody hell,' I sobbed. 'What have I done?'

As good first impressions go this was pretty abysmal, and after my reputation had closed the car door firmly behind it, I started noticing a steady stream of mechanics and technicians making their way out of the garage. They seemed like a happy bunch, which was nice, although I had a sneaking suspicion the person they were laughing at looked a lot like me. They spoke in a mixture of English and German, yet I could tell they were all saying the same thing: 'Look, some idiot has driven into the back of a van. OH MY GOD, IT'S JOHNNY HERBERT!' I may not have won a world championship, as Fernando Alonso once very kindly reminded me, but I bet you a pound to a penny I was the first Formula 1 driver to crash his car when arriving at a test. Yet again I was breaking new ground – the limping pioneer, achieving things other drivers could only dream of.

One thing the shunt did was break the ice between myself and the team – not that it needed breaking. The Sauber crew seemed like a great bunch, and the family atmosphere I'd been promised was there in abundance. They also seemed to have a similar sense of humour to mine, which was great, but most importantly of all they were fanatical about racing, and that really shone through. Compared to Benetton this seemed like heaven, and, prangs not-withstanding, I think our first impressions of each other were extremely positive. The test itself was hampered by one or two mechanical issues so I only managed to do about thirty laps, but it was enough to convince me that Sauber were the team for me. Fortunately, Peter Sauber agreed.

As far as I know, Mark Blundell was in the running right until the end, but apparently what gave me the edge were the two Grand Prix wins. Sorry, Mega.

Within a few weeks I'd signed a three-year contract with Sauber, so against all the odds my future, which had been very much in doubt, had been sorted out before the end of the year. Happy? You bet I was.

On the face of it, though, you might be forgiven for thinking that I was about to jump out of the frying pan and right back into the fire. Think about it: I'd just left a team that was enjoying a not inconsiderable amount of success with a very talented German driver who had been established at the team for a number of years. And where was I going to? OK, at first glance it might have seemed like I was in danger of allowing lightning to strike twice, but Peter and Heinz-Harald couldn't have been more different to Flavio and Michael, and if I'd had even a whiff that I might end up being a support driver I'd have quite happily walked away. Peter's English wasn't good at the time – in fact it was about as good as my German – so a lot of the time we had to speak through an interpreter. To me this made very little difference. Even though Peter's naturally a quiet man and likes to conduct himself in a very business-like fashion, I always felt his door was open, and I have a lot of respect for the man. Masses, in fact.

Heinz-Harald was even more laid-back than me. He too

always functioned best within a family environment. This, so I've been told, is why he flourished at Sauber and Jordan, which were family teams and not especially corporate, but struggled at Williams, which was a very ordered team, which to Heinz-Harald probably felt a bit cold. He once told me that on his first day of testing for Williams, which is where he went after leaving Sauber at the end of 1996, he split part of the monocoque after going over a kerb and technical director Patrick Head was so incensed that he sent him home. Knowing Heinz-Harald like I do, that would have affected him badly. Sure enough, he ended up having a hard time there. Some might say it should have been up to him to adjust to Williams' way of doing things, but if a driver can only operate under certain conditions then that's just the way it is. You can't change that. Teams should be prepared to compromise where they can, especially with people as talented as Heinz-Harald Frentzen. He's one of the most natural drivers I've ever seen in a racing car – so from that point of view I knew I was going to be in for a real battle in 1996, just as I had been at Benetton in 1995.

There was one fundamental difference at Sauber, though: it would all take place on a level playing field. As far as I was concerned there was no favouritism and no games being played. I have to give Peter Sauber credit for this because it must have been very tempting for him to concentrate more on Heinz-Harald, who had finished a very respectable ninth in 1995 with 15 points. He didn't, though, and because we were left to race fairly we ended up pushing each other, which in my humble opinion is exactly how it should be. It wouldn't always be like this, and there was a point which I'll come on to later when Peter and I came close to falling out, but as you'll see it was understandable and on a different scale to what happened with me and Flavio.

I'm not sure what they're like today, but back in the 1990s

the Sauber car launches were, shall we say, creative, and they always drew a large yet often somewhat confused crowd. For 1996 they hired a theatre just outside Zurich, and as well as a very impressive laser show, which must have cost them a mint, they'd also hired a theatrical troupe. They'd even commissioned some music which I remember had lots of chanting in it. I didn't understand a single word of this, nor did I really know what was going on, but I learned the words nonetheless, and when some of the journalists I knew looked at me as if to say, 'What is this, a car launch or a sacrificial ceremony?' I just smiled and carried on chanting. I thought it was all great fun. The fact that it wasn't corporate or run-of-the-mill suited me down to the ground.

Despite the brand-new Zetec-R V10 engine, which had performed well in testing, we had an absolute stinker of an opening race in Melbourne. Many of you will remember it as the one where motorsport's very own Evel Knievel, Martin Brundle, flew through the air at 180mph, landed on his nosecone and then barrel-rolled into the gravel, before running back to the pit lane – heroically waving to his adoring public on the way – and jumping into the spare car. All that was missing was a cape and somebody singing 'BATMAAAAAN!' What you probably won't remember is whose car he used as a launch pad. To be fair to Martin there was absolutely nothing he could have done about it because, going into turn three, David Coulthard had veered left after a shunt and when I slammed on the brakes to avoid him Martin was right behind me. Heinz-Harald had already had problems on the parade lap so by the time Martin took me out, the spare car was already in use.

In Brazil my electrics failed on lap 28, and in Argentina in April I only had front brakes for the majority of the race and finished ninth. Not a good start, and with Heinz-Harald not faring much better, Sauber were already being seen as a lower-mid-table team, which was worse than the previous season. The following two races, at the Nürburgring and Imola, all but confirmed our position, and going into Monaco Heinz-Harald had an eighth and four retirements to his name whereas I had three retirements, a seventh and a ninth. Qualifying had also been disappointing with both of us starting on about the sixth or seventh row. We just didn't have the speed we needed.

The Monaco weekend started off just the same as the previous races, with Heinz-Harald qualifying ninth and me thirteenth. We weren't fast enough to be able to overtake many cars on the grid, but the potential advantage Monaco gave us was that nobody could overtake *us*. With strategy playing more of a role, not to mention the weather and even luck, the race would hopefully be a lot less predictable than the previous five.

On race day, heavy rain started falling shortly after the first session so we were given an extra fifteen minutes to try to acclimatize. I'm not sure it did much good because if memory serves about six or seven cars spun off, and although everyone started the race, one or two cars did so carrying damage. I was fourth fastest in that session, well in front of the Williams and the Ferraris. It didn't mean anything, but it still gave me a boost going into the race.

After a good start and a few retirements, including Michael Schumacher, I was up into ninth after the first lap and there I stayed until lap 21. By this time there had been no fewer than nine retirements, and when Gerhard Berger went out with a gearbox problem I was up to eighth. Come lap 24 the track had started drying up a bit, but Heinz-Harald then got a little bit overconfident and ended up bumping Eddie Irvine's Ferrari and having to pit, which moved me up to seventh. Between laps 28 and 30 there was a sudden rush of pit stops with everybody wanting to change to slicks, and after putting in some fast laps just prior to that I came out of it running sixth – the first time I'd been in the points all season.

Everything was going well, then, a lot better than I'd hoped, and when Olivier Panis in the Ligier made an audacious move on Eddie Irvine at the Loews hairpin, with Irvine losing control and going off, I was up to fifth, which is when I started thinking that I might be in with a chance of a podium.

Damon Hill, who just a few months later would be crowned world champion and who had won four of the previous five races, brought me one step closer to that wish on lap 40, when his engine failed. I caught a quick glimpse of him coming to a rather smoky halt on one of the escape roads, and asked for confirmation of my position. 'You're now running fourth, Johnny,' said Gil, my engineer, 'behind Alesi, Panis and Coulthard.'

Poor Jean, who was on course for his second Grand Prix win, had to come in with a suspension problem on lap 54, which meant I'd provisionally made it on to the first step of the podium. By this point only ten cars remained on the track, and it wouldn't be too long before that number was reduced to just four. By lap 71, the penultimate lap, this was still the state of play, so Heinz-Harald, who was running fourth but a long way behind me, came into the garage early, safe in the knowledge that with nobody running behind him he would retain his position.

Panis won, with DC in second and me third, so for the first time in 1996 things had gone exactly how we'd predicted they would – the only issue being that our prediction had been 'Anything could happen!' so there wasn't a great deal we could take from it. It was still a brilliant result for the team, though, and we hoped it might act as a springboard for the second half of the season.

The only hangover from Sauber's previous season that annoyed me was that Heinz-Harald still enjoyed the majority of the testing. This was just a habit, I think, as opposed to being premeditated, and after a couple of chats with Peter the situation changed and I started spending more time in the car.

From the team's point of view this paid dividends, as even if you're not in the running for the Constructors' Championship you're still going to have more chances of getting sponsors on board if you have two drivers out there doing well rather than just one. From here on in I started to out-qualify Heinz-Harald regularly, which for an old-timer like me was a big boost, as he was regarded as one of the sport's biggest talents.

That springboard we'd hoped for post-Monaco never really materialized. Apart from a few minor advancements, we played out the second half of the season pretty much the same as we had the first, with a mixture of mid-table qualifying positions, retirements and finishes that were just outside the points. Once again Sauber ended up seventh in the Constructors' Championship, but with far fewer points than was either hoped for or anticipated.

The Cosworth deal was now at an end, and for the last two years Peter had been working on a deal with Ferrari whereby they would design Sauber's engines and gearboxes, which would then be built in-house by a newly formed company called Sauber Petronas Engineering. It was a hugely controversial move initially and all kinds of accusations were made on the subject of fairness. All I knew was that for the first year of the deal, or at least until Sauber had the experience to build the engines from scratch, I'd be driving a car powered by the Grand Prix-winning Ferrari F310B engine and with a brand-new chassis that had been developed with my help – not necessarily to my specifications, but with my help. That was going to make a huge difference. I'd always wanted a car in which I could be aggressive on the turn-in but be able to control the understeer going through the corner, which would allow me to get on the power coming out, but the most important thing was that entry. At Benetton, Michael always preferred a very sharp turn-in, and one where the car did most of the work, whereas I always wanted to be in control, to be able to attack a corner with absolute confidence. The Sauber C16, which was designed by Leo Ress, gave me just that. The back of the car was solid too, and when I first started testing it did feel like it had been designed just for me.

I was still very much a confidence driver in those days, in fact I don't think that ever changed. How much of that was down to what had happened to me in the past I'm not entirely sure, so I'll let you make up your own mind on that. It's certainly no coincidence, though, that I felt at my best in the cockpit when I was surrounded by people who inspired me. At the end of the 1996 season Peter Sauber hired Josef Leberer, who today is the most experienced driver trainer in Formula 1 and is best known for having looked after Ayrton Senna and Alain Prost. Almost twenty years on, Josef is still working with Sauber. When I first met him, at the beginning of 1997, he was, from a motivational point of view, exactly what I needed. Some trainers can be quite reserved when it comes to communicating with drivers and tend to concentrate on fitness, but Josef, who I already knew slightly through his work with Ayrton, seemed to be all things to all people and could turn his hand to anything. He has an instinct for knowing exactly what a driver needs, both physically and mentally, and everything he does is tailored specifically to a driver's needs, so there's nothing generic about anything he does. It's almost as if he can see inside you, and in me he saw somebody who was quite fit physically (apart from the obvious blemishes) but who, in order to perform to the best of his ability, needed one or two rules putting in place and some inspiration that didn't just amount to a few high-fives and a 'You can do it, Johnny'.

It got to a point with Josef where he got it into my head that during qualifying I only needed one lap. We had an hour, but I'd always go into the session thinking, *It only takes one lap. Just one lap.* At Benetton I never enjoyed qualifying (I can't think why) and often used to feel quite sick before the session began. It was the hour from hell as far as I was concerned. What Josef taught me to do was compartmentalize the hour and take things one lap at a time. If one didn't work out I would eradicate it from my mind and simply start again. There were no hang-ups from any previous laps, no worries about any future ones. I was completely focused on the present moment. He's a very clever guy, Mr Leberer.

As part of the deal with Ferrari, one of their test drivers, Nicola Larini, was named as the replacement for Heinz-Harald, who had taken Damon's seat at Williams, but after just five races he hadn't impressed and was sent home. For the remainder of the season the other car was shared between Norberto Fontana and Gianni Morbidelli. Even though I had a lot of attention and was seen very much as the senior driver, I missed not having a team-mate who could really give me a run for my money.

As the season progressed Ferrari's influence at Sauber became more and more apparent, to the point where, at Spa in August, I was told that if I was in front of Michael, and Ferrari said so, I'd have to let him past. I think if this had been made public at the time it would have put Ferrari in a bad light, which is perhaps why it never happened. It was strange just being aware of it. I remember at the time thinking, *Why can't you just leave me alone?*

I found out long after leaving Sauber that their main concern prior to signing me, apart from the public war of words I'd had with Flavio, had been the difference between mine and Michael's performances. Their fears had been allayed when I first tested for them, of course, but not their curiosity. I had no idea this was happening, but the matter was settled once and for all at Ferrari's Fiorano Circuit during a test in September

1997. Michael was also there testing with Ferrari, and because of that 'special relationship' I talked about he'd been asked to spend half a day testing the Sauber. After Michael had left the track, I took the same car out on the same number of laps. According to Beat Zehnder, who was Sauber's team manager at the time, we posted almost identical times and our feedback too was practically indistinguishable. It means nothing of course, because Michael wasn't used to the car, but I have to admit that I smiled when I was told. I'm a confidence driver, remember, and being told you've just matched one of the best there's ever been on the track is always going to give you a boost.

I'm not going to take you through the 1997 season race by race, nor even pick out one or two highlight races, I'm just going to give you a bit of a summary. Why? Well, believe it or not, we had some awful luck in 1997 and if I expand on any of this, which I'd have to, you'd end up thinking I was either a Jonah or a whingeing pain in the bum, and I promise you I'm neither. Actually, I will give you one Jonah story, for the simple reason it's quite funny.

It was 15 June and I was running third in the Canadian Grand Prix at Circuit Gilles Villeneuve. Qualifying had been appalling and I'd started thirteenth, but once the race had begun I came alive and, even though I say so myself, I'd driven an absolute blinder. It was another one of those races where I could and should have been on the podium, but unfortunately it all went belly-up during my pit stop. I was on a one-stop strategy, and when I came in I encountered an electrical problem that resulted in me speeding on my exit and incurring a ten-second stop-go penalty.

The pit stop itself had gone beautifully, despite my flapping, and I'd rejoined the race still in third but only just behind Jean Alesi. It was all there for the taking! A lap or so later the team came on the radio and told me about the penalty, so before I could make a move on Jean I was back in the pits to serve my time. All this took place, by the way, after my team-mate, Gianni Morbidelli, had crashed into me, ripping off one of my rear wings. This had happened earlier in the race during a red flag and even though Gianni was a lap down on me he was behind me in the queue. Ironically enough, Gianni's excuse for shunting me was that he was trying to adjust his brake balance. You really couldn't make it up, could you? Anyway, I finished fifth, which wasn't too bad I suppose.

From a reliability point of view, 1997 was quite a good season. I suffered mechanical issues on only two or three occasions. There was a podium too, at Hungary, and it was probably one of my best races for Sauber. The weekend had started badly, when the team were hit with a $25,000 fine after the FIA discovered that the fuel we were using was illegal. This was an oversight on Shell's behalf as they had supplied us with two different kinds. Both were legal if kept separate but when mixed together the chemical fingerprint was not the same as the one held by the FIA, and they came down on us like a ton of bricks. From then on things just got better and better, which made for a nice change. It was only Sauber's third ever podium finish.

I remember I was in quite a boyish mood that weekend and had been winding people up left, right and centre. In that respect the fine should have been manna from heaven, but Peter was furious so I thought better of asking him if he could lend me a few quid until payday, which is what I'd planned to do. In the end I turned my attentions on my race engineer, Gil Aligeot, who is very nice but had been known to panic a bit. A few minutes before the start of the parade lap I decided I needed to have a wee so I told Gil, pulled myself out of the cockpit and nipped off behind some advertising hoardings. Can you imagine doing that nowadays? You'd get someone like me or Martin following you and asking what you thought your chances were.

As I was standing there relieving myself I got chatting to one of the marshals, and as time ticked on I could see Gil growing more and more nervous. He kept looking around to see if I was coming back, so I decided to hold my position a little bit longer. With only about a minute to go I walked leisurely back on to the track and climbed very slowly into the cockpit, almost as if I were getting into bed.

'Where the hell have you been, Johnny?' asked Gil. 'Zee parade lap is starting in a matter of seconds!'

I looked at him with the dumbest, most childlike expression I could manage. 'Been wee wee,' I said, and then proceeded to look at the steering wheel and all the controls as if I hadn't a clue what they all did.

By this time all the other drivers were beginning to rev their engines in preparation for the start, and Gil, who was now bright red, began screaming at me: 'Don't do this to me, Johnny! Vot is happening? VOT IS GOING ON?'

When the cars began moving, I pointed to the car in front of me and looked at Gil blankly again, as if to say, 'Should I just follow them, then?' The poor man was close to tears by now so I thought it was probably time for me to set off. As I pulled down my visor and started to move off, I gave him a little wave, but he still looked very angry. I think he was placated by the podium, thank God. Otherwise there could have been a murder.

I also managed a couple of fourths, another fifth and a sixth, but that was about it for 1997 and I ended up tenth in the Drivers' Championship with 15 points. Not bad, all things considered, but we were going to have to work hard in the close season. The engine, although quite good at the start, had obviously become more obsolete as the season had gone on and because we weren't in a position to do much development work, we ended up falling away a bit. With a team like Sauber it can often be difficult to plan ahead because your financial situation can change almost daily. You've just got to make the best of it. But what softens it all and keeps everybody positive is that family atmosphere I keep harping on about. I was getting very well paid as a driver – in fact the change in engine manufacturer had triggered a clause in my contract that meant I got an even better deal – but with the likes of Sauber money is not the primary motivation. The primary motivation is a passion for racing. They're unlikely ever to win a world championship but they will always be an extremely popular team for that very reason.

Mark my words, the celebrations you see when a smaller team wins a point or two easily match those you'll see after one of the big teams wins a Grand Prix. Why? Because there are usually few external pressures to consider and there's often little or no expectation involved – just dedication, hope, and a huge amount of endeavour. Does anyone remember Mark Webber making his Formula 1 debut for Minardi back in 2002? It was in Melbourne so it was his home Grand Prix, not to mention that of the Minardi team owner, Paul Stoddart, and when Mark finished fifth, bagging two gigantic points, the entire team acted like they'd just won the world championship. Mark had scored points on his debut, which was fantastic, but he knew just how much that meant to the team as a whole. Financially the points were worth a fortune – hundreds of thousands of pounds probably, which can mean life or death to a smaller team – but that was only half of it. Those two points were a little bit of recognition for the years and years they'd been battling against the odds. In my opinion there's something very pure about a victory like that, and I feel genuinely privileged to have been involved in one or two of them.

I have no idea what the future holds for the Saubers of this world but at times it does feel like F1 doesn't care very much. Opportunities for the smaller independent teams to compete with the big boys appear to be decreasing by the year and many people are suggesting that Formula 1 is fast becoming a closed shop, with the dominant factory teams basically calling the shots. This isn't the time or the place to start pontificating about the state of Formula 1, but I will say this: should we ever lose the likes of Sauber, Formula 1 will be a much poorer place.

Fifteen

By the end of 1997 Peter Sauber had decided to ditch Italian drivers in favour of moody little French ones. When I was first told that my team-mate for 1998 would be Jean Alesi, I was thrilled. He'd had two good-ish years at Benetton, equalling my own record of fourth in both seasons. We'd known each other for years and got on well together, but Jean is to this day one of the most competitive drivers I've ever known so I knew it was going to be a very different season for me. If I wanted pushing, and I did, he'd do it all right.

The 1998 Sauber car launch remains the most bizarre I've ever attended, in any capacity. I first got an inkling that Peter might be going 'all-out peculiar' when somebody mentioned he'd commissioned an Austrian composer to write a Symphony of Luck, together with a narrative running alongside that would be performed, once again, by a strangely attired troupe of theatrical performers. Though to be fair, that's a normal day for Peter.

The launch took place at the historic Schönbrunn Palace in Vienna, which probably had something to do with Red Bull, who were the team's main sponsor. Unlike your average racing driver, I know an awful lot about culture; in fact I've often been referred to as the Melvyn Bragg of motorsport. It wasn't lost on

248

me, then, that in the year 1762 a six-year-old musical prodigy by the name of Wolfgang Amadeus Mozart played the clavichord at the Schönbrunn Palace, and from that moment a star was born. Would the venue have the same effect on Sauber, I mused? We'd have to wait and see.

During the show, almost like an insurance policy, somebody from the theatrical troupe presented Peter with this ginormous papier-mâché heart which, like the music, was supposed to provide us with some luck. Poor old Jean thought he'd landed on another planet. I remember watching the expression on his face when the troupe started doing their thing. It went from surprise, to confusion, to fear, and then back to surprise again. He was probably thinking, *What is all zis rubbish? What's wrong with a few models and a smoke machine?*

I started the 1998 season by creating a bit of a shock and qualifying fifth. It was common knowledge that we hadn't made a great deal of progress over the close season and we were expected to start roughly where we'd left off. The race itself was controversial for two reasons, both involving McLaren. First, there were allegations of 'radio tapping' when Mika Häkkinen came into the pits without being asked to do so by the team. Then, shortly before the end of the race, the leader, Mika's team-mate David Coulthard, allowed Mika to pass him on the straight, thus surrendering the win at the last minute. This put the contentious subject of 'team orders' right back into the limelight, and it's stayed there, via a variety of different teams, pretty much ever since.

I finished sixth in Melbourne, which was a great start for the team, and over the next eight races it was pretty much even-stevens between Jean and me, both in qualifying and racing. Then, when we got to the A1-Ring in Austria at the end of July, everything changed. It had been raining shortly before qualifying but by the time the session got underway the track was starting to dry out. After my first run I was about eighth and ahead of Jean, and it was the same state of play after my second. By the time I went out for my final run the track was almost dry and with no more rain forecast it was obvious I should be on slicks, but I immediately noticed that this wasn't the case.

'What tyres am I on, Gil?' I asked over the radio.

'Wets, Johnny,' he said. 'You're on wets.'

'But why am I on wets when the track's clearly dry?'

'OK,' replied Gil, 'you'd better come back in.'

By this time there was seven minutes left to the end of the session and I was going to have to get a move on if I was going to post a good time. I felt frustrated with what had happened but because the team were normally so professional I just let it go. Once I was back out again and on the right tyres I tried to concentrate on qualifying, but before I could do a thing Peter Sauber came over the radio.

'Let past Jean,' he snapped, almost as if I were holding him up.

I assumed Jean was a few hundred yards behind me so I prepared to let him through, but half a lap later he was nowhere in sight. After another half a lap Peter came on the radio again and said the same three words, but once again there was no bloody sign of Jean. 'What the hell's going on?' I asked, but again he just repeated himself. After about two laps Jean eventually did pass me, although because he'd already completed his fast lap there'd been absolutely no need for me to slow down.

Now I had about one minute left, and providing I crossed the start line within those sixty seconds I could still finish the lap. There was one slight problem, though: my tyres were now freezing bloody cold so the fast lap I'd been hoping to post ended up being dreadful and I qualified eighteenth. Jean, on the other hand, had put in a blinder and qualified second.

I wanted some answers. According to Peter, he'd acted

overcautiously, and as well as apologizing he thanked me for doing it for the team. This made me feel better – NOT!

Poor old Jean went off during the race after colliding with Giancarlo Fisichella and I ended up finishing just outside the points in eighth.

At the following race, in Hockenheim, Jean and I qualified eleventh and twelfth respectively, so apart from the fact that we'd both have liked to be higher up the grid, there were no problems. I was on a one-stop strategy for this race and Jean was on a two, and after getting a good start I was ahead of him going into the first corner. Then, probably five or six laps before Jean was due to come in for his first stop, Peter came on the radio.

'Let past Jean. Let past Jean.'

This time I'm afraid it made no sense whatsoever so I got back on the radio and said, 'No, I will not let past Jean. He's on a two-stop, I'm on a one, I'm in the lead, so I'm sorry, Peter, I won't.'

Peter wasn't happy. 'No, Johnny,' he said. 'Let past Jean!'

This argument went on for at least two laps with Jean just behind me, and in the end I got so worked up that I pulled over to let Jean pass me, but when I did I ended up spinning off into the gravel. The marshals pushed me out, which they were allowed to do, but by this time I was raging and instead of continuing the race I drove straight back into the pits, got out of the car and went to cool off. You can probably count the number of times I've lost my temper over the years on the fingers of one hand, but if I'd gone to see Peter straight after getting out of the car I might have attacked him.

After calming down a bit I went to have it out with the team boss, but by the time I found him Jean was already there bending his ear, so I left them to it. We did talk later but Peter failed to convince me that what he was doing was for the good of the team. Had Jean been fighting for the championship at the time, fine, I'd have understood, but we were both in a similar position;

in fact, all things considered, I had my nose just out in front. Once again I probably didn't handle it very well because when Peter and I couldn't agree I just went into my shell and let it fester. That is the worst thing you can do in such circumstances and, unsurprisingly, it affected my performances for the rest of the season. I left Sauber not under a cloud, exactly, but not on a high either.

I suggested earlier that Peter's actions might have been understandable, and although this is just a theory, I'll tell you what I mean. Peter has always been a big Ferrari fan, hence their continued involvement with Sauber, and I think he had a soft spot for Jean, who was an ex-Ferrari driver, the same as Peter Collins had a soft spot for me. I have no problem with that because I've been on the receiving end, but what Peter Sauber failed to consider was the effect it might have on me personally. At the time, though, he genuinely couldn't understand what my problem was. We've spoken about it a few times since and I think he now realizes it wasn't the right thing to do, but I'm satisfied that his actions were the result of misplaced enthusiasm rather than anything more Flavio-esque. In addition to being a racer, Peter is a good, honest human being, and although it did spoil the latter half of that third season a bit, I still look back on my time at Sauber with a massive amount of fondness.

We used to get up to some crazy things, things that back then you could never do with one of the big teams. At the start of 1998, for instance, we made a short silent comedy film for a Swiss TV company that involved me and a fake pit crew consisting of nothing but beautiful women. It was a little bit Benny Hill I'm afraid, with just a smidgen of Charlie Chaplin. After the girls make a mess of preparing the car for me, I crash it, then the real Sauber pit crew turn up looking horrified. After that I stand there in the middle of the two pit crews and I have to choose which one to go with. Naturally I choose the girls, and with the Sauber crew standing there with their arms folded, looking grumpy, I go waltzing off into the distance surrounded by lovely ladies. That's about it really. It didn't win any awards, and when I watched it back recently I found it definitely of its time, but we had such a great laugh making it, and it epitomized the atmosphere and camaraderie we had at the team. (The film is easily found, by the way. Just go to Sauber's YouTube channel.)

We're back to old sayings again now, and the one I'm going for this time is 'One door closes, another one opens'. Had my contretemps with Peter Sauber not taken place, then I would never have been contacted by Sir Jackie Stewart – or plain Mr Stewart as he was then – and so would probably never have won a third Grand Prix. More importantly, I would never have acquired that beautiful tartan suit Jackie had made for me, which, as you can imagine, I still wear on a regular basis.

Just like Peter Sauber – and Flavio Briatore, it should be said – Sir Jackie Stewart is a very astute businessman who has a knack for making things happen. There's no better example of this than when he persuaded Ford and HSBC to help him start Stewart Grand Prix. When he offered me the drive I was over the moon. I knew Jackie fairly well and had spent quite a bit of time with him, but only socially. For example, back in 1989 when I couldn't walk, he very kindly invited me to his home in Switzerland where we, his family and some other guests all watched the Bruno v. Tyson fight. I remember this well because instead of using a wheelchair around the house I just dragged myself around on my bum!

Working with him was going to be a genuine thrill and because he said his approach was going to be very hands-on I was looking forward to what lay ahead.

The first test took place in Barcelona, and when I arrived Jackie shook my hand and reaffirmed his commitment to forging close driver–owner relationships. I do a pretty good Jackie Stewart impression but it's obviously no use here so you'll just have to imagine it. It's exaggerated slightly, and very high-pitched.

'I like to take a very keeeeeeeeeeeeen interest in what my drivers dooooooooooooo, Johnny,' said the great man. 'So if there's anything I can do to help, just yoooooooou say.'

'Thank you very much indeed, Jackie.'

After being introduced to everyone at the team, many of whom I already knew, I was all ready to go. About two-thirds of the way round the first lap, just on the back straight, I spotted this little tartan-clad figure sitting up in the grandstand. I could almost hear him shouting as I drove past: 'You'll be sure to bring the car back safe and sound, won't you now!' A few laps later I was flying down the home straight doing about 170mph when all of a sudden my rear wing came off. This was far from ideal given the speed I was travelling, and after doing a 180-degree turn I hit the barrier, became airborne and started travelling backwards. Luckily for me the car clipped a wall on the left-hand side, otherwise it would have continued rising with me in it. After another few hundred yards what remained of the car eventually smashed into a different wall at the first turn. Damon was testing for Jordan that day and he claimed that because of the speed at which I hit the wall he thought I was a goner. It's still one of the most frightening things he's ever seen. I was unhurt, fortunately, although for a good few hours I was definitely a little bit dazed.

The following day started in exactly the same way, with me going out and spotting Jackie in the grandstand on the back straight, although this time the rear wing stayed on so we were able to do the full test.

After the first session I was sitting in the cockpit, waiting to go again when, out of the blue, I felt a tap on the top of my helmet. It was Jackie.

254

'I've been watching you out there, Johnny, and one thing I will say is that you're' – at this point he squinted his eyes and his voice went into a kind of hissing whisper – 'veeeeeeeeeeeeeeeery aggressive with the car. You've got to be smoooooooooooooth with the car, Johnny. Smoooooooooooooooooth. Treat it like you would a lady, OK? You do like ladies, don't you, Johnny? Well, treat it like one of them. Right, I'm going back to the stand now, but I'll be watching you, Johnny. I'll be watching yooooooooou.'

There was an element of truth in what he was saying, but even though I was still adapting to the car I carried on – *except*, that is, when I approached the back straight. Then I drove like a geriatric vicar, although Jackie still popped his head in the cockpit afterwards and squinted at me. 'You're still driving ever so slightly too aggressively, Johnny. Now what have I told you about being smoooooooooth? Good driving is smoooooooooth driving, Johnny, and you'll do well to remember that.'

I know I take the mickey a bit, but it was a great privilege driving for Jackie Stewart, and being coached by him was also something else. I didn't always agree with everything he said, but then I don't think he expected me to. He was just trying to get the best out of me for the good of the team, and why not? In mechanical terms it was like being fine-tuned, I suppose, and he often went to enormous lengths to support a driver. It's a shame, but not everybody saw it like I did. One of his drivers, who shall remain nameless (Jos Verstappen), found it difficult to accept Jackie's advice in the spirit in which it was offered and even refused to attend a one-to-one driving session with him up at Oulton Park. As you can imagine, this went down like Jenson Button at an Iron Maiden concert, and it wasn't long before he was looking for alternative employment. I, on the other hand, had a great time there, and as an added bonus I came very close to killing us both.

Jackie took a lot of drivers out at Oulton Park, and the day

I turned up he was also due to take out the American stock car racer Danica Patrick. The car Jackie used for these sessions was a Ford Escort rally car which I have to say threw me slightly when I found out. I'm not sure what I was expecting, but that certainly wasn't it. The idea was that I'd take the wheel first for a few laps so he could analyse what I did and make a few notes, after which he'd take the wheel and demonstrate any bits of advice he had for me.

On my very first lap – it was damp, by the way – I locked up the rear wheels going into Lodge Corner. I then locked up the front wheels too, and I remember seeing the barrier flashing by on my left-hand side, not to mention a very worried-looking former Formula 1 world champion who just happened to be my new boss. The corner went right, and it would have been great to have been able to follow it, but unfortunately Jackie and I were going in a straight line, and after ploughing into the gravel we bounced three times over about a hundred yards before coming to a sharp halt. After that, silence prevailed for what must have been about twenty seconds. Then Jackie looked over at me and said, 'Well, we'd better get out then.' To this day I'm *convinced* there was a little puddle of wee on his seat when he got out. There certainly was on mine.

When we got back to the garage Jackie set about giving me his feedback. Given what had just happened, he began – with a squint, of course – exactly where he'd left off at the test. 'My word, Johnny, that was very *aggressive*. Veeeeeeery aggressive. There was nothing smooooooooth about that run, was there?'

I had to admit that he was absolutely on the button and held my hands up. 'No, Jackie,' I said, 'there wasn't. In fact it was anything but smooth.'

He then took a slightly more serious tone. 'You do realize you almost had us both killed just then, don't you? I like you, Johnny, but not enough to want to die with you.'

'Yes, I am sorry about that, Jackie.'

'Never mind,' he said. 'Now, would you like me to take you out and show you how it's done?'

'Yes, that'd be great, Jackie, thank you.'

As we set off again with Jackie behind the wheel, I was expecting smoothness personified – cashmere on wheels, basically – but he was worse than me! When we came in I said as much, but Jackie was having none of it. 'Noooooooo,' he said, 'that was as smooooooooth as you'll get, Johnny. It's all in the hands, you know. It's all in the hands.' If it was, I think he'd just borrowed Nigel Mansell's.

My team-mate at Stewart GP was Rubens Barrichello, who is one of my favourite ever team-mates, both in terms of personality and professionalism, and he was a joy to work alongside. He has quite a warped sense of humour, which I like, and just exudes happiness. He was quite a bit younger than me at the time (he still is, apparently) and Stewart was very much his team, in the same way that Sauber was very much Heinz-Harald's, and I suppose mine during my second season there. It can be daunting coming into a team where there is already a driver who is younger than you are and doing everything right both on and off the track, and you have to be very careful in terms of how you behave. Try too hard to impose yourself on the team and you might end up alienating people. It's the same on the track. It's very easy to think, *Right, I'm the more experienced driver, so I need to make my mark*, but the chances are you'll end up trying too hard and either making mistakes or underperforming. The best way to approach this situation is to keep your head down, keep smiling, and just get on with the job.

Jackie and his son Paul, who both owned the team, were clearly very fond of Rubens and a strong bond existed between them, so although the family atmosphere was definitely present at Stewart GP, it was so strong that anybody new to the team was initially going to feel like a distant cousin. What made it easier for me was the relationship I already had with Ford, whose van I'd attacked at Paul Ricard several years earlier, and the fact that I got on so well with Rubens. He's probably one of the most competitive yet contented people I've ever met, and even then he had a mature head on his shoulders. Perhaps that's why he was the perfect partner for Michael Schumacher. At Ferrari he accepted his supporting role, knew that all things were not going to be equal, yet always conducted himself impeccably and drove out of his skin.

Anyway, enough about Mr Perfect. It's me you want to read about. And believe it or not, my car is about to catch fire.

On the whole, pre-season testing had been encouraging and we arrived in Australia feeling confident and quite competitive. The results during the first session at Friday free practice supported our mood: after ironing out one or two technical glitches, Rubens and I finished sixth and seventh respectively. *Not too bad*, we thought. *Not bad at all.* The second session went better still, with Rubens moving up to third and me fifth, by which time we couldn't wait for Saturday. That started off even better for me as after morning practice Rubens and I had swapped our final positions from the day before, which put me third. It was all academic, of course, as qualifying was yet to come, but everyone at the team felt good.

An hour or so later our luck finally ran out, or at least some of it, because after Rubens put in a blinder to qualify fourth, I experienced some suspension problems which meant the best I could manage was thirteenth. But I knew what the car was capable of so I wasn't too worried.

After completing the warm-up lap, and just a few seconds before the red lights came on, I noticed smoke coming from underneath my car so I put my hand up to signal I had a problem. What a time for your car to catch light, five seconds before the start of the first race of the season. As I got out of the car the fire marshals came rushing in. With my engine now covered in foam I'd have to use the spare car and start from the pit lane. If only! Just as the fire marshals were taking care of my mini inferno I looked forward and saw that Rubens was having exactly the same problem. Unbelievably, both the Stewart cars had suffered exactly the same fate and within just a few seconds of each other (it turned out that both cars had suffered oil leaks). Because Rubens was the established Stewart driver and further up the grid, he got the spare car. This was fair enough, but unfortunately it meant I didn't get to drive even a yard in anger.

The next six races went as follows: retirement (hydraulics), a tenth (at Imola), two more retirements (engine, then suspension), a fifth (in Canada), and another retirement (gearbox), which, to put it mildly, was a bit of a bugger. All the promise from the start of the season had just about evaporated, and by the time we arrived at Silverstone I was feeling pretty flat. That wonderful day in 1995 seemed like a hundred years ago and, reliability issues notwithstanding, I wasn't performing as I knew I could. Qualifying in general had been poor for me, and with Rubens bagging podiums here, there and everywhere, not to mention a pole position at the previous race at Magny-Cours, I felt like I was letting everybody down.

My feet had started to become even more of a problem again, but, as before, it was something I had to deal with on my own as I was afraid of what people might say. 'Isn't it about time you retired, Johnny? You've had a good run.' Even Becky had to remain in the dark because she too might have suggested the inevitable. My limp had also returned which meant I was often painfully self-conscious, not to mention paranoid. I was convinced for a time that Jackie thought it was all linked. It wasn't linked – not physically, at least – but mentally I think everything contributed.

I finished that British Grand Prix in twelfth, and the following five races were only marginally better, although including the British GP I did manage a run of four without suffering a retirement, which was encouraging. This did my confidence some good and enabled me to improve on my speed, which so far in 1999 had been my Achilles heel. It's not just drivers who become frustrated by a lack of form or by unreliable cars, everybody does, and I've never known a team try so hard to put things right. It was going to be Jackie's final season as team owner so naturally we wanted to finish on a high. The best the team had managed so far in the Constructors' Championship was eighth, and whatever happened in the final three races we were guaranteed to finish above that. How far above would remain to be seen, but with Rubens having already secured two podiums and a pole position, the only thing missing was a win.

Sixteen

THE FOURTEENTH ROUND of the 1999 Formula 1 season took place at a circuit notorious for unpredictable weather patterns, the Nürburgring. Sure enough, after being fine during final practice it rained just prior to qualifying, which meant that the times posted in the early part of the session were quite slow. Eventually the rain stopped and the circuit began to dry out, but the dilemma the teams then faced was whether or not to wait to see if the rain continued to hold off. Some teams took the gamble of leaving it as late as humanly possible, which paid off, others didn't, which meant the final qualifying order was as unpredictable as the weather itself.

Heinz-Harald in the Jordan probably dished out the biggest surprise as he got pole, beating DC and his McLaren by a mere two-tenths of a second. Rubens and I played it safe, which meant we qualified in damp conditions and ended up fourteenth and fifteenth. It was the first time that season that I'd out-qualified my young team-mate and, given what had happened in the previous races, it surprised pretty much everybody. Even I was a little bit taken aback. Still, I may have been an old campaigner and I may have had a poor season to that point, but when my head was in the right place and my confidence was high I'd still have a pound on myself racing anybody on that grid. Time was running out for me, I knew that, but I was adamant I still had something left to offer, a performance that would make people forget about the injuries and the retirements and the poor run of form, and remind them all that I was in fact a bloody good driver. How's that for conceited?

Unlike qualifying, which was full of spins and changeable weather, the warm-up lap took place on a dry track in bright sunshine and featured all twenty-two cars. Best of all, not one of them caught fire, so come the red lights we were all good to go. This had the makings of a very interesting start given that some of the faster cars, such as the Ferraris and the Williams, were starting further down the grid than usual. They'd all have both the speed and the inclination to make up places before the first corner, so prior to the race the team had reminded me and Rubens that it was probably going to be even more chaotic than usual and it was imperative that we try to stay out of trouble. 'Be patient,' was the last thing Jackie said to me before the race, and it turned out to be very good advice.

On the very first lap an accident involving Damon's Jordan led to a chain-reaction that saw a number of cars going out of the race, and Pedro Diniz in the Sauber barrel-rolling off the circuit. After that the safety car came out for a few laps while they cleared up the debris, and when the race restarted I was lying tenth and Rubens eleventh.

By lap 18 the rain had begun to fall, after which chaos broke out. Frentzen, who was in the lead, stayed out on slicks hoping it would pass, as did DC, who was third. Mika Häkkinen, on the other hand, who was running second, got called in for wet tyres only for the rain to pass having covered just half the circuit. Once Mika had gone in to change back to slicks, Rubens was running fifth and me eighth, and after the two drivers separating us also went into the pits to change back, that had us running fifth and sixth. We were being patient, just like Jackie had said, and we were being careful – which in my case must have surprised him somewhat.

A few laps later, just after the halfway mark, Heinz-Harald came into the pits for a scheduled stop but never made it out again after his Jordan suffered a problem. This now put Rubens on the podium with me just a place behind, but there was still a long way to go and only a fool would have bet money on who was going to win.

The thing I was most conscious of at that point during the race was the wind direction, which was coming right down the straight. When you line up on the grid at the Nürburgring, about ninety miles in front of you lies Spa, and at Spa it's *always* raining. Except when it's not. When we'd lined at the start I'd noticed a cloud in the distance and I remember being quite taken by it as it was shaped exactly like a teardrop. It was roundish, wide, and had a little tail running off it, and I can recall thinking, *Wow, look at that*. Now that cloud was a lot closer and as well as noticing how dark it was, I could also see that it was moving quite quickly. A couple of laps later I looked up again and not only was it closer to the circuit but it was holding the same line. I made the decision there and then to come in and go on to wets. It was a huge gamble as there was no guarantee that the cloud would make it to the circuit, let alone bring rain, but the shape of it made me think, *Teardrop equals crying, equals rain. Get the wets on!* Thinking back, it's ridiculous, and I know I'm going to receive all kinds of abuse, but sometimes these things happen, and if you believe in fate, like I used to, you tend to just go for it.

The general consensus in the paddock was that even if my teardrop cloud did arrive and bring rain, it would only be a shower, so I'm pretty sure I was the only driver out there on wets when the rain did start. This, for as long as the 'shower' lasted, gave me an advantage of about five seconds a lap, but in addition to this there were cars spinning off everywhere. I managed to overtake Rubens almost immediately, straight after which he went in to change to wets. So, with about twenty laps to go, I was running third, Ralf Schumacher (Williams) second and Giancarlo Fisichella (Benetton) first.

Once the rain had stopped and calm was restored I pitted for slicks, and because I had a good twenty seconds on Jarno Trulli in fourth I maintained my podium position and set my sights on Ralf. He is one of the very few Formula 1 drivers I never really cared for; in fact I'd go so far as to say that I thought he was a bit of a wally. Why? Well, during the 1997 Italian Grand Prix he was trying to overtake me going past the pits, and as we approached the first chicane he pulled right into my path and left me with nowhere to go. He then clipped me, which sent me flying into the tyre-wall at over 200mph. Needless to say I wasn't too happy. How I wasn't seriously injured I'll never know. After the race his team boss at the time, Eddie Jordan, ordered him to apologize to me, which he did, but with a big smirk on his face as if to say 'I couldn't give a shit'. If you mess up like he did you have to do the right thing. Ralf always struck me as rather spoilt, though, so for him it was probably normal behaviour.

With fifteen laps remaining Giancarlo lost control of his Benetton, which elevated Michael Schumacher's brother to first with me just behind him. As the largely German crowd began going crazy at the prospect of witnessing a home win, I started dreaming about what I was going to do with my magnum of champagne on the podium: spray it in his face or shove it up his . . . And then, less than a lap later, poor old Ralf suffered a puncture, and after pitting he rejoined the race in fourth, a good fifty seconds behind the eventual race winner.

Me.

I've watched the race back, and as I come round the final right-hander, Jackie can be seen hugging members of the team, draped in a Scottish flag, and when the camera switches back to me I'm pumping my fist in the air. The Germans might have been disappointed but there was a Scotsman and a small but imperfectly formed Essex boy who were anything but. Three races before the end of his career as a team owner, Jackie Stewart had done the impossible and won a Grand Prix. What's more, I'd helped him to that victory by driving an almost perfect race after a pretty tough season, so it was a special day all round. I did feel sorry for Rubens, who had been at Stewart since the beginning and, as I said, was very close to Jackie and Paul. Had they been able to choose which driver won their only Grand Prix they'd have naturally gone for him; but with both of us on the podium that day – Rubens finished third, behind Trulli – there wasn't really much not to like. Jackie said afterwards that the win meant more to him than any of his own, which, bearing in mind who he is and what he achieved, is pretty special.

There are two questions people usually ask when they meet me: who is your all-time favourite driver, and what's the best race you've ever driven? Before I get on to the latter, which forms the next part of my story, let me just answer the former.

The first drivers I remember being a fan of were James Hunt and Niki Lauda, but that was more by reputation. They were the ones everybody used to talk about and that was when I was getting interested in Formula 1, so they were a good place to start. In the mid-to-late 1970s you used to get these Tag Heuer helmet clocks – a different one for each F1 driver – and for Christmas one year I remember asking Mum and Dad for Niki's. Come Christmas morning I was like a coiled spring, but when I opened the box, instead of seeing the name Niki Lauda, I saw Mario Andretti. No offence, Mario, but at the time I was following an English playboy and a highly dedicated Austrian driver who gave absolutely nothing away, not a fast, cheery Italian-American. I ended up buying a Niki clock on eBay a few years ago so now I have them both, and I must say I've grown to love Mario as I do Niki and James.

The first driver I remember liking purely because of the way he drove – and I've already mentioned him – was Gilles Villeneuve, a man Jody Scheckter regards as the fastest driver in the history of motor racing, and I think I agree with him. Villeneuve always drove on the edge. It didn't matter what he was driving or in what race or circumstances, that was what he did, and there was no compromise. I remember seeing him drive back to the pits once after getting a puncture and instead of driving like he probably should have, he went flat out. First the tyre flapped around a bit, then it started to fall off, and by the time he reached the garage there were enough sparks flying around to fill a foundry. I can recall thinking, *That's exactly what I'd do!* Sod protecting the car, all he was thinking about was getting out there and racing again. In that respect he was far from being the perfect driver, but boy was he the perfect racer.

Gilles' attitude was never, ever give up and always drive without fear of the unknown. World championships never seemed to be a priority with him, or even races for that matter. It was almost as if he were programmed to attempt to set lap record after lap record, and if he didn't manage it he'd try again; if he did, he would simply attempt to break it again. He was definitely the first driver I wanted to *be* as opposed to the first driver I simply admired. When I think of how Gilles died it always reminds me of what Bruce McLaren wrote after the death of the American driver Timmy Mayer: 'To do something well is so worthwhile that to die trying to do it better cannot be foolhardy. It would be a waste of life to do nothing with one's ability, for I feel that life is measured in achievement, not in years alone.' I'm not sure if Gilles ever read that quote but I'm pretty sure he'd have agreed with it.

The older I got the more fascinated I became with that kind of 'living on the edge' mentality. It was something I always tried to emulate, especially in my early days. A few years ago Jacques Villeneuve told me a story about a bet he and Ricardo Zonta had when they were driving for BAR. They were at Spa and wanted to see who could go through Eau Rouge flat out. Jacques tried first, but when he got to the top he lost it and slammed into the barrier. After that Ricardo had a go, and when he got to the top he also lost it and slammed into the barrier. I don't know how much the bet was for, but that wasn't the point. They were trying to get to the very edge of what was possible, and what makes you do that is wanting to know what lies beyond. It's all part of exploring the unknown, and to do it while you're only partly in control is addictive.

I remember doing something similar myself in Japan after my first stint at Benetton. I'm pretty sure it was with Thomas Danielsson, although I can't say for certain, but during qualifying we had a bet to see who could go off at the first corner without actually hitting the barrier. Looking back, it was a daft thing to do, but the adrenalin you felt was just spellbinding. Pleasure and terror in equal measure, you might say. We both managed to come off without making contact with the barrier, and I missed it by just a few centimetres. Pure ecstasy!

A few years before that, when I was racing in the Formula Ford 2000 Championship, I remember trying to demonstrate to Mike and the mechanics how fast we should be going through Dingle Dell at Brands Hatch. As I'm sure you can recall, that car was very uncompetitive, and I think out of frustration one day I said, 'Right then, I'm going to drive through Dingle Dell at the same speed as the Van Diemens and the Reynards and you see what happens.' So I stood them all on the inside of Dingle Dell, drove through at the same speed as the others, and ended up going straight into the barrier. Even though I knew

I'd crash, that didn't register for a single second. I was trying to make a point. Did I also get a kick out of it? Massively! In fact, if I could have done it a second time, just to make sure, I would have. Some drivers are far more calculated, people like the aforementioned Jackie Stewart and the great Alain Prost. There are a few drivers who still have that gung-ho ingredient – Lewis Hamilton, Fernando Alonso, Romain Grosjean and Max Verstappen spring immediately to mind – but there are so many restrictions these days that the opportunities are few and far between.

Anyway, on to question number two.

After the European Grand Prix, we made our way to Sepang for the inaugural Malaysian Grand Prix, which was the penultimate race of the 1999 season. This race produced a volcano of emotions for me, as in addition to all the excitement of driving a brand-new circuit and going there off the back of a win, it was also the only time since the accident that I experienced a sense of complete oneness with a racing car, that feeling of effortless synergy that I honestly thought had gone for ever. Why it happened there I have no idea, and it only stayed with me for that one weekend. Perhaps it was a reward for winning the Grand Prix: one last race without being hampered by any of the injuries or the baggage I'd accumulated. I know that sounds far-fetched, but both qualifying and the race itself had this kind of ethereal quality to them, almost as if I'd been taken over by the old me. There was no pain in my feet or ankles, and all the thoughts, concerns and worries I normally carried with me at the start of a race weekend were absent. I was free, for the first time in over eleven years.

Qualifying for the race went brilliantly, and the unfamiliarity of the Sepang International Circuit complemented my mood and situation perfectly. Everything felt new and nothing fazed me. I qualified fifth in the end, behind the Ferraris and the McLarens, and was less than four-tenths off Mika who was in fourth. I remember feeling a tiny bit put out by this but I honestly don't think I could have squeezed another thousandth out of that car. I was at my peak again, and enjoying every second.

What's slightly frustrating about that weekend is that I don't remember much about the race; even watching the highlights has failed to refresh my memory, which makes me think that perhaps I did become possessed. It was definitely far less tactical than the previous Grand Prix, for me anyway, and after DC went out with a fuel problem on lap 14 it was left to Michael Schumacher, Eddie Irvine, Mika Häkkinen and me to battle it out between us. The actual details might elude me but my God, I felt confident, and, watching it back, there was an urgency to my driving I hadn't noticed before, yet at the same time I was as smooth as a cashmere codpiece. There's a theory that all the best drivers in the world look like they're driving at about 50mph, which is what I think Jackie was alluding to when he suggested I try and be smooooooooth. Well, if that is what he meant, I certainly managed it that day. I may even have watched those highlights more than once.

With two laps to go before the end of the race I was running third behind Eddie and Michael and I had Mika right behind me. I'd been fending off his amorous advances for about ten laps or so, and given the fact he was the reigning world champion and fighting to keep the title, I'd done a bloody good job. If there was anyone from my past who I could have chosen to be in a dogfight with at that particular moment, Mika would have been top of my list, partly because he was the world champion and therefore the best Formula 1 had to offer, but also because he's such a nice guy. Nice guy or not, that horrible Finnish swine pushed me into making a small mistake at turn nine, which meant that he managed to get past me and bag that final podium place. I didn't begrudge him it one little bit as he was four points behind Eddie Irvine at the time with one race to go, so every point mattered. Mika went on to secure the championship in Japan, beating Eddie by just two points, and although that extra point he got from me didn't win him the title, I like to think that my ineptitude went some way towards preparing him for the final push.

With Rubens finishing one place behind me in fifth, we bagged five points between us in Malaysia. Given that the season was reaching its climax and there was still so much to play for, that was a bloody good show, so the high the Stewart team had been on since Germany was sustained for a while longer. These were to be Stewart Grand Prix's last ever points, though. By the time we got to Japan, where I finished seventh and Rubens eighth, the synergy and oneness had gone, never to be seen again, and the post-Brands Johnny had returned. I wasn't too disappointed, in fact I was relieved to feel normal again. After lowering myself gingerly into the cockpit before first practice at Suzuka the first thing I noticed were my bloody feet. My God, they were sore, but instead of them reminding me of all the negative things that had befallen me, which is what they usually did, they now made me think of all the positive things that had happened, and those final three races with Stewart, not to mention the conclusion to the Constructors' Championship, were up there with some of the best. In the end we finished fourth, behind Ferrari, McLaren and Jordan, and in front of Williams, Benetton and Sauber, which for an independent team barely three years old was an unbelievable achievement.

While Rubens and I had been busy racing, Jackie and Paul had been busy talking to Ford, who were interested in buying the team. Long before the 1999 season came to an end a deal was announced with Ford planning to rebrand the team Jaguar Racing. The new regime, which included the likes of Wolfgang

Reitzle, certainly talked a good game, and in addition to keeping Gary Anderson on to design the new car they brought in Eddie Irvine, fresh from his heroics at Ferrari, with Rubens going in the opposite direction.

Despite finishing the season strongly, I'd come to a point in my F1 career where I felt like I needed constantly to prove myself to other people, which took away most of the enjoyment and left me with a little bit of a chip on my shoulder. The fact is I had too much baggage, good and bad, and that hindered my ability to focus fully on the racing side. I was thirty-five and I'd now been racing competitively for well over twenty years. What I should have done at the end of 1999 was hang up my helmet and leave the scene on a high, but that's easier said than done. One of the hardest parts of any sporting career is knowing when to give up, but what's even harder is accepting the fact and acting on it. Formula 1, if you haven't already realized, can be pretty addictive. I knew deep down that it was over at the end of 1999, but I suppressed the notion and carried on. My entire career – everything I had ever done professionally behind the wheel of a car – had been built on a foundation of pure determination and a dogged refusal to give in, so even when I knew that walking away was the right thing to do, it was diametrically opposed to each and every one of my natural instincts.

Perhaps predictably, my final season in Formula 1 was a poor one. Instead of building on the progress that had been made at Stewart, in 2000 the new team floundered somewhat and ended up finishing ninth in the Constructors' Championship with just 4 points. Gary's new car, the Jaguar R1, wasn't a big improvement and suffered from some engine problems and a recurring glitch with the oil system. It was fast-ish when it worked, but that wasn't very often, and the best I could manage all season was a seventh in Austria and the same in Japan.

Ironically, my worst experience that year happened at the same location as my best the previous season, in Malaysia. It was the final race of the 2000 campaign, and of my F1 career, and after my seventh in Japan I was at least hoping for the same again, perhaps even to get into the points. But by this time neither my heart nor my head was in it and my addiction to a sport which had given me so much pleasure since 1989 had all but disappeared. I hated not enjoying Formula 1: being involved was nothing less than a privilege and I should have been grateful, not resentful. I knew I still wanted to drive, but it had to be in a new environment, somewhere I wasn't seen as yesterday's man (which I have to admit I was in F1), and somewhere I didn't feel like I had to justify my presence on the grid to every Tom, Dick or Harry who looked at me not as Johnny Herbert, experienced racing driver, but Mr Damaged Goods (which, once again, I suppose I was).

I'm possibly overdramatizing this a little bit, but you know what it's like in these situations: there's a snowball effect, and the one or two people who *have* looked at you strangely or questioned your desire or ability suddenly become twenty or thirty. I was tired, to be honest with you; tired of fighting against myself and tired of fighting *for* myself, which was my own fault for not confiding in anybody. My wife and daughters had suffered a bit through 2000 and I don't mind admitting I'd been a right royal pain in the bum at times. All I wanted to do now was race with as few preconceived ideas, perceptions or opinions as possible and dedicate myself anew to motorsport, whether it be endurance racing, touring cars or miniature bloody scooters.

The whole thing came to an end on lap 49 of that 2000 Malaysian Grand Prix when I suffered a suspension failure, and then after losing my rear wing I ended up ploughing into a tyre-wall at about 150mph. It's a pity I was retiring as I was getting good at that particular trick! The worst bit about the crash was the fact that I had to be carried out of the cockpit by the marshals, just as I'd had to be carried into the cockpit at Rio back in March 1989. This rather gloomy little irony wasn't lost on me, and thank God I had my helmet on because as they lifted me out the tears were streaming down my face. It wasn't the first time I'd cried in a Formula 1 car but it was the first time I'd cried tears of sadness and regret rather than simply of pain. You see, even a happy little man like me who'd been known to laugh off having his feet mutilated isn't completely immune to having a moment.

It wasn't the end to my F1 career I'd been hoping for, but it was the end all the same. When the fact eventually dawned on me, shortly after I left the medical centre, I felt like the weight of a thousand elephants had been lifted from my shoulders. My time in that medical centre had been quite a strange experience as when the local doctors removed my overalls to examine me and caught a glimpse of my feet – both of which are permanently deformed, the left particularly badly – everyone in the room jumped back in disgust, and one of them almost fainted. There was no pressure on me any more, though – I was now an *ex*-Formula 1 driver. As Michael, DC and Rubens celebrated their podium finishes with their teams and their families, I was able to float back to the garage unnoticed and start saying my goodbyes.

I'd announced my retirement from F1 a few months earlier. The team had even put on a little *This Is Your Life*-style leaving party for me at the start of the weekend featuring people like Jackie and Paul, Murray Walker, Rubens, Eddie Irvine, Giancarlo Fisichella and several others. It still felt strange, though, saying goodbye. Very strange, in fact. Most importantly of all, however, it felt right, and because of this I had no regrets and am now able to look back on my time in Formula 1 with a sense of pride and gratitude. As I said earlier in the book, I've been labelled unlucky many times over the years – thousands of times, probably. But I am a lucky man, make no mistake about it. My eleven years working at the heart of this amazing sport – the sport I love more than any other – are testament to that.

Seventeen

THE CLOSEST THING I had to a plan, or indeed an ambition, after leaving Formula 1 was to drive in the Indianapolis 500. Graham Hill had been the last British driver to win the race back in 1966, the year after Jim Clark, but since then we'd drawn a blank. Nigel had been unlucky once or twice but had still won the IndyCar World Series so I didn't feel too sorry for him. The 500, a Grand Prix and Le Mans had always been at the top of my 'bucket race list', so to speak, and there was only one left to fulfil.

Gerhard Berger, who was working for BMW at the time, had already approached me about becoming the Williams test driver for 2001, and although I was extremely flattered to be asked, I was in no doubt that I needed to be away from the sport for a while. I also wanted to continue racing full-time, so if I had said yes it would have been for all the wrong reasons and I don't think I'd have enjoyed it. (Incidentally, at Sky Sports F1 during our coverage of the 2016 British Grand Prix we talked to Gerhard and he got through an entire interview without swearing. I don't know what it is with these Austrian racing drivers but they do tend to turn the air blue the moment a microphone appears. Gerhard's word of choice begins with an f, by the way. Niki Lauda's starts with a b and rhymes with the words 'full skit'.)

Another rather pleasant approach that came my way towards the end of 2000 was from the BBC. They were planning to relaunch *Top Gear* in 2002 with somebody called . . . Clarkson, was it? And they were looking for co-presenters. Knowing what I do now about working in television, and knowing how popular the programme went on to become, I should perhaps have entertained the idea a little bit longer than I did. Then again, we may never have seen the classic Clarkson–May–Hammond line-up and that would be unthinkable. I'm pretty sure they didn't want me for the Stig, as has been suggested, as I have a feeling that my height and my limp might well have given the game away.

So, the first thing I did when the season had finished and everything had calmed down was go over to the States and speak to one or two team owners. My agent had been out there earlier in the year and there was some interest. Whether it would still be there now he couldn't say, but I was still willing to go over and give them a bit of the old flannel.

I'm afraid that my legendary charm was completely lost on our American cousins. I arrived all guns blazing, banging the Herbert drum, but they didn't want to know. In fact I'd go so far as to say they couldn't wait for me to leave. Was it bad breath? I wondered. Whiffy pits? I'd turned on the Herbert charm big-time, and I was not without experience. And there, I'm afraid, lay the problem. According to one or two journalists, the sport wasn't keen on being seen as a retirement home for ex-Formula 1 drivers, and although I was disappointed by this, I could understand the reasoning. It wouldn't be impossible to get a drive, they said, but it was going to take a lot more than just a cosy chat with an owner. I'd probably have to look at it long-term.

Come 1 January 2001, then, I didn't have a single race arranged for the year ahead. But enquiries were now coming in thick and fast. The first call that made me sit up a bit was from Thierry

Boutsen, who was now helping out a Florida-based sports car racing team run by Kaye Wilson called Champion Racing. He wanted to know if I'd be interested in doing Le Mans with the team in an Audi R8, and I bit his hand off.

You know how I hate blowing my own trumpet, but during that 2001 Le Mans I was at times in the wet twelve seconds a lap faster than the two works Audis (which eventually finished first and second), and it felt like 1991 again, just with fewer flames spilling from the car and more hydration. Unfortunately, the driver who went in after me burned the clutch out and spun off so we never got back out again. My God, it was good to be back, though. I'd been so preoccupied trying to get a drive in IndyCar and at the Indy500 that I'd forgotten how much I loved endurance racing.

Ironically, it was this new relationship with Champion Racing that finally got me a drive in America, but more on that in a second. First I've got to tell you what I did at the start of the year, before all this came about, and it includes me becoming Britain's fastest racing car driver.

My first concrete offer in 2001 came from my old boss Tom Walkinshaw who owned and ran the Arrows Formula 1 team. He, like Gerhard Berger, wanted me as a test and development driver, but because I'd still only had about three months out of F1, I wasn't keen. I explained all this to Tom but he looked at things in a different way. 'Surely this is the perfect solution?' he said. 'You get to drive the car all day but without any of the pressure or the politics. And you can still race elsewhere and near as damn it full-time.' He had a point. It would only be a part-time position, which would leave me to race at Le Mans and perhaps in America.

'OK, then,' I said to him, 'I'll do it.'

Tom was right, it was the perfect solution, and when I arrived at Silverstone on 3 March to test the Asiatech-powered A22 I felt as good as I ever had turning up to a circuit. OK, I wasn't racing, but I knew that would still happen somewhere down the line so it didn't bother me. Until then I think it's fair to say I'd always had a kind of love-hate relationship with that side of the sport. It was something I found interesting yet at the same time I considered it a little bit of a necessary evil. You need patience to test effectively, and while I was racing in F1 that was something in which I was often found lacking. Now both my situation and my priorities had changed, which meant I was able to give the job my full attention.

About a month after my first test for Arrows, I finally got the chance to drive an open-wheeled car around an oval track, but not where you might think. It took place on this side of the Atlantic and rendered me, according to a couple of motorsport journalists, Britain's fastest racing car driver. The venue was the newly opened Rockingham Motor Speedway in Northamptonshire which included a 1.48-mile banked oval. It is to this day the fastest circuit in Europe, and Nigel Mansell had set the first lap record (33.008s) just after it had opened. As part of its inaugural year, the owners of Rockingham were planning to host an IndyCar race there in September, and to help promote the event one of the American teams taking part in the race, Dale Coyne Racing, were coming over to do a test for Firestone. I can't remember who, but somebody asked me if I wanted to take part in the test (probably to add a bit of glamour to proceedings) and I said yes. In addition to their Lola-Ford Champ Car, the team also brought with them their star driver, a chap called Alex Barron, and after going out twice and changing the tyre compounds and fuel levels to simulate all the different race conditions, Alex recorded a best time of 27.7s. Never having driven one of these cars before, that at least gave me something to aim for, and on my first run I managed to match Alex's time. *Not bad*, I thought. *I could get used to this.* On my second run I managed to beat Alex's time and went into full-on smug mode. Modesty naturally forbids me from divulging the exact margin of my triumph. Let's just say it was somewhere between 0.459s and 0.458s and with an average speed of around 198.223mph.

It was such a thrill, like an unremitting adrenalin rush with no let-up. What surprised me was how easy it was to adapt to. I was sure I'd be spending the majority of the test simply finding my feet and wasn't expecting to get anywhere near Alex. For starters I thought the speed might scare me a bit, not to mention the wall; I'd assumed these things alone would require the majority of my attention. Not a bit of it. After just a few laps I felt completely at home and was able to hold my speed and concentrate on making the track work for me, using the banking and the undulations. By the end of the test I think I'd become slightly obsessed by all things IndyCar, and had a drive materialized in 2001 I might even have become a pay driver. Actually, on second thoughts . . .

After driving for Champion Racing at Le Mans – and, it has to be said, enjoying every second – the team's owner, Dave Maraj, asked me if I'd like to drive for the team in the second half of the 2001 American Le Mans Series, partnering Andy Wallace. American Le Mans was hugely popular at the time and with my love of endurance racing now officially back on I accepted his offer and packed my bags. Once again I was going to be driving an Audi R8, and with just six races to worry about between July and October that would give me plenty of time to try and satisfy my IndyCar ambitions.

One person who'd been very helpful in this department was a man called Roger Penske, who is a phenomenally successful team owner in the States with a record sixteen Indy500 wins to his name. He'd dabbled in Formula 1 over the years, both as a driver in the early 1960s and as an owner in the 1970s, and we got on really well. He didn't seem to mind the fact that I was a badly injured retired Formula 1 driver approaching his forties and ended up putting me in touch with all kinds of people.

One of these was a man called John Mecom III, whose father, John Jr, had been the winning team owner when Graham Hill won the Indy500. He and his business partner, Jim Rathmann Jr, whose father had won the Indy500 as a driver in 1960, were looking at putting a team together for the 2002 season for their team, Heritage Motorsports, and they wanted me to drive for them. Setting up a new team in any major motorsport requires a massive amount of time and resources but they seemed to have both in abundance. They even went to the press, I remember, and when a test was arranged at the Kentucky Speedway that August it all started to feel very real. The car was an Infiniti-powered G Force chassis, the same model that Bruno Junqueira had driven to a fifth place at that year's Indy500, and the conditions were exactly the same as they had been at the IRL race the day before. I spent about three hours out on the track, and even though I'd accumulated less than a day's worth of experience, I still managed to post a speed of just over 214mph, which would have qualified me on pole for the previous day's race. Age didn't come into this at all. I felt about twenty again, and the more I drove IndyCar the better it felt and the more I wanted.

About a week later Heritage booked me into another test, this time at Indianapolis, and once again I flourished, posting a top speed of 222.366mph and finishing the day. I remember leaving there feeling like I had after my first test in F1, and the next day Heritage pushed my mood higher still by asking me if I'd be interested in driving for them at the Chevy 500. The Chevy 500 is the finale of the IRL season and takes place at the Texas Motor Speedway in Fort Worth. I wasn't expecting to race in either CART (the Champ Car World

Series) or the IRL before 2002, if at all, so it was the best possible news.

Five days before the race the World Trade Center attacks of 11 September took place. In addition to ending so many people's lives and ruining thousands of others', the atrocity put everything that had ever befallen me in motorsport well and truly into perspective. After that, every sporting event in the country was pushed back a few weeks, and when the new date for the Chevy 500 was announced, it clashed with Petit Le Mans (part of the American Le Mans Series), which I was driving for Champion, so basically that was that. It was also the end of the Heritage deal, although I forget why. Once again, it was all chicken feed compared to what had happened in New York, and when I finally boarded the plane home towards the end of October I left a country that was grieving and in a state of shock.

When I arrived back in the States in February 2002 I was amazed at how the country had pulled itself together, and I felt compelled to honour that by trying to show the same kind of spirit on the track. I'd been employed by two teams thus far: Champion Racing again, for races two to ten in the American Le Mans Series; and the Audi works team, for both Le Mans and 12 Hours of Sebring, which was the first race on the American Le Mans calendar. Sebring came first, taking place on 16 March, and myself, Rinaldo Capello and Christian Pescatori finished first, a lap in front of the Champion team featuring Andy Wallace, Jan Lammers and the man who'd be partnering me this year at the team, Stefan Johansson. It was a great way to start the year but I now had over two months to wait before my next race, and that could mean only one thing – lots of meetings about IndyCar!

Finding support for this year had been a lot more difficult

than in 2001 so instead of trying to bag a race or two in either CART or the IRL, I decided to put all my efforts into trying to qualify for the Indy500. That was still my ultimate dream, and what had happened with Heritage (or rather what had not happened) had done nothing to dampen my enthusiasm. I had a backer, Keith Duesenberg, and would be driving a Chevrolet-powered Dallara. The only trouble was that qualifying for the Indy500 took place over the two weeks leading up to the race itself, and on the second of those weekends I'd be two thousand miles away at the Sonoma Raceway in California competing in round two of the American Le Mans Series. It was a nice prospect, as for that particular race I was going to be partnering Tom Kristensen who, at thirty-four, was already one of the all-time greats of Le Mans. This meant that pole day, which took place during the first weekend, was my only chance, and even if I did well, there was still no guarantee I'd qualify.

They used to have a very strange qualifying system at the Indy500 and it all culminated in something called 'Bump Day', which took place on the last day of the second weekend. Basically, out of the thirty-three cars that had qualified for the race, only the top nine were safe, the remaining twenty-four being at the mercy of this rather bizarre but none the less entertaining finale. The cars that hadn't qualified for the race had one day to post a time better than one of the qualified entrants, and every time one managed it, whoever was lying thirty-third would be 'bumped' off. They could always try re-qualifying by posting an even better time, but whoever was lying thirty-third at 5.55 p.m. on Sunday would be suffering from some serious squeaky bumitis.

As it was, Bump Day made absolutely no difference to my qualifying as all three of my attempts had to be aborted due to various engine problems. I was devastated. I'd spent something like forty hours over the previous three days on aeroplanes flying

to and from tests and I'd thought and dreamed about nothing
else for months. I phoned Dave Maraj at Champion just to see if
there was any chance of him letting me do the second weekend
but he needed me, so once again that was that.

For some reason the Indy500 and I were never destined to be,
and I don't mind admitting that it took me a long time to get
over it. If I hadn't had the guts to do it, like some drivers, or I
simply hadn't taken to the sport, then fine, I'd have been OK.
I loved it, though, and would have given my eye teeth, not to
mention my Tag Heuer Mario Andretti clock, to have lined up
as one of the thirty-three at the Indy500.

Try not to feel too sorry for me, because when I wasn't flying
around ovals at 220mph I was having a fantastic time racing sports
cars all over America and at Le Mans. I'll come to Le Mans in a
moment, but first I want to go into a little bit more detail about
my time racing for Champion – or should I say getting drunk
with J. J. Lehto. To be fair, that was only in 2003, but it was quite
a year. In total I spent four years racing for Champion in the
American Le Mans Series, from 2001 to 2004, and in addition
to six wins, including that victory at the 12 Hours of Sebring, I
managed a further fourteen podiums and finished fourth in the
championship in both 2002 and 2003.

Dave Maraj runs the biggest Porsche dealership in America
and is probably one of the most passionate team owners I've
ever worked for. He had the same approach to endurance racing
as Mazda had in 1990 and 1991, which is why he hired a lot of
ex-Formula 1 drivers like me and JJ. He'd invested heavily in the
cars, about $5 million maybe, and it was all his own money. What
I used to like most of all about Champion was the fact that come
race weekend, everyone who worked either for the team or the
dealership – whether as a salesman, a mechanic or a receptionist
– would come together as one and just enjoy the racing. There
was no hierarchy as such, just a bunch of people who did their

jobs well and loved being together. It was my foundation stone, I think, as, because I felt happy and comfortable, I was able to do a good job for Dave as well as go off and do other things.

The vast majority of the races in the American Le Mans Series happened at established circuits like Sebring, but there was one race in Miami that took place on a street circuit that went through the centre of the city. It was only held twice, I believe, in 2002 and 2003, but in the second of those years we did a very good impression of what had happened to Jos Verstappen at Hockenheim back in 1994. Many of you will remember this. When he came into the pits the refuelling guy had some problems attaching the nozzle to the car and petrol went all over the place. Then, when he tried to pull the nozzle away from the car, some fuel spilled on to the engine and within a millisecond it was a blazing inferno. They managed to put the fire out in a couple of seconds and Jos was unhurt, but it looked astonishing. Well, that's almost exactly what happened to JJ and me in Miami, except our story's even more eventful.

We were leading the race at the time, and by quite some distance, and when JJ came in to hand over to me, the pit team set about refuelling the car and changing the tyres. When JJ got out, I jumped in, then he set about strapping me in, which is what happens during a changeover. While he was doing this the refuelling rig went a bit mad and spat all over the car, including, of course, the engine. Fortunately for me only half of the car set alight which meant I was able to unstrap myself and get out.

'No, no, stay in the car,' said JJ, and he began pushing me back in.

'But it's on bloody fire!' I screamed.

'No, no, no, you'll be OK,' he insisted, as calm as you like.

This all happened in just a few seconds but I remember seeing the flames spread slowly around the car, and while JJ's standing there with his hand on my crutch looking, quite frankly, a little bit bored, I was on the verge of being burned alive. Mr Lehto was actually right to restrain me as a second or so later the fire was out and I was on my way to winning the race, but at the time I was terrified.

As well as winning the race that day, we made it on to CNN's 'Play of the Day' in the evening, but that was only the start of it. I said 'getting drunk' with JJ earlier, didn't I? You see, what I should have said was 'getting absolutely paralytic'. After watching ourselves on CNN, JJ said to me, 'You do trust me don't you, Johnny? I mean, you do *really* trust me?'

I thought, *God Almighty, what's he going to do?*

Fortunately, all he had in mind was a drink – although the drink in question was a pint of vodka each with a drop of orange. It was horrible, but he downed it in one and then stood there and made me drink every last drop of mine. After more vodka we decided it was time for a swim and broke into the swimming pool at the hotel where we were staying. The last thing I recall seeing before passing out was a naked Finn standing on the edge of the pool sideways on and then just falling in. Some of the dreams I had that night were on a par with the ones I'd had in hospital after the accident, and when I woke up the next morning I vowed never to watch CNN or drink vodka with JJ again.

JJ and I got on like a house on fire – or should I say car? He'd had a good run in Formula 1 back in the early 1990s but, after breaking his neck during a test, he'd been forced to retire from F1 and so moved over to sports cars. By the time I started working with him he'd already won Le Mans and would go on to win it again in 2005. He's Finnish, like Mika, but he's like the badly behaved older brother, and for whatever reason we just clicked. Driving together as a team wasn't easy, though, as he's about six feet tall whereas I'm . . . not. This meant that I had to sit on a cushion when I was driving and even then could only just see over the steering wheel, and he had all kinds of problems when it came to the pedals. That sums up sports car racing, though: it's all about compromise.

The one other 'Johnny & JJ' escapade I'd like to tell you about – or perhaps I should say the one I'm prepared to tell you about – involves a swim in Lake Michigan followed by some pole-dancing. We were at a track called Road America in Wisconsin, which is just a few blocks away from the lake, and had just won a race called the Road America 500. JJ and I were in buoyant mood because of our victory and after drinking several cans of something brown and liquidy we decided to go for a dip. Starkers, of course. The sans clothes bit was JJ's idea but I was game, and after downing a few more cans we disrobed and went to explore some of the fifty-eight thousand square kilometres of water that lay before us.

After about ten minutes swimming around in the lake I turned to say something to JJ but he was nowhere to be seen. *Bloody hell*, I thought, *the silly bastard's drowned!* After a while I started flapping a bit and began calling out his name. 'JJ? JJ? JJ? Where are you, JJ?'

'I'm here,' came a voice.

I looked round and there he was, bobbing up and down about an inch from my face.

'You absolute—'

'Now, now, now, Johnny,' said JJ, 'don't get overexcited. Let's swim back and have another beer.'

What a thing to do to somebody. But that's JJ.

After getting our kit on we made our way back to the club where the rest of the teams were, and by this time we were in quite an advanced state of refreshment. But then so was everybody else, and once JJ threw himself into the mix things became quite riotous. Not wanting to be left out of the proceedings, I decided to put on a little bit of entertainment. The question being, what? There was no stage or anything, just a pole in the middle of the bar that went from the floor up to the ceiling.

That's it! I thought. *I'll put on a display of pole-dancing!*

At the time I was talking to one of the mechanics at Champion as well as to his girlfriend, and because we'd been having a bit of a laugh I decided to ask if I could borrow a piece of her clothing.

'You mean my underwear?' she asked.

'If you don't mind,' I said.

'Here, try this,' she said, and out of her handbag she pulled a leopard-skin-patterned thong, pretty much like the one DC wears on Channel 4.

'Thank you very much,' I beamed, and off I ran to the toilets to change into my costume.

It's thinking back to times like this that I thank God we didn't have mobile phone cameras or social media, because had they been in existence at the time I think it's safe to say I'd have been working for Peter Stringfellow now, not Rupert Murdoch. The show I put on was sensational, and by the time I'd finished gyrating in front of my adoring public, a total of three dollars had been stuffed inside my thong. What happened after that I don't quite remember, but from my audience's point of view I think I'd provided a repulsive end to what had been an otherwise perfect day.

After driving well but failing to finish Le Mans with Champion Racing in 2001, I had four more attempts at winning the race for a second time before finally calling it a day in 2007. This included a run of three consecutive runners-up positions in 2002, 2003 and 2004, the most memorable of them 2003 when I partnered David Brabham and Mark Blundell in the stunning Bentley Speed 8. I've often cited the Bentley Speed as the best car I've ever driven, and although I fluctuate from time to time, it's certainly the best-looking. As well as winning the race in

2003 (although not with us at the wheel, more's the pity) it won all kinds of awards. If you've never seen the car, Google it now.

The other Bentley, which was driven by Tom Kristensen, Rinaldo Capello and Guy Smith, qualified on pole with us alongside it, and after just one lap our headrest came unstuck, which meant David had to make an early unscheduled stop. After that we suffered a battery problem that we couldn't get to the bottom of, so every three or four hours, regardless of what was going on, we had to come in for a new one. Each one of these cost us thirty or forty seconds, and even though we always managed to make the time up, we were always dragged back again. In the end we lost by a lap, which was so, so frustrating, but that's Le Mans. We'd also lost by a lap the previous year, and by just twenty seconds in 2004. That one was probably the most annoying as it was purely down to bad luck as opposed to mistakes. I only wanted one more win. Just one!

The last bit of serious racing I did before joining the team at Sky Sports F1 was the short-lived but extremely enjoyable Speedcar Series which took place primarily in the UAE and south-east Asia between 2008 and 2009. It was like a Middle East version of NASCAR, I suppose, and because there was a lot of money about at the time, the organizers decided to fill the cars with as many former F1 drivers as possible. They did a good job in that respect: in that first season alone they had, in order of popularity, ME, Christian Danner, Heinz-Harald Frentzen, Gianni Morbidelli, Pedro Lamy, Ukyo Katayama, Alex Yoong, Stefan Johansson, J. J. Lehto (God help us), Jacques Villeneuve and Jean Alesi. That's not a bad line-up, is it? You must have about five hundred Grands Prix worth of experience there, and to top it off we all got on really well.

Jean and I did the majority of the testing as well as all the initial media so it was like being back at Sauber again, just with slightly less refined machinery. The cars themselves were probably the rawest I've ever driven, and in addition to the 600bhp V8 engines you had an H-box gear-box, a huge steering wheel and a lot of noise. At the start of the season it was absolute carnage, crashes everywhere. We all treated it more like banger racing. Pretty soon, though, people realized they weren't going to earn any cash that way, so after the first meeting we all cottoned on and began taking it a bit more seriously.

There were ten races in all, spread over five different locations, and four of these were support races for the Malaysian and Bahrain Grands Prix. I've heard that Bernie used to stop his poker games so he could come and watch us, and to be fair, the racing was often awesome. It was very close and there was always plenty of banging and argy-bargy going on. Yes, we were all mates, but nobody wanted to lose so there was as much competition on our grid as there was anywhere else, including F1.

When it got to the business end of the season there were three drivers in contention: me, the Frenchman David Terrien, and a super-fast German driver called Uwe Alzen. To clinch the championship I had to win both races at the final meeting in Dubai, as did David, whereas Uwe only had to finish in the top six. I managed to win the first race fairly easily, with David coming second and Uwe fourth. It was all down to the final race then, and after qualifying on pole I just had to pray that Uwe suffered a stinker. Luckily for me he clashed with Stefan Johansson and ended up finishing eleventh. This meant that I, John Paul Herbert III, became the inaugural Speedcar Series champion. Not that I knew it at the time. I hadn't a clue what had happened to Uwe, so when Luciano Secchi, one of the founders of Speedcar, came up and told me that I'd won, I thought he meant the race.

'Yes I know I've won the race,' I said, with mild indignation.

'No, Johnny, you've won the championship!' said Luciano, with his hands held aloft. 'Uwe finished eleventh.'

Never before in the history of motorsport has a driver of my diminutive stature made it on to the roof of a racing car as quickly as I did that day in Dubai. I went completely berserk, in fact. The last thing I'd won of any note was the European Le Mans Series back in 2004, which I'd driven after taking a break from American Le Mans, but Speedcar had been so much fun and I'd won it surrounded by all my old mates. The money was nice, I shall not lie, but competing against the likes of Jean, Jacques, JJ, Heinz-Harald and the rest of them, and having a laugh at the same time, was very special.

I came second in the 2009 Speedcar Series, losing to Gianni Morbidelli in the final race of the season by half a car. After that the money dried up and sadly the series folded. It was a shame really, because had it carried on I think I'd have kept on going over there for many years to come, as I'm sure would many of the other drivers. Those cars were so amazing though, almost agricultural, and that seemed to suit me. Believe it or not, the rear suspension was held on by chains, so when you were braking all you could hear in the back were these things rattling around. It made about as much noise as that V8 engine.

I did do one or two things after Speedcar but nothing where I was going to be particularly competitive so to me they don't really count. If the truth be told, once Speedcar came to an end I started to lose my desire to race, which I have to say surprised me somewhat. I'd always pictured myself carrying on until I dropped – the body weak but the spirit strong – and had been half expecting myself to appear in the inaugural Motability Scooter Grand Prix somewhere along the way.

I don't know what changed. I just woke up one morning and it had gone, the same way some of my ability had after the accident. I must admit, however, that I'm quite relieved it's all over. When I finally did hang up my helmet and take stock for a moment or two, I realized that I was absolutely knackered. I'd either been driving, talking about driving, thinking about driving, or travelling to do some driving every day for nearly forty years, and as much as I'd enjoyed myself I just couldn't do the first bit any more. These days I still do the talking, the thinking and the travelling bit, but apart from crashing hoverboards and going dune buggy racing with Lewis Hamilton and Nico Rosberg as part of a Sky Sports F1 piece, or driving to the shops or to an event, I've given up the driving bit for good. You wouldn't believe the difference it makes. In fact, as you'll see if you watch me on Sky, I'm probably in better shape now than I ever have been, although please take into account the fact that the camera puts on at least two stone.

By far the best thing about being retired is at last being able to spend time with my family, something that I'm afraid to say rarely happened while I was racing. My wife, Rebecca, who I first met during my Formula Ford days back in 1986, has been totally selfless over the years, and in addition to bringing up our two daughters almost singlehandedly has backed every decision I ever made as a racing driver. When our eldest daughter, Chloe, was born in 1990 I was away in Japan for much of that year trying to get my career back on track and Rebecca went through what can often be a very difficult time – not to mention one that should be shared with your partner – almost completely alone. We did manage to snatch a bit of time here and there, but that really was about it. In fact, not long after Chloe was born, I remember coming home from Japan, staying a few hours and then flying back. By the time Aimelia came along in 1992 I was at Lotus and although they were mixed days for me professionally, Rebecca always made sure there was a warm welcome when I arrived home and without that love and security there's no way I would have coped. It was always the same though, through every triumph and every hardship; home was always a haven (it still is) and was somewhere I could feel happy and safe regardless of what was going on in my professional life. Words alone cannot express the admiration I have for Rebecca, nor the love I feel for her, Chloe and Aimelia and catching up on all that lost time is something I'm savouring. They're my world and I'm a very lucky man.

I never thought I'd end up doing a book on my career, though, for the simple reason that I didn't think anyone would want to read it. Whether they do or not remains to be seen, but remembering all the stories and the characters I've met and then writing it all down has been a strangely therapeutic experience and I'm very glad I did it. The title of the book, *What Doesn't Kill You . . .*, obviously refers to the injuries I sustained and the fact that I gained strength from what I experienced. I'd add, though, that if you can also put a bit of a smile into the mix when you're going through the mill, perhaps even a little pole-dance here and there, it'll make you stronger still.

Acknowledgements

First of all I'd like to say a big thank you to James Hogg who has spent the last few months translating 'Broken Herbert' into the Queen's English, or something there or thereabouts. It's been quite a task. Two other people who deserve a round of applause here are Giles Elliott at Transworld and Tim Bates at Peters Fraser & Dunlop who helped bring the book to life. It's been a whole new experience for me and one that I've enjoyed.

Moving on to my day-to-day existence, I'd like to send my appreciation to Mr Benny Lawrence, my old buddy Mr John Hayes and everyone at Champions plc. Poor Benny has the unenviable task of trying to make sure I'm always in the right place at the right time and it can't be easy. We always get there in the end, don't we Benny?

From 1994 until 2014 I ran a charity karting day each year with a friend of mine called Roy Craig. We raised an awful lot of money over that time and had lots of fun, but it wouldn't have happened without you Roy and I'd like to express my gratitude.

Even though many are mentioned in this book, I would still like to say thank you to all the journalists who have supported me over the years. I don't know if it's quite the same in other sports, but in motor racing they and the people they write about every day very often become friends and regardless of how things were going I was always grateful for their support. I still am, in fact. I won't try and name them all at the risk of missing somebody out but they know who they are. Thank you, gentlemen.

All of the following feature very favourably within this book. Nevertheless, I think it necessary to acknowledge their contribution here too, as without any one of them my story would probably be very different. In order of appearance: my late uncle Pete, Bill Sisley, Mike Thompson, Eddie Jordan, Peter Collins, the late Ohashi-san, Dave Maraj, Peter Sauber and Sir Jackie Stewart. Thank you.

Moving back to the present day, the team at Sky Sports F1 is like a surrogate family and they make going to work a pleasure. I won't name check them all as it'll just inflate their egos but I love them dearly. Oh, go on then: Barney Francis, Martin Turner, Billy McGinty and the rest of the team behind the scenes, not forgetting my co-workers Simon, David, Natalie, Ted, Martin, Anthony, Rachel, Paul and Damon.

On a personal level, I'd first like to thank Stuart and Di Spiers, who, in addition to being godparents to our daughters, have been friends of ours for many years and we think the world of them. The same goes for Mark Perkins and Jane Allavena who, when we moved to Monaco, moved heaven to make sure we were happy and well looked after. You really couldn't wish for better friends.

Next I'd like to thank my mum and dad, who, all those years ago in Cornwall, saw a glimmer of talent, bought an old kart from a vicar, and backed me every step of the way. Love you both very much.

Finally I would like to pay tribute to my wife, Rebecca, and to our daughters, Chloe and Aimelia. Their patience and love over the years has known no bounds and regardless of what's been going on they've always been there for me. I'm so proud of them and can't tell you how grateful I am.

Picture Acknowledgements

All images have been supplied courtesy of the author unless otherwise stated.

First section

Page 1 (bottom left) photo supplied by Bill Sisley

Page 2 (1985 Formula Ford win), page 3 (Brands Hatch crash), both supplied courtesy of Sutton Images (www.suttonimages.com)

Pages 4, 5, 6 and 8 all © PA Photos as follows:

Silverstone race victory © Claire Mackintosh/EMPICS Sport

Celebratory kiss, podium, trophy, tambourine all © Steve Etherington/EMPICS Sport

Monza cornering, podium, dance all © Steve Etherington/EMPICS Sport

Briatore, Schumacher, Japan all © Steve Etherington/EMPICS Sport

Damon Hill, Nigel Mansell both © John Marsh/EMPICS Sport

Second section

All except Le Mans breakfast (page 15) and JH's daughters (page 16) © PA Photos as follows:

Page 9 (Sauber launch) © John Marsh/EMPICS Sport; (singing, banner) both © Steve Etherington/EMPICS Sport

Page 10 (100th Grand Prix) both © John Marsh/EMPICS Sport; (Hungary) © Claire Mackintosh/EMPICS Sport; (minute's silence) © Steve Etherington/EMPICS Sport

Page 11 (Australia) © Claire Mackintosh/EMPICS Sport; (Italy) © Steve Etherington/EMPICS Sport; (Canada) © John Marsh/EMPICS Sport

Pages 12, 13, 14 all © John Marsh/EMPICS Sport

Page 15 (fire) © Terry Renna/AP/Press Association Images; (Mazda) © Vincent Michel/AP/Press Association Images

Page 16 (Vettel, Hamilton) both © XPB Images/Press Association Images; (crowd-surfing) © James Moy Photography/PA Images

Index

ABOUT THE AUTHOR

Johnny Herbert is one of only nine British drivers to win a Grand Prix since the 1970s, tasting success with Benetton at Silverstone and Monza in 1995, then delivering a one and only top podium place for Jackie Stewart's team at the 1999 European Grand Prix at the Nürburgring. He also became the first active Formula 1 driver to win the endurance classic 24 Hours of Le Mans, with Bertrand Gachot and Volker Weidler in 1991, and has been a champion at karting, the Formula Ford Festival, Formula 3, the American Le Mans and the Speedcar Series in his long and varied career.

As one of the lead pundits on Sky Sports' Formula 1 channel, he remains high-profile and hugely popular. Johnny is widely admired for his encyclopaedic knowledge of motor-racing, as well as for his extraordinary driving skills, legendary sense of humour and love of the sport.